TRANSACTIONS

OF THE

AMERICAN PHILOSOPHICAL SOCIETY

HELD AT PHILADELPHIA
FOR PROMOTING USEFUL KNOWLEDGE

NEW SERIES—VOLUME 65, PART 6
1975

JUSTICE IN MEDIEVAL RUSSIA: MUSCOVITE JUDGMENT CHARTERS (*PRAVYE GRAMOTY*) OF THE FIFTEENTH AND SIXTEENTH CENTURIES

ANN M. KLEIMOLA

Assistant Professor of History, University of Nebraska

THE AMERICAN PHILOSOPHICAL SOCIETY
INDEPENDENCE SQUARE
PHILADELPHIA

October, 1975

TO MY PARENTS

506
A512 Ptn
v. 65
pt. 6
1975

PREFACE

Studies dealing with medieval Russian legal and administrative history have tended to picture the Muscovite judicial system of the fifteenth and sixteenth centuries as guilty of arbitrariness and class justice. But my examination of the judgment charters (*pravye gramoty*), the records of trial and statements of decisions of the courts, has led me to reappraise this generally accepted view of how the medieval Russian judicial system worked. These documents are the fullest, but hitherto largely neglected, source of information on trial procedure, types of evidence, the roles of judges and litigants, and, generally, the processes by which the courts reached their decisions. Although there is abundant evidence of shortcomings in a legal and administrative system still in the early stages of centralization and standardization, my analysis of these charters shows that the decisions in most cases were in accord with the evidence presented in court and the traditional rules of procedure that had evolved over the preceding centuries.

Translation of medieval Russian legal terminology has presented difficulties. Some Russian terms have no standard English equivalents, while in other cases the superficially analogous Western legal term has connotations that do not apply in the Russian situation. The Russian term has, therefore, been given in parentheses after the first reference.

This study was begun as a Ph.D. dissertation at the University of Michigan. Its completion was made possible by the award of a postdoctoral year fellowship at the Center for Advanced Study, University of Illinois, and summer fellowships from the Summer Research Laboratory of the Center for Russian and East European Studies at the University of Illinois, and the University of Nebraska Research Council.

I wish to express my gratitude to Professors H. W. Dewey and John V. A. Fine, Jr., of the University of Michigan, and Professors Ralph T. Fisher, Jr., Benjamin Uroff, and Henry Kahane of the University of Illinois at Urbana-Champaign, for their assistance and encouragement over the years. My colleagues at the University of Nebraska-Lincoln have been helpful and encouraging.

I wish also to express my appreciation to the many librarians who assisted me in locating materials, particularly Miss Mary E. Rollman at the University of Michigan and Professor Laurence Miller and Mrs. Marianna Choldin at the University of Illinois.

A.M.K.

3

JUSTICE IN MEDIEVAL RUSSIA:
Muscovite Judgment Charters (*Pravye Gramoty*)
of the Fifteenth and Sixteenth Centuries

ANN M. KLEIMOLA

CONTENTS

I. THE JUDGMENT CHARTER AS A DOCUMENT OF MEDIEVAL RUSSIAN LAW

The Russian word *gramota,* which is of Greek origin, was the term used to designate a written document from the time of Russia's first contacts with Greece until the fifteenth century. Various types of records, whether legislative, administrative, procedural, or private-law documents, were called *gramoty.* The term applied to princely decrees and orders, last wills and testaments, all possible varieties of transactions and agreements concerning property or personal obligation, and even to correspondence. In the seventeenth century the diminutive forms *gramotka* and *gramotitsa* were often applied to letters. Other terms designating a written document, such as *krepost'* (document strengthening the holder's claim to land), *ukaz* (order or decree), *zapis'* (record), and *pamiat'* (memorandum), appeared only in the fifteenth and sixteenth centuries, and then were used almost interchangeably with *gramota.*[1] Yet a certain degree of differentiation among all these *gramoty* was possible, since an adjective was often added, indicating the content.[2] For example, a *zhalo-vannaia gramota* was a charter of grant, a patent (usually bestowing privileges and/or immunities on the recipient), a *kupchaia gramota*—a deed of purchase, an *ustavnaia gramota*—an administrative charter, and a *pravaia gramota*—a judgment charter.

Judgment charters, which record trial proceedings and the court's decisions, are a basic source for the study of Muscovite legal history. These documents, which were issued by medieval Russian courts from the thirteenth to the seventeenth centuries, are perhaps most important for the light which they throw upon the actual operation of the legal system.[3] The judgment charters record the method used in trying cases, the types of evidence presented, the role of litigants, witnesses, and judges, and the decision reached. Where the law codes allude to these matters, usually in connection with setting fees or strict procedural requirements, the judgment charters provide illustrations of the court in action. Thus, in many cases, the judgment charters supplement knowledge gained from the law codes, filling gaps or adding detail. Yet, as in the case of the law codes, the laconic nature of the documents leaves many questions unanswered. Scribes apparently saw no reason for recording those things which everyone knew. Most extant judgment charters from the fifteenth century, for example, name the disputed land, on which the trial was generally held. While the judge's name is given, there is usually no designation of his rank or indication as to the extent of his jurisdiction. Boiar judges are identified most frequently only by given name and patronymic. Despite such limitations, however, the judgment charters remain our only source for much basic data concerning the realities of medieval Russian law.

A judgment charter (*pravaia gramota*) was a written trial record and statement of the court's decision which was awarded to the victorious litigant. In form and content it was closely related to two other Muscovite trial documents, the *sudnyi spisok* (trial record) and *dokladnoi spisok* (trial record including *doklad* proceedings, when a case was referred to a court of higher instance). Muscovite trial documents actually include,

---

[1] Maks Fasmer, *Etimologicheskii slovar' russkogo iazyka,* trans. O. N. Trubachev, ed. B. A. Larin (4 v., Moscow, 1964–1973) 1: p. 451; S. A. Shumakov, "Obzor gramot kollegii ekonomii," *Chteniia v imperatorskom obshchestve istorii i drevnostei rossiiskikh pri Moskovskom universitete* (264 v., Moscow, 1846–1918), 1917, no. 2, pt. 1: p. 1; I. I. Sreznevskii, *Materialy dlia slovaria drevnerusskogo iazyka* (3 v., St. Petersburg, 1893–1903) 1: pp. 578–584.

[2] For English definitions of various kinds of *gramoty,* see *Dictionary of Russian Historical Terms from the Eleventh Century to 1917,* comp. Sergei G. Pushkarev, ed. George Vernadsky and Ralph T. Fisher, Jr. (New Haven and London, 1970), pp. 24–27.

[3] For English translations of representative judgment charters from these centuries, with commentary and analysis, see *Russian Private Law XIV-XVII Centuries,* trans. and ed. H. W. Dewey and A. M. Kleimola, Michigan Slavic Materials no. 9 (Ann Arbor, Mich., 1973), pp. 41–211.

for the most part, only (1) that which was said during the trial, or (2) that plus the court's decision, and (3) in rare instances the execution of judgment.[4] The content of a particular document can therefore be used in determining its classification.

The trial record (*sudnyi spisok*) served as the basic document in the sequence. It was a detailed record of the court proceedings, in which everything that had occurred during the trial was reported, including what had been said and what evidence had been presented. Yet the trial record merely provided material for the court's decision. It did not include the decision itself, and was not issued to the litigants.

The judgment charter (*pravaia gramota*) consisted of two parts, the trial record (*sudnyi spisok*) and the decision given by the court. The content of Muscovite judgment charters in the fifteenth and sixteenth centuries took the following form. First came an introductory section, naming the judge and the litigants, almost always stating the place where the trial was held, and sometimes indicating the date. The main body of the text presented a detailed report of the trial itself, beginning with a statement of the plaintiff's complaint and defendant's answer to the charge, followed by a step-by-step procedural account, in which the testimony of both litigants and their witnesses, texts of documentary evidence presented, and requests for oath-taking or judicial duel as a means of proof were recorded. This represents a word-for-word report of the statements by the judge, parties, and witnesses, preceded by a laconic identification of the person speaking. Traditional formulae accompany each stage of the trial. These set phrases, which had become remarkably consistent by the early sixteenth century, are frequently marked by alliteration, assonance, syntactical parallelism, and metonymic imagery.[5] When description of the court procedure was completed, the trial record *per se* ended. Names of witnesses present might be stated at this point, or given after recording of the court's decision. The concluding section of the judgment charter declared the decision of the court, sometimes a simple statement of fact, sometimes listing the reasons for deciding in favor of (or against) one of the parties. Then followed a list of the officials present at the trial, noting the names of the secretary who signed the document and the undersecretary who wrote it. After adding its official seal, the court awarded the

judgment charter to the victorious litigant.[6] Judgment charters were documents of public law "with private-law significance," since, in the case of lawsuits involving land, the judgment charters certified the rights of the litigants to whom they were awarded, and served as proof of those rights in case of their violation.[7]

On some occasions the judge who originally heard the case was unable to give a decision, either because the case did not fall within the limits of his jurisdictional grant, or because he was unsure of the law governing a particular matter. The case was therefore sent to his superiors on *doklad,* i.e., referred to a court of higher instance, usually the boiar court in Moscow or even the court of the Grand Prince himself. The record of subsequent trial in a higher court was usually called a *dokladnoi spisok* (trial record including *doklad* proceedings in a court of higher instance). Again the *sudnyi spisok* (trial record) formed the first part of the document. After incorporating the report of the case as heard in the court of first instance, the record continued with an account of proceedings before the higher judge. His decision was rendered in the form of an order from the upper court to the original judge, who was to hand down the decision as decreed by the higher court and grant a judgment charter to the victorious party.[8] In effect, however, there was little real

---

[4] D. M. Meichik, *Gramoty XIV–XV vv. Moskovskago arkhiva ministerstva iustitsii. Ikh forma, soderzhanie i znachenie v istorii russkago prava* (Moscow, 1883), p. 27.

[5] For a detailed discussion of formulae in fifteenth-century judgement charters, see A. M. Kleimola, "Formulae and Formalism in Muscovite Judgment Charters," *Canadian-American Slavic Studies* **6**, 3 (Fall, 1972): pp. 355–373. See also L. V. Cherepnin, "Iz nabliudenii nad leksikoi drevnerusskikh aktov," *Voprosy istoricheskoi leksikologii i leksikografii vostochno-slavianskikh iazykov* (Moscow, 1974), pp. 211–218.

[6] To be official, judgment charters required both signature and seal; 1497 Sudebnik, articles 15, 16, 17, 22, 23, 24, 25, 40; 1550 Sudebnik, articles 33, 34, 35, 38, 39, 40, 42, 65. For the texts of these two law codes, see *Sudebniki XV–XVI vekov,* ed. B. D. Grekov *et al.* (Moscow-Leningrad, 1952), pp. 19–29, 135–177. For English translations of the Sudebniki, see *Muscovite Judicial Texts 1488–1556,* trans. and ed. H. W. Dewey, Michigan Slavic Materials no. 7 (Ann Arbor, Mich., 1966), pp. 7–21, 45–74. See also *Akty iuridicheskie, ili sobranie form starinnago deloproizvodstva, izd. Arkheograficheskoiu kommissieiu* (St. Petersburg, 1838), nos. 5 and 6 (hereafter cited as *AIu*). For a discussion of seals, see Shumakov, "Obzor gramot kollegii ekonomii," p. 2; A. S. Lappo-Danilevskii, *Ocherk russkoi diplomatiki chastnykh aktov* [Petrograd, 1920], pp. 101–105. Chronological dating came into use from the fourteenth century, but was done as a general rule only from the sixteenth. Years were counted according to the Byzantine system "from the creation of the world," i.e. 5508 years before the birth of Christ, and the year started on the first of September (in most documents). Thus, in calculating dates for documents written between the first of September and the first of January, it is necessary to subtract 5509 from the year recorded; see E. I. Kamentseva, *Khronologiia* (Moscow, 1967), pp. 52–53; Lappo-Danilevskii, *Ocherk russkoi diplomatiki,* pp. 130–132.

[7] Lappo-Danilevskii, *Ocherk russkoi diplomatiki,* pp. 42–44. For a discussion of the mixture of "public law" and "private law" elements in medieval Russian documents, see *Russian Private Law,* pp. xv–xvi.

[8] Many scholars have commented on the characteristics of these trial documents; see, *inter alia,* I. D. Beliaev, "Spiski sudnye i dokladnye i gramoty pravyia i bezsudnyia v Moskovskom gosudarstve," *Arkhiv istoriko-iuridicheskikh svedenii, otnosiashchikhsia do Rossii,* ed. Nikolai Kalachov (3 v., Moscow, 1850–1861) **2**, pt. 1, sect. 3, no. 4: pp. 115–128; L. V. Cherepnin, *Russkie feodal'nye arkhivy XIV–XV vv.* (2 v., Moscow-Leningrad, 1948–1951) **2**: pp. 226–230; M. I. Gorchakov, *O zemel'nykh vladeniiakh vserossiiskikh mitropolitov,*

difference between a judgment charter and a trial record including *doklad* proceedings. The decision recorded in the latter document could not be changed, and the issuance of a subsequent judgment charter was often prescribed specifically by the upper court, rather than merely being assumed as a consequence.[9]

A special type of judgment charter was the default judgment (*bessudnaia gramota* or *bessudnaia pravaia gramota*). If one of the litigants failed to appear either for the original trial or for the trial conducted before the higher court, his opponent received a default judgment charter, entitling him to recover "whatever loss shall occur to him in this matter through deliberate delay" or at least the costs of "summons, judgment charter, and default judgment." Judges did not even take part in granting these decrees. The court secretary (*d'iak*), after checking the trial date set in the summonses, issued the default judgment charter on the eighth day after the designated trial date.[10]

The provisions of the Muscovite Sudebniki (law codes) of 1497 and 1550 clearly show that the trial record,[11] judgment charter,[12] trial record including *doklad* proceedings,[13] and default judgment charter[14] each played a specific role in judicial procedure, but since these codes were concerned mainly with procedural matters, specific fees and fines, and elimination of judicial corruption, the trial documents themselves are

our only source for determining their form and content.

Diuvernua asserts that judgment charters were issued only at the request of the victorious party. This is clear, he argues, from a reconciliation agreement (*mirovaia*), where the parties were obliged not to take a judgment charter from the judge,[15] and from a judgment charter which states, "Prince Vasilii ordered that judgment be found in our favor, and, Sire, ordered us to *request* a judgment charter from the judge."[16]

Diuvernua's evidence is, to say the least, inconclusive. When litigants reached a settlement among themselves before conclusion of the trial, both Sudebniki provide that court officials shall receive fees only for those procedural steps through which the trial had already progressed.[17] Since the litigants in Diuvernua's first example became reconciled, their agreement brought an end to court proceedings; no decision would be given and it seems very unlikely that a judgment charter could be issued. The texts of the law codes also give no indication that the issuance of a judgment charter was optional; it seems to be an assumed consequence of trial, the only restriction being that judges without full jurisdictional grants are not to issue (*dati*) judgment charters in certain cases without referring the matter to their superiors.[18] The judgment charters themselves do not usually record such requests by the victorious party, and considering the highly formal nature of Muscovite court procedure, it seems improbable that such a step would have been so consistently eliminated from the documents.[19] In addition, complaint could be brought against a judge who erred in issuing a judgment charter or who refused to give a decree.[20]

Before 1550, the only way to confirm the authenticity of a judgment charter was to check it against the trial record or record of trial on *doklad*, which had served as a basis for issuing the charter in question. Frequently such comparison proved quite difficult: the judge who had granted the judgment charter kept the trial record with his personal papers, and it remained among the family possessions even after his death.

patriarkhov i sv. sinoda, 988–1738 gg. (St. Petersburg, 1871), pp. 17, 304–306; Meichik, *Gramoty XIV–XV vv.*, pp. 26–34; N. N. Pokrovskii, *Aktovye istochniki po istorii chernososhnogo zemlevladeniia v Rossii XIV-nachala XVI v.* (Novosibirsk, 1973), pp. 20–46; and Shumakov, "Obzor gramot kollegii ekonomii," p. 9.

[9] See Meichik, *Gramoty XIV–XV vv.*, p. 29; Pokrovskii, *Aktovye istochniki*, p. 21. Two trial records which include *doklad* have the seal of the lower-court judge, and apparently are copies of the upper-court documents, issued with a seal as judgment charters by the judge involved; Meichik, *Gramoty XIV–XV vv.*, p. 33.

[10] 1497 Sudebnik, articles 27, 32; 1550 Sudebnik, articles 42, 49, 50. According to the 1550 code, default judgment charters were to be issued on the seventh day after failure to appear in court for litigants within one hundred versts, with corresponding time limits for further distances. The default judgment was not a hasty, arbitrary procedure, since a Muscovite citizen who had been summoned to court had the right to postpone the trial date twice, if he paid the required fee. And the court could not issue a default judgment until a week after his third, unauthorized, failure to appear. The default judgment was thus a device for protecting the litigant who came to court as summoned, and the 1550 Sudebnik made the defaulting party responsible for all losses, fees and subsistence expenses incurred by his opponent. See I. D. Beliaev, "O vyzove v sud po drevnim russkim zakonam do Ulozheniia 1649 g.," *Zhurnal ministerstva iustitsii* 3 (1860), bk. 2, sect. 3: pp. 127–128.

[11] 1497 Sudebnik, article 64; 1550 Sudebnik, articles 4, 62, 69.

[12] 1497 Sudebnik, articles 15, 17, 19, 20, 22, 23, 32, 40, 41; 1550 Sudebnik, articles 2, 33, 35, 38, 40, 42, 43, 63, 65, 66, 67.

[13] 1497 Sudebnik, articles 16, 24; 1550 Sudebnik, articles 34, 39.

[14] 1497 Sudebnik, articles 25, 27, 32, 36; 1550 Sudebnik, articles 20, 21, 41, 42, 49.

[15] N. L. Diuvernua, *Istochniki prava i sud v drevnei Rossii* (Moscow, 1869), p. 411. The source cited by Diuvernua is *AIu*, no. 269.

[16] "Kniaz' Vasilii velel nas opraviti i gramoty nam, gospodine, pravye velel *prositi* [italicized N.D.] u sud'i." The source cited here by Diuvernua is *AIu*, no. 11.

[17] 1497 Sudebnik, articles 4, 5, 38, 53; 1550 Sudebnik, articles 9, 10, 31, 62.

[18] 1497 Sudebnik, articles 20, 41; 1550 Sudebnik, articles 63, 66, 67.

[19] For another discussion of the question, see D. S., "Dopolnitel'noe zamechanie o pravykh gramotakh," *Arkhiv istoriko-iuridicheskikh svedenii*, 2, pt. 1, sect. 3, no. 6: pp. 135–137.

[20] 1497 Sudebnik, article 19; 1550 Sudebnik, articles 2, 7; F. M. Dmitriev, *Istoriia sudebnykh instantsii i grazhdanskago appelliatsionnago sudoproizvodstva ot sudebnika do uchrezhdeniia o guberniiakh* (Moscow, 1859), p. 292.

Consequently difficulties arose in searching for the record.[21]

The second Sudebnik, however, recorded steps which had been taken to eliminate the problem. Secretaries became personally responsible for making sure that documents were compiled and kept in administrative offices. Moreover, the code decreed flogging with the knout for any undersecretary caught with court records in his possession either outside the city or in his private residence.[22] This article of the Sudebnik probably served to record officially and make standard a practice which grew up as the Muscovite administrative system became more centralized.[23] Documents came to be stored in boxes (iashchiki), under the name of the secretary who signed them. Every secretary in charge of a prikaz (chancery) left behind one of these boxes, containing documents about matters decided by him and authenticated by his signature during the period of his administration.[24]

Although the Muscovite courts continued to issue judgment charters well into the seventeenth century, approximately one-half of the published documents are texts of judgment charters which were issued between ca. 1480 and 1505.[25] Most of the surviving judgment charters from the fifteenth century are accounts of lawsuits involving some type of rights to land.[26] The majority of the sixteenth-century documents likewise record trials over land, but some litigants also brought suit for restitution in other matters: arson,[27] theft,[28] assault and robbery,[29] runaway slaves,[30] a loan,[31] appropriation of the right to toll-gate fees,[32] and even the question of precedence among the tsar's servitors (mestnichestvo).[33] As some of these documents show, the norms and practices of criminal law could suddenly appear in the middle of a civil lawsuit.

In the fifteenth and sixteenth centuries judgment charters seem to have been one of the standard judicial records issued by Muscovite courts. From the brief, often cyptic notations concerning early trials, they developed into much longer, more detailed, and increasingly complex accounts. By the middle of the seventeenth century, however, the nature of these documents appears to have changed. The 1649 Ulozhenie of Tsar Aleksei Mikhailovich is much more detailed than the earlier codes of law, being composed of 25 chapters, divided into 967 articles,[34] as opposed to the 68 articles of the 1497 Sudebnik and the 99 (100) articles of the 1550 Sudebnik.[35] It reflects the growing administrative centralization of the Muscovite state, the development of the system of chanceries (prikazy), the replacement of regional vicegerents (namestniki) by military governors (voevody), and the subsequent changes in judicial procedure.

Apparently many of the cases which had formerly been heard by the Grand Prince or his agents were now handled by chancery courts, where the procedure was somewhat different. A prikaz undersecretary (pod'iachii) wrote down everything said in court, in record books (zapisnye knigi) which each prikaz kept specifically

[21] Dmitriev, Istoriia sudebnykh instantsii, p. 269.

[22] 1550 Sudebnik, article 28, and commentary in Sudebniki XV–XVI vekov, p. 214.

[23] For recent literature on the problem see, inter alia, A. V. Chernov, "O klassifikatsii tsentral'nykh gosudarstvennykh uchrezhdenii XVI–XVII vv.," Istoricheskii arkhiv, 1958, no. 1: pp. 195–201; idem, "O zarozhdenii prikaznogo upravleniia v protsesse obrazovaniia russkogo tsentralizovannogo gosudarstva," Trudy Moskovskogo gosudarstvennogo istoriko-arkhivnogo instituta 19 (1965): pp. 273–293; S. V. Iushkov, Obshchestvenno-politicheskii stroi i pravo Kievskogo gosudarstva (Moscow, 1949); idem, Istoriia gosudarstva i prava SSSR (Moscow, 1950); A. K. Leont'ev, Obrazovanie prikaznoi sistemy upravleniia v Russkom gosudarstve (Moscow, 1961); P. A. Sadikov, Ocherki po istorii oprichniny (Moscow, 1950), pp. 212–417; S. O. Shmidt, "Chelobitennyi prikaz v seredine XVI stoletiia," Izvestiia Akademii nauk SSSR, Seriia istorii i filosofii 7, no. 5 (1950): pp. 445–458; A. A. Zimin, "O slozhenii prikaznoi sistemy na Rusi," AN SSSR. Doklady i soobscheniia instituta istorii 3 (Moscow, 1954): pp. 164–176.

[24] Judgment charter of 1519–1520, Akty sotsial'no-ekonomicheskoi istorii severo-vostochnoi Rusi kontsa XIV–nachala XVI v. (3 v., Moscow, 1952–1964) 3, no. 390 (hereafter cited as ASEI); N. P. Likhachev. Razriadyne d'iaki XVI veka (St. Petersburg, 1888), pp. 45–48. See also Lappo-Danilevskii, Ocherk russkoi diplomatiki, pp. 59–62, and D. Ia. Samokvasov, Russkie arkhivy i tsarskii kontrol' prikaznoi sluzhby v XVII veke (Moscow, 1902).

[25] For a study of peasant attempts to retain or regain rights to land, based upon this concentrated group of judgment charters, see L. I. Ivina, "Sudebnye dokumenty i bor'ba za zemliu v russkom gosudarstve vo vtoroi polovine XV–nachale XVI v.," Istoricheskie zapiski 86 (1970): pp. 326–356; A. D. Gorskii comments on this article in "Iz istorii bor'by krest'ian za zemliu na Rusi XV–nachala XVI v.," Vestnik Moskovskogo universiteta. Seriia IX, Istoriia, 1972, no. 3: pp. 38–57. See also A. D. Gorskii, Bor'ba krest'ian za zemliu na Rusi v XV–nachale XVI veka (Moscow, 1974).

[26] One exception, a case in which a servant is accused of inciting slaves to flee across the border, adds little to our knowledge, since the defendant admits his guilt immediately; ASEI 3, no. 357.

[27] ASEI 3, no. 390.

[28] S. M. Kashtanov, Ocherki russkoi diplomatiki (Moscow, 1970), no. 40: pp. 409–414.

[29] Akty feodal'nogo zemlevladeniia i khoziaistva (3 v., Moscow, 1951–1961) 1, nos. 1a, 2a, 222 (hereafter cited as AFZKh).

[30] AIu, nos. 21, 22.

[31] Aleksandr Iushkov, ed. and comp., Akty XIII–XVII vv., predstavlennye v razriadnyi prikaz (Moscow, 1898), no. 128.

[32] AIu, no. 24.

[33] Sobranie gosudarstvennykh gramot i dogovorov (5 v., Moscow, 1813–1894) 2, no. 47; V. B. Kobrin, "Iz istorii mestnichestva XVI veka," Istoricheskii arkhiv, 1960, no. 1: pp. 214–219; N. P. Likhachev, ed., Mestnicheskiia dela 1563–1605 gg. (St. Petersburg, 1894); A. M. Kleimola, "Boris Godunov and the Politics of Mestnichestvo," Slavonic and East European Review 53, no. 132 (1975): pp. 355–369.

[34] For the text of the 1649 Ulozhenie, see Sobornoe ulozhenie tsaria Alekseia Mikhailovicha 1649 goda, Pamiatniki russkogo prava, 6, ed. K. A. Sofronenko (Moscow, 1957); M. N. Tikhomirov and P. P. Epifanov, Sobornoe ulozhenie 1649 goda (Moscow, 1961).

[35] Sudebniki XV–XVI vekov, pp. 19–29, 135–177.

for legal matters.[36] From his notes on the proceedings, which had to have the authenticating signatures of the litigants, the undersecretary then compiled a brief extract (the trial record or *sudnyi spisok*), on the basis of which the judge made his decision. The secretary (*d'iak*) added his authenticating signature to the trial record, after comparing it with the notes in the record book, and the notes were then returned to the undersecretary for safekeeping on the chance that argument might arise.[37] The judges of the *prikaz* had to reach a decision jointly; this decision (*prigovor*) was signed by all, and if anyone were not present, the reason for his absence was noted. The litigants (or their representatives) were thereafter required to appear in court, where the decision was declared orally.[38]

The records of such legal cases (*sudnye dela*) differ considerably in form from the earlier judgment charters.[39] A case of this sort was usually the record of proceedings in a specialized chancery, rather than a document issued by a tsar, boiar, or other judge with broad jurisdiction. It might include a series of separate documents, such as petitions, surety bonds, contracts, decrees, and so forth. Records of testimony are given in third-person reported speech rather than as dialogue in direct discourse. Appearance of the litigants to hear the decision is recorded, and there may be a notation that a judgment charter had been issued. Such judgment charters were probably quite condensed in form.[40] An examination of late sixteenth-century judgment charters, which incorporate the texts of numerous documents and official memoranda in addition to repetitive word-for-word testimony, suggests that the continuous recording of an entire legal case in a single document simply became too unwieldy.

The judgment charter as a legal document seems to have lost much of its significance, perhaps owing to the improved recordkeeping of the government *prikazy*. Judgment charters appear to become progressively less important. Only three articles (Chapter XVIII, article 58; Chapter XX, articles 81 and 82) of the Ulozhenie's 967 refer to *pravye gramoty*, as opposed to 9 of 68 in 1497 and 11 of 100 in 1550. It is not even clear that judgment charters had to be given to the winner in 1649. Two of the three articles deal with the rights

which a judgment charter conferred on a master over a slave, and the text of the third (Chapter XVIII, article 58) is unclear: "And to whomever judgment charters shall be given, to any people, concerning inherited land and concerning any matters, and from the Bondage Chancery in [questions of] bondage, the whole trial shall be written in the charter as in the original: and these documents will be sealed with the Sovereign's seal, and the seal fees will be taken according to the decree."[41] Two interpretations of this provision have been suggested: that for granting judgment charters in cases concerning inherited land and cases concerning bondsmen, fees were taken for application of the seal if the entire trial record was set forth in the document;[42] or, that judgment charters were given only upon request of the litigants themselves.[43] In Chapter X of the Ulozhenie, the main section of the code devoted to court procedure, no references to judgment charters can be found. The code mentions no fee to be paid to secretaries or undersecretaries for writing and signing such documents.

Furthermore, the Ulozhenie contains no reference to the default judgment charter (*bessudnaia gramota*). Yet the principle was still very much in effect: if one of the litigants failed to appear in court at the designated time, he lost the case.[44] No reference follows, however, to the issuance of a document to the winner. It would appear that, since the fact was on record in the *prikaz*, a judgment charter was not considered necessary.

Two other types of documents, similar in nature to judgment charters, appeared in the seventeenth century. Shumakov mentions one of them, a document of the seventeenth and eighteenth centuries known as a *pravaia vypis'*, which he considers a "modernized" equivalent of the old *pravaia gramota*.[45] The other document, known as a *pravaia pamiat'*, seems very similar in form to a *pravaia vypis'*. Both types were summaries of trial proceedings and decisions, written completely in the third person, with paraphrased notations concerning documentary evidence presented in court.[46] Despite

---

[36] 1649 Ulozhenie, **10**: art. 128; see also the commentary on procedure as decreed by the Ulozhenie in K. D. Kavelin, *Osnovnyia nachala russkago sudoustroistva i grazhdanskago sudoproizvodstva v period vremeni ot ulozheniia do uchrezhdeniia o guberniiakh,* in *Sobranie sochinenii K. D. Kavelina* (4 v., St. Petersburg, 1897–1900) **4**: pp. 322–328.

[37] 1649 Ulozhenie, **10**: arts. 11–12; Kavelin, *Osnovnyia nachala,* p. 327; Grigorii Kotoshikhin, *O Rossii v tsarstvovanie Alekseia Mikhailovicha* (4th ed., St. Petersburg, 1906), chap. 7, p. 42.

[38] "A prigovor po tem sudnym delam skazyvati isttsom i otvetchikom na otsrochnoi srok"; 1649 Ulozhenie, **10**: arts. 23, 113.

[39] For texts of some *sudnye dela,* see A. Iakovlev, *Kholopstvo i kholopy v Moskovskom gosudarstve XVII v.* (Moscow-Leningrad, 1943), pp. 318–562.

[40] Tikhomirov and Epifanov, *Sobornoe ulozhenie,* p. 331.

[41] Chapter 18, article 58 reads as follows: "A komu dany budut pravye gramoty, vsiakim liudem, o votchinakh i o vsiakikh delekh, i iz Kholop'ia prikazu v kholopstvakh, a napisano budet v gramote vse sudnoe delo podlinno: i te gramoty pechatati Gosudarevoiu pechat'iu, a pechatnye poshliny imati po ukazu."

[42] Commentary to article 58 in *Pamiatniki russkogo prava* (8 v., Moscow, 1952–1963) **6**: p. 303 (hereafter cited as *PRP*).

[43] Kavelin, *Osnovnyia nachala,* p. 328.

[44] 1649 Ulozhenie, **10**: arts. 108, 117; Kotoshikhin, *O Rossii,* chap. 7, p. 40.

[45] Shumakov, "Obzor gramot kollegii ekonomii," p. 9.

[46] For texts of pravye pamiati, see *Sbornik gramot kollegii ekonomii* (2 v., Peterburg, 1922–1929) **1**, no. 596 (hereafter cited as *SGKE*); *Akty, otnosiashchiesia do grazhdanskoi raspravy drevnei Rossii,* comp. and ed. A. Fedotov-Chekhovskii (2 v., Kiev, 1860–1863) **2**, nos. 125–132, 134–135, 143, 151. For *pravye vypisi* see, in the same volume, nos. 154, 159, 160, 163, 171, 174, 175, 181. For an example of a transitional judgment charter, with third-person narration and paraphrased notes of

the differences in form, however, both *pravye pamiati* and *pravye vypisi* clearly show the underlying structure of the old *pravye gramoty*.

Differentiation among the types of documents is not as clear as the above definitions would indicate, even when discussion of the terms is limited to their use in the fifteenth and sixteenth centuries. In clerical practice of the time the terms *sudnyi spisok* and *pravaia gramota* at times coincided.[47] Later copyists came to call a *pravaia gramota* a *sudnyi spisok*.[48] Scholars who edited and published these documents were likewise inconsistent in attaching labels to them.[49] The confusion is even greater, however, because the term *delo* is mixed in with the others, and is certainly the least specific of the group. In modern Russian *delo* has many meanings: affair, business, pursuit, concern, cause, deed, act, work, matter, situation, case, file, dossier, record, or, in the plural, things, state of affairs. Wide applicability has been characteristic of the word for centuries. From the early fourteenth century, the word *delo* began to be used in juridical documents in the sense of "argument," "suit," or "trial."[50] Article 62 of the 1550 Sudebnik uses the term *sudnoe delo* as an equivalent for *sudnyi spisok,* both referring to the trial record written by the local-government secretary (as opposed to the copy—*protiven'*—written by the

vicegerent's secretary).[51] By the middle of the sixteenth century the term *sudnoe delo,* as a result of ellipsis, was frequently written simply *delo,* with an expanded meaning "documents relating to a trial."[52] In the 1649 Ulozhenie, *sudnoe delo* is used to indicate the trial record prepared by the undersecretary on the basis of his notes (*zapiski*).[53] Toward the end of the seventeenth century the word *delo,* firmly established in clerical terminology as "a complex of documents relating to a trial," acquired the broader meaning of "a collection of documents on any question whatsoever," and has been used in that sense ever since.[54]

Despite the terminological jungle, judgment charters are one of the most important sources on Muscovite legal history, providing information not only about judicial procedure of the fifteenth and sixteenth centuries, but also about the court hierarchy and personnel, and even giving some indications of the development of the Muscovite administrative language.

II. COURTS AND OFFICIALS

The 1497 Sudebnik, which refers specifically to a number of different courts, indicates that the Muscovite legal system was already quite complex by the end of the fifteenth century. Surviving judgment charters from the period, however, suggest that this structure was still rather loosely organized, not yet having developed a set hierarchy or rigid framework. Most of the extant judgment charters were issued by one of the central courts in Moscow—the court of the Grand Prince, of his sons (*deti*), or of the boiars. Our sources make it possible, in a general way, to trace some aspects of the gradual evolution of the Muscovite central court system, but the precise nature of its development remains a subject of speculation.

One must keep in mind that during the early period of Muscovite history the hierarchy of courts was not rigidly fixed. All came to the Grand Prince with their disputes, expecting to receive justice from him. The Grand Prince then had three choices: he could send such petitioners directly to the judge within whose competence their case lay, or send them to a specially designated judge, or hear the parties himself.

The Grand Prince acted as a judge in several capacities. As a private landholder, he possessed administrative and judicial rights over the peope living on his domains, and received the income from manorial courts. As the sovereign, he was the supreme authority for the central court system and for the system of regional vicegerents (*namestniki* and *volosteli*) who

---

documents, see the judgment charter of 1595 published in Gorchakov, *O zemel'nykh vladeniiakh,* no. 6, pp. 65–73.

[47] L. V. Cherepnin, "Akty kontsa XIV–XV vv., ikh raznovidnosti i znachenie v kachestve istoricheskogo istochnika," *ASEI* 1: p. 649; N. A. Kazakova, "O 'sudnom spiske' Maksima Greka," *Arkheograficheskii ezhegodnik za 1966 god* (Moscow, 1968), p. 28.

[48] *PRP* 3: p. 243.

[49] See, for example, Meichik's complaint, *Gramoty XIV–XV vv.,* pp. 26, 33–34; the editors of *PRP* 3 point out (p. 243) that the *sudnyi spisok* published on pp. 234–237 is a *dokladnoi spisok;* Shakhmatov calls one judgment charter a *sudnaia gramota,* although the term *pravaia* is found in the text itself; A. A. Shakhmatov, "Izsledovanie o dvinskikh gramotakh XV v.," *Izsledovanie po russkomu iazyku,* izd. Otdeleniia russkogo iazyka i slovesnosti Imperatorskoi akademii nauk (St. Petersburg, 1903) 2, pt. 3: pp. 34–35, 108–109. This text has also been published as a judgment charter in *PRP* 2: p. 195. The document published as a *sudnyi spisok* of 1505–1511 in *AIu,* no. 12, was republished as a *pravaia gramota* of 1495–1499 in *AFZKh* 1, no. 129. To cite just one more example, a document published as a judgment charter of 1547 is much closer in content to a temporary injunction order, since it merely prohibits the defendant from entering the disputed land until the court officials can conduct an investigation; N. Serebrianskii, *Ocherki po istorii monastyrskoi zhizni v Pskovskoi zemle* (Moscow, 1908), p. 574. For a discussion of the methods used and problems encountered in classifying documents, with particular emphasis on formulae and internal evidence, see Lappo-Danilevskii, *Ocherk russkoi diplomatiki,* pp. 80–90, 97–99, 139–163.

[50] S. S. Volkov, "Razvitie administrativno-delovoi terminologii v nachale XVII veka," *Nachal'nyi etap formirovaniia russkogo natsional'nogo iazyka,* ed. B. A. Larin *et al.* (Leningrad, 1961), p. 148; for a discussion of *delo,* see also Sreznevskii, *Materialy* 1: 786–789.

[51] Volkov incorrectly states that in article 62 *sudnoe delo* means the trial record, while *sudnyi spisok* means a copy of the trial record with the decision of the case, given to the litigants; "Razvitie administrativno-delovoi terminologii," p. 148.

[52] Volkov, "Razvitie administrativno-delovoi terminologii," p. 148.

[53] 1649 Ulozhenie, **10**: arts. 11, 12.

[54] Volkov, "Razvitie administrativno-delovoi terminologii," p. 149.

administered the state lands. And although the court of the Grand Prince often made the final decision in matters referred to it by the lower courts, it could also serve as a court of first instance.[1] The ruler's personal justice was considered one of the highest privileges which could be bestowed upon a subject, and was included in many charters of grant (*zhalovannye nesudimye gramoty*). In medieval Muscovy, several categories of people gradually came to be exempt, by reason of the Grand Prince's charters of grant, from the regional courts: the clergy (as a special religious class and as a specially protected group of landholders), servitors and peasants of priests and monasteries, peasants subject to manorial courts or specially privileged state peasants, guild merchants, foreign merchants and their people, and in later years foreigners who entered the Muscovite military service and the Muscovite military men and artisans who were subject to the *prikazy* rather than local authorities.[2]

Such charters of grant were also issued by other people possessing "sovereign" judicial authority. A judgment charter of 1505, presented as evidence by an estate manager of Dmitrii Vasil'evich Shein (Morozov), incorporates the text of a charter of grant issued about 1466 by Grand Princess Mariia. After listing the various fee and assessment exemptions granted to Dmitrii Vasil'evich and his mother for their villages and hamlets, the charter declares:

And the vicegerents and their deputies of the Volskaia [canton] shall not take their subsistence dues from them (the village residents), nor send [anyone] to them for anything, nor judge them in any matter, except murder and brigandage with material evidence and theft. And sergeants-at-arms and bailiffs shall not take their assessments from them, nor come to them in any matter. And Stefanida or her son Dmitrei shall administer and judge those people of theirs. And [if] a joint-court trial takes place [between] those people of theirs and cantonal people, and the Volskaia [canton] vicegerents [or] their deputies try [the case], [then] Dmitrei, or whomever he orders, shall try [the case] with them; and they shall divide the judges' fees in half. And [if] anyone brings suit against Dmitrei or his estate manager for anything, I, the Grand Princess, or my boiar deputy, shall judge them.[3]

The existence of these charters of grant complicated the matter of issuing judgment charters. Holders of such documents were directly under the jurisdiction of the princes who granted them; thus these princes were the only judges competent to try cases in which charter grantees were litigants. Yet, owing to custom of the time, land suits required a local trial, so special judges were sent out to compile trial records on the spot, and then present the evidence in that form to the higher authority. The princes then proceeded to give judgment in their own name, making a decision on the basis of the trial record and recording that decision in the form of a judgment charter. On the surface, such a judgment charter looks like a *doklad* case: the record contains an account of proceedings in both courts and verification of the trial record in the court of higher instance.[4]

In addition to judicial activity arising from the charters of grant and through regular legal channels, the Grand Prince often received direct requests for his personal intervention.[5] Petitioners considered it an obligation of the sovereign to right wrongs, and the deluge of such requests eventually resulted in the establishment in the mid-sixteenth century of a special chancery to handle petitions submitted to the Grand Prince (the Chelobitnyi Prikaz).[6] In addition, there was pressure from the clergy, who tried to spur the princes onward in judicial activities, since personal judgment by the prince was considered the best security for the rights of his subjects; as Kiril of Beloozero wrote to Prince Andrei of Mozhaisk early in the fifteenth century, "Sire, do not shirk from giving justice to the peasants thyself; that, Sire, is a higher responsibility given to thee from God than prayer or fasting."[7] Thus the sovereign Grand Prince of All Rus'

---

[1] See, for example, *ASEI* 3, nos. 31, 357.

[2] For a study of the charters of grant, see S. M. Kashtanov, *Sotsial'no-politicheskaia istoriia Rossii kontsa XV-pervoi poloviny XVI v.* (Moscow, 1967); see also S. B. Veselovskii, *K voprosu o proiskhozhdenii votchinnogo rezhima* (Moscow, 1926); *idem, Feodal'noe zemlevladenie v severo-vostochnoi Rusi* (Moscow-Leningrad, 1947), pp. 110–145. On the legal situation of the merchants, see Samuel H. Baron, "Who Were the *Gosti?*" *California Slavic Studies* 7 (1973): pp. 1–40. On the legal position of foreigners in Russia, see I. Andreevskii, *O pravakh inostrantsev v Rossii* (St. Petersburg, 1854), and A. S. Muliukin, *Ocherki po istorii iuridicheskogo polozheniia inostrannykh kuptsov v Russkom gosudarstve* (Odessa, 1912).

[3] *ASEI* 1, no. 658; see also charters of grant incorporated in a judgment charter of 1543, N. P. Likhachev, *Sbornik aktov sobrannykh v arkhivakh i bibliotekakh* (St. Petersburg, 1895), no. 10. Grand Princess Mariia Iaroslavna was the wife of Grand Prince Vasilii II Vasil'evich Temnyi, daughter of

Prince Iaroslav Vladimirovich of Serpukhov-Borovsk. She entered holy orders under the name of Marfa in 1478 and died July 4, 1484. By the terms of Vasilii II's will, written in 1461 or 1462, she held as a life estate the Sreten'e half of Rostov, in addition to scattered holdings in other principalities and one half of the Moscow and Nizhnyi Novgorod customs. When Ivan III purchased the second half of Rostov in 1474/1475, he gave it to his mother for her lifetime; see *ASEI* 1: p. 617; R. C. Howes, *The Testaments of the Grand Princes of Moscow* (Ithaca, N.Y., 1967), pp. 24–26, 43, 44, 46, 92. For some charters of grant issued by Grand Princess Mariia, see *ASEI* 1, nos. 246, 247, 248, 327, 341, 349, 399, 451, 502.

[4] For examples and discussion, see Meichik, *Gramoty XIV–XV vv.*, p. 34.

[5] See, for example, *AFZKh* 1, no. 249, where Metropolitan Gerontii asked the Grand Prince to intervene.

[6] For a study of the development and functions of this chancery, see S. O. Shmidt, "Chelobitennyi prikaz v seredine XVI stoletiia," *Izvestiia Akademii Nauk SSSR, Seriia Istorii i filosofii* 7, no. 5 (1950): pp. 445–458.

[7] Letter of 1408 or 1413, *Akty istoricheskie* (5 v., St. Petersburg, 1841–1842) 1, no. 16. See also Dmitriev, *Istoriia sudebnykh instantsii*, pp. 144–146. A brief statement on the responsibility of the tsar to establish justice accompanies reference to the decree on local-government reforms and the abolition of the old system of vicegerents in 1555–1556; *Polnoe sobranie russkikh letopisei* (31 v., St. Petersburg-Moscow, 1846–1968)

was the highest legal authority in his realm, acting as legislator, judge, and court of last resort.

Until the second half of the fifteenth century Muscovite governmental administration was marked by its "personal" quality. As the state's territory grew, however, and administrative complexity increased, personal administration of justice by the Grand Prince became impossible.[8] More and more judicial responsibility was delegated to the sovereign's agents—his sons, his boiars, his scribes, his secretaries. In charters granting the right to trial by the sovereign, the Grand Prince usually declared that he himself, his trusted boiar (*boiarin vvedennyi*, member of the inner circle of advisers), or whomever he should appoint, would act as judge.[9]

In addition to the court of the Grand Prince, the Sudebniki refer to the court of the Grand Prince's sons.[10] Evidence from the judgment charters suggests that this court was established well before 1497. Ivan Molodoi, eldest son of Ivan III, served as a judge from 1485 until his death in 1490.[11] A judgment charter from this period provides some indication as to Ivan Molodoi's role as his father's agent. The lower-court judge, Kuzma Klimentiev, had agreed to refer a case concerning deserted land to higher authorities for de-

cision. When Kuzma Klimentiev and the litigants appeared in the upper court before Mikita Vasil'evich Beklemishev, Klimentiev was ordered to arrange a time for both litigants to appear before Grand Prince Ivan Ivanovich (Molodoi), after he returned from Tver', "because Grand Prince Ivan Vasil'evich of All Rus' had ordered that land trials be deferred until his son, the Grand Prince, [arrived]."[12] Ivan Molodoi gave the final decision in other *doklad* cases,[13] and judgment charters have survived in which his was the court of first and only instance.[14] The Sudebnik provided that the court of the Grand Prince's sons be staffed with a secretary, undersecretary, and seal-keeper. As noted above (Chapter I), the men who wrote the judgment charters were frequently remiss in recording these details, particularly in the early period. We do have the names of two secretaries from Ivan Molodoi's court—Fedor Kuritsyn and Vasilii Dolmatov—both of whom were later entrusted with great responsibilities by Ivan III. In addition to the Grand Prince's secretaries, the boiars Vasilii Fedorovich Saburov and Vasilii Fedorovich Obrazets were present at Ivan Molodoi's court. Despite the incompleteness of the records, the court of Ivan Molodoi appears to have been equal in authority to that of his father. We have no evidence of cases from it going on *doklad* to his father's court; presumably, however, Ivan III could have stepped in if he had so desired.

Other sons of the Grand Prince also tried cases: Vasilii Ivanovich, eldest son of Ivan III and Sophia,[15] and Ivan Molodoi's son Dmitrii Ivanovich.[16] Apparently this was a right of the heir to the throne rather than a right of the Grand Prince's "sons" in general. Surviving judgment charters from Ivan Molodoi's court were issued between 1485 and 1490. During this period he was co-ruler with his father. Vasilii presided in the court sometime between 1495 and 1497, and again from March, 1499, while extant judgment charters issued by Dmitrii are all dated 1498, the year in which his grandfather named him co-ruler.

As we have seen, the Grand Prince found it increasingly necessary to delegate a large part of his judicial work to others for execution, and even provided for this eventuality in his charters of grant. References in the Sudebniki and data from the judgment charters provide

13, pt. 1, pp. 267–268. Vernadsky believes that the author of this essay was the priest Sil'vestr, or Metropolitan Makarii in collaboration with Sil'vestr; George Vernadsky, *The Tsardom of Moscow* (2 v., New Haven and London, 1969): p. 84. Zimin suggests the author may have been Adashev; A. A. Zimin, *Reformy Ivana Groznogo* (Moscow, 1960), pp. 429–431.

   [8] For a study of the Muscovite state's response to the new pressures and problems resulting from expansion, with emphasis upon the delegation of authority, see Gustave Alef, "Reflections on the Boyar Duma in the Reign of Ivan III," *Slavonic and East European Review* **45**, no. 104 (January, 1967): pp. 76–123. On the military aspects of Muscovite centralization, see Alef, "Muscovite Military Reforms in the Second Half of the Fifteenth Century," *Forschungen zur osteuropäischen Geschichte* **18** (1973): pp. 73–108. For more general studies of Ivan III's reign, see J. L. I. Fennell, *Ivan the Great of Moscow* (London, 1961); K. V. Bazilevich, *Vneshniaia politika Russkogo tsentralizovannogo gosudarstva* (Moscow, 1952); L. V. Cherepnin, *Obrazovanie Russkogo tsentralizovannogo gosudarstva na Rusi v XIV–XV vekakh* (Moscow, 1960).

   [9] For examples of such charters of grant, see *ASEI* **2**, nos. 169, 266, 278, 300, 301, 359; *ASEI* **3**, nos. 72, 75, 82, 92, 96, 97, 98, 101, 109, 179, 187, 240, 241, 243. See also M. F. Vladimirskii-Budanov, *Obzor istorii russkago prava* (6th ed., St. Petersburg-Kiev, 1909), pp. 632–633, n. 2.

   [10] 1497 Sudebnik, articles 21, 22, 24; 1550 Sudebnik, articles 28, 37, 38, 39.

   [11] See Cherepnin, *Russkie feodal'nye arkhivy* **2**: p. 237 Early judgment charters were frequently undated. In order to ascertain the approximate time a charter was issued, the researcher may have to turn to extrinsic evidence. The cases tried by Ivan Molodoi have been dated in accordance with the years during which he was a Grand Prince. Since Ivan died in 1490, that year is the latest possible date. A case of 1493/1494 (7002) is recorded as being tried on *doklad* before "Grand Prince" Ivan Ivanovich "when he was in Kostroma"; *AFZKh* **1**, no. 248. Perhaps the date became confused by later copyists, and the document should be dated 1490 or before.

   [12] *ASEI* **1**, no. 523.
   [13] See, for example, *ASEI* **1**, nos. 524, 525, 537, 538, 539; *ASEI* **2**, nos. 481, 483.
   [14] *ASEI* **1**, nos. 521, 522.
   [15] *ASEI* **1**, no. 628, and p. 635, n. 628; *ASEI* **3**, nos. 208, 209.
   [16] *AFZKh* **1**, nos. 117, 259, 308; *ASEI* **2**, no. 416; Dmitrii Ivanovich "ordered that the seal of his grandfather the Grand Prince be attached to the [trial] record in the year 7000 and six (1498)." In a judgment charter of 1505/1506, incorporated as evidence in a 1511 trial, the plaintiff refers to an earlier suit against the same defendants, which had been heard on *doklad* by "the Grand Prince's grandson, Dmitrei Ivanovich," who had appointed Fedor Kozhin as judge in the court of first instance; *AFZKh* **1**, no. 309.

some clues about the early stages of delegating authority, although the precise lines of subordination remain unclear.

The development of an organized judicial hierarchy was a very slow and seemingly haphazard process, for which we have much less specific evidence than would be desirable. The Grand Prince turned over some of his judicial work to his sons. In other instances, it would appear, judicial matters came to be handled on a pattern established in other areas of administrative practice. For example, no unified system was developed to collect Moscow's taxes from the former patrimonial principalities incorporated into the central state. Income from each former principality was obtained separately, the collection being entrusted to a special land administrator. Gradually, in accord with the general system of the time, all affairs of a given principality reached the sovereign through the particular official in charge of the territory, and subsequently even the lawsuits of that area's privileged people were dealt with by that same administrator.[17]

The Grand Prince might select his agent on a purely personal basis. He often turned over some of his judicial duties to the leading boiars. From among the boiars in general, a special category of trusted boiars, those "admitted to the palace" (*boiare vvedennye*) who formed the Grand Prince's council, took form in the first half of the fifteenth century. These men served constantly as advisers of the ruler, and carried out commissions entrusted to them connected with any and all questions of state administration. Various matters might also be tried before these boiars: cases involving privileged people with charters of grant, cases referred to them from the lower courts, cases referred to them for final decision or arbitration in those instances when the two judges of a joint court remained at variance.[18]

Apparently the Grand Prince appointed boiar judges for particular cases on an *ad hoc* basis, probably for reasons of convenience at the moment. We find an indication of this in a 1494 case, decided on *doklad* by Prince Ivan Iur'evich Patrikeev. Plaintiffs from the Simonov Monastery, appearing before the lower-court judge Vasilii Chubar, declared that their archimandrite had petitioned Ivan III, complaining that the defendants had sown grain in the monastery's land and mowed the monastery's meadows. "And the sovereign Grand Prince ordered Prince Ivan Iur'evich [Patrikeev] to give thee as a judge [in our suit]."[19] Since many of the extant documents cannot be dated precisely, however, the question remains open. It is possible that certain boiars were appointed to hear cases for limited periods of time. Yet nowhere do we find an explicit statement that a particular boiar was in charge of *doklad* cases for a certain month or year, or had been designated to handle all cases of a certain kind or from a particular area.

At first the Grand Prince judged together with his boiars, but apparently the boiars' judicial competence became independent to some extent during the fifteenth century, since the 1497 Sudebnik distinguishes the Grand Prince's court from that of the boiars. In a recent Soviet interpretation, the boiar court is given a very definite structure, three different levels with varying competence. There was the boiar court conducted at the end of the 1490's by I. Iu. Patrikeev with the participation of the Grand Prince's secretaries; this court decided cases in the final instance. Then there was the boiar court which gave decisions after referring cases to the Grand Prince. Finally there was the court of a judge to whom a case had been especially entrusted, with decisions reached after reference to the boiar court headed by Prince Patrikeev.[20]

At first glance this scheme appears to show a clearly defined and established judicial hierarchy. Yet it tells us nothing about the actual operation of the system. Judgment charters are cited as the basis for this court outline; but in each instance, the examples of cases tried at all three levels involve the same men as court officials and judges. Thus, while the judgment charters can be pigeonholed according to the categories outlined above, the documents themselves do not provide enough data to support a fixed classification of the court structure or judicial hierarchy. The documents never state that a case was tried in a particular court. One can merely make assumptions on the basis of the judges' identity and the level at which a final decision is given. The judgment charters include no explicit statements concerning the competence of a particular court, and do not indicate why a boiar could make final decisions in some cases while others, seemingly of the same nature, were referred to the Grand Prince. All we know

[17] Dmitriev, *Istoriia sudebnykh instantsii*, p. 121.

[18] The boiar council (Boiarskaia Duma) was the chief advisory body which assisted the Grand Prince in governing his realm. Despite much scholarly attention to the problem, the question of the responsibilities and functions of the Duma remains controversial. The classic study is V. O. Kliuchevskii, *Boiarskaia duma drevnei Rusi* (5th ed., Petrograd, 1919). Even the personnel of the Duma has not yet been identified completely, and much research remains to be done in order to determine the functions of the various members. For initial studies in this direction, see S. B. Veselovskii's works, particularly his "Explanatory Notes to the Documents" in *ASEI* 1: pp. 590–637, *Issledovaniia po istorii oprichniny* (Moscow, 1963), and *Issledovaniia po istorii klassa sluzhilykh zemlevladel'tsev* (Moscow, 1969); A. A. Zimin, "Sostav boiarskoi dumy v XV–XVI vekakh," *Arkheograficheskii ezhegodnik za 1957 god* (Moscow, 1958), pp. 41–87, supplemented by Alef, "Reflections," *passim*, especially pp. 110–123; A. L. Stanislavskii, "Opyt izucheniia boiarskikh spiskov kontsa XVI-nachala XVII v.," *Istoriia SSSR*, 1971, no. 4: pp. 97–110; S. P. Mordovina and A. L. Stanislavskii, "Boiarskie spiski kontsa XVI-nachala XVII veka kak istoricheskii istochnik," *Sovetskie arkhivy*, 1973, no. 2: pp. 90–96; R. O. Crummey, "The Reconstitution of the Boiar Aristocracy, 1613–45," *Forschungen zur osteuropäischen Geschichte* 28 (1973): pp. 187–220.

[19] *ASEI* 2, no. 409.

[20] *Sudebniki XV–XVI vekov*, pp. 42–43.

is that some cases were decided in the final instance by the boiar court. In fact, the documents used as evidence for the above interpretation would lead to an opposite conclusion: apparently, under varying circumstances, the same court officials would have different degrees of authority.

Beginning in the 1490's, the trial of land cases was on occasion entrusted to the scribes who were in charge of drawing up the land cadastres.[21] The cases might be decided by one scribe independently, with no report to the sovereign,[22] the decision might be made after referring the case to the Grand Prince,[23] or the case might be decided "upon instructions of the Grand Prince."[24]

The delegated judges (sometimes known as *dannye sud'i*) formed yet another category. These officials were designated as judges of the central or local administration for examining a stated matter. They might be important members of the judicial hierarchy, but more often were officials of lower rank, whom the higher judges instructed to investigate a case. On occasion they conducted only a part of the trial, for example, a personal examination of disputed land or a local inquest; in other circumstances they might hear the entire case. Yet, after carrying out such tasks, they placed the entire matter for decision before the judge who had appointed them.[25]

A case tried sometime between 1473 and 1489 provides a good illustration, since it is one of the few which contain any information on pre-trial procedure. The judgment charter incorporates the text of Ivan III's order to Ivan Sukhoi, instructing him to go to the land in question and try the case between the metropolitan's people and the people of Prince Boris, "and having tried [the matter], tell me, the Grand Prince." At the conclusion of the trial, Sukhoi set a time for both litigants to appear before the Grand Prince. On the designated date, he presented both parties before Ivan III "and told the Grand Prince about the trial which he had conducted (*i sud svoi velikomu kniaziu skazal*)." Ivan III thereupon gave his decision.[26] The clarity of the judge-Grand Prince relationship in this case is a rare exception. In general, the judgment charters simply do not provide such information.

The activities of one judge around the turn of the century indicate that the same man could perform a number of different services for the sovereign, with the degree of authority granted him varying from one instance to another. Vasilii Ivanovich Golenin was a descendent of the Rostov princes who entered the service of Grand Prince Ivan III and his son Vasilii.[27] He served the Muscovite ruler in a number of capacities: as a military servitor,[28] as scribe (*pisets*) in charge of drawing up the land cadastres for the Pereiaslavl' and Moscow districts,[29] and, for a brief period beginning in 1500/1501, as a palace-land adminstrator (*dvoretskii*).[30] Upon Ivan III's orders, Prince Golenin also measured off the boundaries of Dmitrov, Ruza, and Zvenigorod, which the Grand Prince bestowed upon his son Iurii.[31]

In addition to his other duties, Golenin was entrusted with a variety of judicial responsibilities. Judges who tried cases "upon written instructions" usually received them from the Grand Prince. In 1498, however, the scribe Prince Vasilii Ivanovich Golenin instructed Danilo Krotkii to try a case, later heard the case on *doklad*, and ordered a judicial duel to decide the matter. When one witness failed to appear for the duel, the case was heard on *doklad* for the second time by Grand Prince Dmitrii Ivanovich.[32] Golenin decided certain

[21] See Cherepnin, *Russkie feodal'nye arkhivy* 2: p. 237.
[22] *ASEI* 1, no. 581; *ASEI* 3, no. 105; *AFZKh* 1, nos. 114, 254, 258.
[23] *ASEI* 3, no. 50; Likhachev, *Sbornik*, no. 10.
[24] *ASEI* 1, no. 658; *ASEI* 2, nos. 309, 310; *ASEI* 3, nos. 221, 223; *AFZKh* 1, nos. 306, 309; *AIu*, no. 15; *Akty, otnosiashchiesia do iuridicheskago byta drevnei Rossii*, ed. Nikolai Kalachov (3 v., St. Petersburg, 1857–1884) 1, no. 6 (hereafter cited as *AIuB*).
[25] For an example of a document ordering the appointment of a judge from among the Novgorod petty nobles (*deti boiarskie*) to hear a case, see *Dopolneniia k aktam istoricheskim* (12 v., St. Petersburg, 1846–1875) 1, no. 51, pt. 1, p. 72. See also Dmitriev, *Istoriia sudebnykh instantsii*, p. 151.
[26] *AFZKh* 1, no. 249.

[27] *Vremennik imperatorskogo obshchestva istorii i drevnostei Rossiiskikh* 10 (1851), Materialy, pp. 38, 140–141, 229; A. V. Ekzempliarskii, *Velikie i udel'nye kniaz'ia severnoi Rusi v tatarskii period* (2 v., St. Petersburg, 1889–1891) 2: p. 43.
[28] *Polnoe sobranie russkikh letopisei* 6: p. 245, 20: p. 337; *Razriadnaia kniga 1475–1598 gg.*, ed. V. I. Buganov (Moscow, 1966), pp. 38, 42.
[29] The land cadastres were drawn up at various times between 1491/1492 and 1503/1504: see *ASEI* 1, no. 643, and notes to documents 624 and 628 on pp. 634–635; *ASEI* 2, nos. 25, 26, 46. For data on Golenin's work in land surveying, see Kashtanov, *Sotsial'no-politicheskaia istoriia*, pp. 206–211.
[30] *Drevneishaia razriadnaia kniga*, ed. P. N. Miliukov (Moscow, 1901), p. 28; *Razriadnaia kniga*, p. 31; *ASEI* 1, p. 635. He probably served in Tver', since he was sent there with Grand Prince Vasilii Ivanovich, within whose jurisdiction Tver' lay, and Ivan III's will refers to a separate Tver' *dvoretskii*; *Dukhovnye i dogovornye gramoty velikikh i udel'nykh kniazei XIV–XVI vv.*, ed. L. V. Cherepnin and S. V. Bakhrushin (Moscow and Leningrad, 1950), p. 363. For a discussion of the duties of the *dvoretskii* and the development of this administrative office, see A. A. Zimin, "O sostave dvortsovykh uchrezhdenii russkogo gosudarstva kontsa XV i XVI v.," *Istoricheskie zapiski* 63 (1958): pp. 180–205.
[31] *Sobranie gosudarstvennykh gramot i dogovorov* 1, no. 140; *Opisi tsarskogo arkhiva XVI veka i arkhiva Posol'skogo Prikaza 1614 goda*, ed. S. O. Shmidt (Moscow, 1960), p. 55. Golenin is mentioned in a land-exchange charter of December, 1499, as the scribe who had surveyed land in Dmitrov; *ASEI* 1, no. 624. On the Dmitrov principality, see A. A. Zimin, "Dmitrovskii udel i udel'nyi dvor vo vtoroi polovine XV-pervoi treti XVI v.," *Vspomogatel'nye istoricheskie distsipliny* 5 (Leningrad, 1973): pp. 182–195.
[32] *AFZKh* 1, no. 117. Golenin also gave initial instructions to a lower-court judge in a trial held in 1500/1501; *ASEI* 1, no. 635. This was the prerogative of a *dvoretskii* (see *ASEI* 1, p. 635) and the 1498 instance suggests that Golenin may have held the rank earlier or that he had this administrative

cases on his own, either conducting the trial through-out[33] or hearing the matter on *doklad*.[34] A judgment charter issued between 1499 and 1502 records that Golenin conducted the trial on the land, but referred the matter to the Grand Prince for decision.[35] In April, 1502, Prince Golenin heard a case on *doklad*. After the trial record had been read aloud, both litigants agreed that the trial had been as recorded. At this point the record often states that the upper-court judge ordered that judgment be given in favor of one party. In this case, however, we find: "And upon instructions of Grand Prince Ivan Vasil'evich of All Rus', Prince Vasilei Ivanovich ordered the judge, in accordance with this [trial] record, to give judgment in favor of the plaintiff. . . ."[36] Apparently Golenin had consulted the Grand Prince, although there is no indication that Ivan III heard the trial record or questioned the litigants. Prince Golenin heard another *doklad* case in August, 1502. After hearing the trial record, he was instructed by the Grand Prince to search for the original charter of grant (a copy was presented in court); after examining the original in the Grand Prince's archives, Golenin handed down his decision and instructions to the lower-court judge without further reference to the Grand Prince.[37] Golenin was still serving as a judge in 1510.[38] At various times, as we have seen, Golenin apparently enjoyed differing degrees of judicial competence. He acted as an original judge, a delegated judge, and an upper-court judge. His *doklad* decisions were given independently, with consultation, and upon instructions of the Grand Prince. At no point is there a reference to his connection (or lack thereof) with the boiar court or any notation concerning the scope of Golenin's competence. But his activities serve to illustrate a few of the many variations in types of subordinate authority revealed in the judgment charters.

The surviving judgment charters were issued primarily by the central courts in Moscow. There were, however, several other courts in the Muscovite judicial system. Regional judicial authority rested with the Grand Prince's city and rural vicegerents (*namestniki* and *volosteli*).[39] These officials might be appointed

with grants of full jurisdiction (*s boiarskim sudom*) or with limited jurisdictional grants (*bez boiarskogo suda*). Vicegerents with a grant of full jurisdiction had the right to give a final decision in cases involving bondsmen and in matters of higher criminal justice (e.g., arson, murder, theft, or brigandage).[40] Men with limited grants, however, could only hear such cases and send trial records up on *doklad*. They could not release a bondsman, issue a manumission or court decision regarding a thief, murderer, or other felon without referring the matter to a court of higher instance.[41] Their competence to hand down final decisions was thus limited to lesser matters. The vicegerent with a full jurisdictional grant enjoyed roughly the same competence as a boiar judge in Moscow.[42] It has been suggested that the later limitations on the vicegerents—the requirements that they refer cases previously within their competence to the central courts[43]—reflect the sovereign's attempts to strengthen central control over the activities of provincial organs of power.[44] One might suggest in addition that the central courts were probably interested in obtaining the income from the fees entailed.

Any vicegerent could, of course, refer a case to the Grand Prince's court for final decision,[45] while the sovereign himself retained the right of intervention in final decisions by his vicegerents, for example, on *zhaloba* (petition with complaint). In addition, the Grand Prince might entrust cases arising outside of Moscow to his own deputy (*tiun*)[46] or to his scribe (*pisets*).[47] On occasion vicegerents might turn over their judicial functions to deputies.[48] Within the limits set by the jurisdictional grants (for example, obligatory *doklad* in cases involving slaves), deputies could issue judgment charters independently.[49]

privilege as official scribe for Pereiaslavl', where the land in question was located. Kashtanov resolves the issue by suggesting that the 1498 case began not under Golenin but under Ivan III's son Vasilii, the case being decided by Ivan's grandson Dmitrii after Vasilii's disgrace (*opala*); Kashtanov also believes that the 1500/1501 case should be attributed to the early 1490's and that it records a trial heard by Vasilii Ivanovich, the future Vasilii III; Kashtanov, *Sotsial'no-politicheskaia istoriia*, pp. 53–54, 56.

[33] *ASEI* 2, no. 421.

[34] *PRP* 3, p. 234; *ASEI* 1, no. 635; *ASEI* 2, no. 419.

[35] *ASEI* 3, no. 50. See also *ASEI* 1, no. 628, a case tried by Golenin and heard on *doklad* by Grand Prince Vasilii Ivanovich (the future Vasilii III).

[36] *ASEI* 2, no. 336.

[37] *ASEI* 2, no. 337.

[38] Fedotov-Chekhovskii, *Akty grazhdanskoi raspravy* 1, no. 23; A. A. Zimin, *Rossiia na poroge novogo vremeni* (Moscow, 1972), p. 98.

[39] For recent attempts to determine the names of Muscovite vicegerents, see A. A. Zimin, "Spisok namestnikov russkogo gosudarstva pervoi poloviny XVI v.," *Arkheograficheskii ezhegodnik za 1960 god* (Moscow, 1962), pp. 27–42; A. P. Pronshtein, *Velikii Novgorod v XVI veke* (Kharkov, 1957), Appendix 3, pp. 259 ff.; Alef, "Reflections," pp. 83–91. Alef's study indicates that *namestniki* were not generally selected from the Duma.

[40] 1497 Sudebnik, articles 38, 40, 42.

[41] 1497 Sudebnik, articles 20, 43.

[42] *Sudebniki XV–XVI vekov*, pp. 66–67.

[43] 1550 Sudebnik, articles 62, 63. See also commentary in *Sudebniki XV–XVI vekov*, pp. 251–255.

[44] Commentary to article 20 of the 1497 Sudebnik, *Sudebniki XV–XVI vekov*, p. 68.

[45] See *ASEI* 2, no. 451.

[46] *ASEI* 1, no. 557; *ASEI* 2, no. 370; *ASEI* 3, no. 208.

[47] *ASEI* 1, nos. 581, 658; *ASEI* 2, nos. 309, 310; *ASEI* 3, nos. 50, 105, 221, 223; *AFZKh* 1, nos. 114, 254, 258, 306. For two cases involving runaway slaves, heard originally by the sovereign's deputies and decided on *doklad*, see *AIu*, nos. 21, 22.

[48] 1497 Sudebnik, articles 37, 38, 40, 41, 43; 1550 Sudebnik, articles 62, 65, 67, 68, 69.

[49] 1497 Sudebnik, articles 40, 43; 1550 Sudebnik, articles 62, 65, 67. For examples of cases tried by deputies of the Dvina vicegerents, see *Russkaia istoricheskaia biblioteka* (39 v., St. Petersburg, 1872–1927) 14, no. 17 (hereafter cited as *RIB*);

Since the Sudebniki were concerned primarily with fees and regulations for the system of central-government courts and provincial administration, many aspects of local justice receive no attention. Peasant communal courts were not regulated by the state and are not mentioned. No records of their proceedings have survived; in all probability peasants conducted trials among themselves orally and kept no written accounts. There is likewise no reference to courts at which town, district, or canton officials, such as elders, hundredmen, and tenmen, presided. The seignorial courts of the great landholders formed an independent sphere of judicial activity, as did the courts of the patrimonial princes and the holders of charters of grant. Within their areas of private jurisdiction, such people could delegate authority to their own judges and deputies.[50]

In addition to these secular courts a separate, almost parallel, system of church courts operated under the metropolitan's direction. As in other countries during the medieval period, Russian ecclesiastical courts exercised jurisdiction in a number of areas: cases related to marriage, problems between parents and children, questions of morality, wills and estates, religious issues such as heresy and sacrilege. The church courts also settled affairs of a religious nature involving members of the clergy. The metropolitan issued charters of grant to his own "metropolitan's boiars," giving them fiscal, administrative, and judicial privileges. His lands and those of the monasteries had their own system of vicegerents and administrative officials. Court cases could be referred to the metropolitan for final decision, or he could delegate such matters to be tried by others, often a council including abbots or archimandrites. Monasteries also held their own courts to judge the peasants living under their jurisdiction. The ecclesiastical court system's hierarchy was as complicated as that of the secular courts.[51]

When litigation arose between people subordinate to different judicial authorities, e.g., residents of different cantons, or a secular landholder and an ecclesiastical landholder, a joint or mixed court (*sud smestnyi* or *sud (v)opchii* or *obchii*), composed of a representative from each legal power involved, gave the decision. Under such circumstances, both judges presided and split the judicial fees.[52] In case the joint court could not resolve the issue, a third judge was selected to arbitrate the matter.

A trial conducted between 1490 and 1500 provides an illustration. The judgment charter states that Mikita, the deputy of Prince Fedor Fedorovich, and Petr, the deputy of Prince Dmitrii Semenovich, tried the case jointly and handed down the decision without bringing in a third party or referring the matter to either of the princes.[53] No information is given about the court except the names of the men. The term "joint court" does not appear. Unlike some other judgment charters,[54] this document does not indicate the position of the princes. They have been tentatively identified as Prince Fedor Fedorovich Alabysh and Prince Dmitrii Semenovich Kurbskii, who probably served as vicegerents in Velikii Ustiug.[55] The appointment of more than one vicegerent was apparently a common practice.[56] It is also possible, of course, that the princes were vicegerents in different cities or held other positions entirely. Thus the nature of the two jurisdictions involved in this joint court is not clear.

More commonly, a joint court was composed of secular and ecclesiastical representatives. In one instance, the deputy of the Zvenigorod vicegerent Dmitrii Davydovich Morozov and the monasterial deputy Sueto conducted a trial between a Zvenigorod town resident and the abbot of the Savvin Storozhevskii Monastery over rights to a deserted village. For decision, the judges agreed to refer the matter to their sovereign, Prince Andrei Vasil'evich Bol'shoi.[57]

A judgment charter issued between 1456 and 1464 states directly, "This case was tried by the joint-court judges (*sud'i s"ezh'i*)." The men who heard the case were Stepan Zapinkin, deputy of the Suzdal' vicegerent Klimentii Grigor'evich, and elder Iev, representing Archimandrite Isakii of the Efim'ev Monastery. Elder Okul of the monastery was in litigation over the

AIu, no. 19; *SGKI* 1, no. 76. According to the 1497 code, anyone who accepted the position of deputy automatically became a slave (article 66); in 1550, however, slavery did not result without an accompanying full-slavery document or slave document sent on *doklad* (article 76). For a recent study of the judicial-administrative and other functions of slaves in the fifteenth and sixteenth centuries, indicating that in practice many of the vicegerents' functions were generally performed by their deputies, see E. I. Kolycheva, *Kholopstvo i krepostnichestvo (konets XV–XVI v.)* (Moscow, 1971), pp. 54–75.

[50] *ASEI* 1, no. 447; *ASEI* 3, nos. 288, 319, 364, 477. For a discussion of courts and court officials in the 1497 Sudebnik, see Horace W. Dewey, "The *Sudebnik* of 1497" (Ph.D. diss., University of Michigan, 1955), pp. 90–123. For a discussion of judicial procedure in disputes between princes and their servitors, see Veselovskii, *Issledovaniia po istorii klassa*, pp. 476–479. Unfortunately no judgment charters of this type have survived.

[51] For a discussion of the church courts, see Dmitriev, *Istoriia sudebnykh instantsii*, pp. 96–114; Gorchakov, *O zemel'nykh vladeniiakh*, pp. 241–289; I. S., "O tserkovnom sudoustroistve v drevnei Rossii," *Chteniia*, 1865, bk. 1, pt. 1, Izsledovaniia, pp. 1–101; E. Golubinskii, *Istoriia russkoi tserkvi* (2 v., Moscow, 1901–1917) 1, pt. 1: pp. 332–444. For examples of ecclesiastical judgment charters, see *AFZKh* 1, no. 204; *AIu*, no. 16.

[52] 1497 Sudebnik, article 65; 1550 Sudebnik, articles 30, 74. On joint courts, see Veselovskii, *Feodal'noe zemlevladenie*, pp. 125–129.

[53] *ASEI* 3, no. 288.

[54] See, for example, *ASEI* 2, no. 458; *ASEI* 3, no. 390; *RIB* 14, no. 17; *AIu*, no. 19; *SGKE* 1, no. 76.

[55] See *ASEI* 3, pp. 538, 555. Their names do not appear on the list of vicegerents compiled by Zimin. A certain "Fedor Fedorovich" served as vicegerent in Kostroma, October, 1496; Zimin, "Spisok namestnikov," p. 31.

[56] See 1497 Sudebnik, article 65; 1550 Sudebnik, article 74; commentary to article 65 of the 1497 Sudebnik in *Sudebniki XV–XVI vekov*, p. 106.

[57] *ASEI* 3, no. 56.

meadowland of a deserted village with Stepan Nora, a peasant of Prince Semen Borisovich Gorbatyi-Suzdal'-skii.[58]

In a case tried between 1462 and 1464, the metropolitan's peasants were in litigation with the peasants of a village belonging to the Zvenigorod prince Andrei Vasil'evich Bol'shoi. Apparently the joint-court judges —Semen, chief land administrator for Metropolitan Feodosii, and judge Ivan Khvoshchinskii, representing Prince Andrei—doubted that they could reach agreement, since they had already named Grand Prince Ivan III as the third judge before the trial started.[59]

In addition to records of joint-court cases, several of the judgment charters record the presence of more than one judge at a trial. The documents frequently note that one or more boiars were there when the Grand Prince or a boiar heard a case. These men may have served merely as witnesses, but, on the other hand, they may have served as consultants to the judge. The question of judicial collegiality must be considered, particularly in those cases where more than one judge presided.[60] With regard to judicial collegiality, the judgment charters provide much less information than we would like. There are no statements recording a judge's turning to his colleagues for advice, but then, such an occurrence would probably have been considered an off-the-record event rather than an official procedural step. We likewise have no record of litigants conferring among themselves or with the court officials about presenting their evidence or about the procedural step which they should take next, but it seems likely that illiterate peasants, untrained in the law, might on occasion desire such advice.

As noted above, judgment charters for cases tried by a joint court usually give the names and source of jurisdiction for each judge participating, and the record indicates that both judges bore responsibility for the questions asked. Certain other judgment charters state clearly that several judges tried the case, apparently acting as a collegial body. One such set of cases covers the period 1490–1500; the same judges (Mikhailo Dmitrievich Shapkin and Ivan Golova Semenov) appear in each instance, with *doklad* to the same boiar (Prince Daniil Aleksandrovich Penkov). The judges conducted the cases together (e.g., "And the judges asked" . . . "And the judges examined the document"), and both men are named as giving the decision.[61] Records of trials conducted by the Beloozero scribes in 1504–1505 provide a second illustration. Each begins with the statement that the Beloozero scribe Vasilii Grigor'evich Naumov and his colleagues (*s tovarishchi*) tried the case. Thereafter, "the scribes" question litigants and examine evidence. At the end

Naumov alone is named as giving the decision. The other scribes (the same men in all cases) are simply named: "And at the trial with Vasilei Grigor'evich were his colleagues, Grigorei Asanskoi, and Gnevash Stoginin, and Zakhar, son of Mikula Gavinskoi."[62]

The majority of the judgment charters name the presiding official(s) only in the introductory formula, thereafter referring to "the judge(s)." A case of *ca.* 1501 suggests the possibility that more than one "judge" (perhaps the colleagues present) took part in the trial, although only the Grand Prince's scribe, Grigorii Romanovich Zastolbskii, is named.[63] Elder Frol, son of Tokar', and Kopos Bulgakov, representing all the peasants of their borough, were suing Vania, the metropolitan's estate manager of the village Kulikovo, for hamlets and deserted lands in the Kostroma district. As usual, the judge's questions throughout the case merely state "and the judge asked," but on several occasions the testimony suggests that more than one judge was presiding. The mixture of singular and plural forms was probably not a scribe's error, since the singular pronoun (*ty*) was commonly used in addressing the judge. Apparently the litigants at times addressed a particular judge (probably the one asking the question)[64] and at other times spoke to the entire group. For example, when suggesting on-the-spot examination of disputed land, the plaintiffs said: "Ride thou (*ty*), Sire judge, after us, we shall show you (*vam*) where the Triastino hamlet stood." Later, when the judge asked why they had kept silent about the matter for so long, they replied, "Sire, we have petitioned the Grand Prince about those lands many times, and the Grand Prince does not listen, and it is impossible to gain access to the sovereign, and we, Sire, now bring suit before you (*pered vami*)." When both parties called for the testimony of longtime residents, the scribe recorded: "And the longtime residents of both stood before the judges (*sud'iami*)." The plaintiffs' longtime residents, Iakush and his comrades, also declared, "Ride (*poedite*) after us, Sires, we shall show you (*vam*) the boundaries between the Grand Prince's lands and the metropolitan's lands." On the other hand, Iakov Mokeev and his comrades, the defendant's longtime residents, said, "Ride (*poedi*), Sire, after us, we shall show thee (*tebe*) the boundary between the Grand Prince's land and the metropolitan's." The concluding sentences of the case follow the usual pattern. The judge originally named as trying the case, Grigorii Romanovich, gave judgment. "And at the trial with Grigorei Romanovich were his colleagues: Prince Ivan Ivanovich

---

[58] *ASEI* 2, no. 458.
[59] *AFZKh* 1, no. 103.
[60] For a discussion of the collegial principle in Muscovite administration, see Likhachev, *Razriadnye d'iaki*, pp. 6–22.
[61] *ASEI* 2, nos. 285, 286, 287, 288, 289, 332, 334.

[62] *ASEI* 1, no. 658; *ASEI* 2, nos. 309, 310; *ASEI* 3, no. 223; *AFZKh* 1, no. 306.
[63] *AFZKh* 1, no. 258; see also *AFZKh* 1, no. 222; *RIB* 14, no. 17.
[64] Since definite and indefinite articles do not appear in the Russian text, it is impossible to determine if "the judge" or "a judge" is meant.

Ukhtomskoi, and Ivan, son of Kuzma Korob'in, and the undersecretary Iushko, son of Onufei." [65]

Judicial collegiality may have been a practical approach to the everyday operation of a legal system in which custom and tradition played a large role. A pattern of procedural steps and associated formulae had developed over the years. And even if he were well educated by standards of the time, the Muscovite judge had no opportunity for formal legal training. There were no lawyers and no law schools. His only methods of instruction were probably observation, experience, conversation with other judges, and the advice of his secretaries. As Bloch pointed out, however, in his discussion of West European judicial institutions, "the administration of justice was not a very complicated task, though it naturally called for a modicum of legal knowledge. Where written codes existed this amounted to knowing their rules more or less by heart or having them read to one. . . ." If customary law was involved, "it sufficed to have some acquaintance with this diffuse tradition." Finally, Bloch concludes, "it was important to know the prescribed gestures and the necessary phrases, which imposed a rigid formality on procedure. In short, it was all a matter of memory and practice." [66]

To supply such knowledge of practice from memory was apparently one of the functions served by a number of local residents who attended the trial. The judgment charters almost always include a list of the *sudnye muzhi* ("men of court") present. These men were thus easily identifiable if further dispute about the trial should arise in the future. Since testimony of such men was for many years the only method of confirming the authenticity of juridical documents, their presence at court was considered indispensable. For a variety of reasons, therefore, judges hearing land cases on the disputed territory did so in the presence of local residents; the Moscow boiars conducted trials in the presence of their colleagues: scribes did the same; finally, the Grand Prince himself judged cases in the presence of his boiars. [67]

If a case were sent to a higher court on *doklad*, and disagreement arose between the litigants concerning the record of the original trial, the "men of court" listed in the trial record could be called to testify. [68] On the whole litigants who appeared in a higher court for decision of their case tended to state that their trial had been such as the record indicated. In very few of the surviving documents do we find the men of court being summoned to testify. Yet a case tried between 1495 and 1499 indicates the procedure. After the trial record had been read aloud in the upper court, the plaintiff declared in response to the judge's question that the trial had been such, while the defendant disagreed. The judge thereupon summoned the men of court named in the trial record. When the constable presented the men of court before the superior judge, the original judge and plaintiff also appeared, but the defendant, who had been released on surety bond, had run away. Despite the defendant's absence, the judge had the trial record read before the men of court, whereupon he asked: "Did elder Efrem and Stepanko have such a trial in your presence as is written in this [trial] record?" The men replied: "Sire, we see elder Efrem before thee, but we do not see Stepanko; and, Sire, elder Efrem and Stepanko did have such a trial in our presence as is written in this [trial] record." [69]

Men of court not only served as witnesses but, in the provinces, also advised the judge concerning customary law. When the Muscovite government faced the problem of incorporating the former Beloozero principality as a Muscovite province, officials were sent to study local laws and customs. The data were then studied in Moscow and used in preparing the charter defining the competence of Muscovite vicegerents in the area. Article 19 of the Beloozero Ustavnaia Gramota (Administrative Charter) of 1488 requires that hundredmen and "good men" (*dobrye liudi*) from the region should represent the local population in court, so that they could be consulted by the judge. [70] A comment in the Pskov chronicle points up the importance of a vicegerent's familiarity with local custom. The Pskov chronicler remarks, concerning the appointment in 1510 of Prince Petr Vasil'evich Velikii Shestunov, that he had formerly been prince in Pskov, knew all the resi-

---

[65] When testifying, litigants and their witnesses address the judge directly, repeating the term "*gospodine*" (Sire) in almost every sentence. The exception which proves the rule is a case in which the plaintiff's opening "*zhaloba mi*" speech does not contain "*gospodine*"; *ASEI* 2, no. 458. One is tempted to assume that this must be the result of a scribe's error. *Gospodine* may refer to several judges as well as to one; for examples, see *AFZKh* 1, no. 103; G. N. Anpilogov, ed., *Novye dokumenty o Rossii kontsa XVI-nachala XVII v.* (Moscow, 1967), pp. 485–490; *ASEI* 3, nos. 56, 288. It is usually found after the second word in a clause, sometimes the third, and, on one occasion, the fifth ("A posle tekh khristian iaz, gospodine, tot navolok Dolgoi koshu. . . ."; *AFZKh* 1, no. 248).

[66] Marc Bloch, *Feudal Society,* trans. L. M. Manyon (2 v., Chicago, 1965) 2: p. 360.

[67] Dmitriev, *Istoriia sudebnykh instantsii,* p. 43; Iu. G. Alekseev, *Agrarnaia i sotsial'naia istoriia severovostochnoi Rusi XV–XVI vv.* (Moscow-Leningrad, 1966), p. 32. The presence of such men in court also provided a check against corruption

and other abuses. Judicial collegiality could serve the same purpose.

[68] Some judgment charters even have a "roll call" device, listing all those present at court several different times. This may have been done so that the name of each witness would be firmly impressed on the memory of all; for a good illustration, see *ASEI* 3, no. 390.

[69] *ASEI* 1, no. 595.

[70] For the text of the Beloozero *Ustavnaia gramota,* see *PRP* 3: pp. 346–357; for an English translation, see Horace W. Dewey, "The White Lake Charter: A Mediaeval Russian Administrative Statute," *Speculum* 32 (1957): pp. 74–83. See comments in George Vernadsky, *Russia at the Dawn of the Modern Age* (New Haven and London, 1959), pp. 102–104.

dents, and because he was so capable, people who had left Pskov were again assembling in the city.[71]

Whereas the 1497 Sudebnik merely stated that a steward (*dvorskii*), an elder (*starosta*) and outstanding citizens (*luchshie liudi*) must be present at vicegerents' courts,[72] their role was more clearly spelled out in 1550. The second Sudebnik decreed that the steward, elder, outstanding citizens, and wardens (*tseloval'niki*) were to sign cases recorded by the local-government secretary. After the vicegerents' secretary had made duplicate copies of the records, and the vicegerents had affixed their seals, the local representatives were to keep the copies in case of dispute.[73] Vicegerents and their deputies were not to hold court without elders and wardens; if there had been none in the district previously, they were to be elected in the future.[74] In case a court record were declared false during trial on *doklad,* the court was to send for the elders and wardens, who should bring their copy of the trial record, for verification. Their testimony, in conjunction with comparison of the two trial records and the signatures on them, determined authenticity—and the decisive element here was the sworn word of those local representatives who could not read and write.[75] Men for whom there was no bond could not be retained in custody unless they were first presented to the locally elected officials.[76] Since litigants could not bring suit for more than their own property was worth, the elders, wardens, and outstanding citizens also conducted investigations of such matters.[77]

With the local-government reforms of the 1550's and abolition in most areas of appointed vicegerents, the duties of elected officials in the provincial administration increased, since they were entrusted with judicial, fiscal, and police as well as administrative responsibilities.[78]

They handled both civil and criminal cases, in addition to various matters concerning land.[79] A judgment charter of January, 1571, records a case tried by the Dvina elective judges of both the upper and the lower halves of the region. Eleven wardens from both halves were present, and one from each group signed the document. The secretary of the local administration wrote the trial record and judgment charter.[80] A 1574 judgment charter records that the elected judges of the Vazhskoi district, after conferring with the wardens, decided to refer the case to the sovereign, who made the final decision.[81]

The judgment charters add little to our knowledge of the secretary's role during the trial, since, as a general rule, they simply note that secretaries were present or signed the documents. The law codes merely state that, in the majority of cases, the undersecretaries are to write the trial records, which the secretary is to sign. Yet our information about Muscovite secretaries (*d'iaki*) from other sources suggests that many of them were much more influential than the notations in the judgment charters would indicate.[82] Their increased importance may be reflected in the first article of the 1550 Sudebnik, which, unlike the law code of 1497, lists *d'iaki* among those who are to administer the tsar's justice.

During the sixteenth century, the growing bureaucracy provided an avenue of personal advancement. Consider, for example, the case of Ivan Mikhailovich Viskovatyi, who rose from the lower ranks of society to become an undersecretary (1542), secretary of the central office for foreign affairs (Posol'skaia izba; spring, 1549), secretary to the Boiar Duma (1552–1554 on), and then seal-keeper to Ivan IV (February 9, 1561). He was a leading diplomat and close adviser to the tsar.[83] Viskovatyi's place in Ivan's favor

[71] A. N. Nasonov, ed., *Pskovskie letopisi* (2 v., Moscow, 1941–1955) 2: p. 299. Petr Velikii held the rank of second-level Duma member (*okol'nichii*) and served as *namestnik* in Pskov from 1510 to 1514; see Zimin, "Sostav boiarskoi dumy," p. 49; Alef, "Reflections," p. 83.

[72] 1497 Sudebnik, article 38.
[73] 1550 Sudebnik, article 62.
[74] 1550 Sudebnik, articles 62, 68.
[75] 1550 Sudebnik, article 69. Article 62 of the 1550 code provided that elders and sworn representatives of the community, who were present at the vicegerent's court, were to sign the trial record—or to make their mark, if they could not write. Furthermore, the copy of the trial record was to be entrusted for safekeeping to those who could not write, obviously to eliminate tampering with the documents.
[76] 1550 Sudebnik, article 70.
[77] 1550 Sudebnik, article 72. The local officials were responsible for tax and service registers.
[78] There have been numerous studies of the local-government reforms. See, *inter alia,* G. B. Gal'perin, *Forma pravleniia russkogo tsentralizovannogo gosudarstva XV–XVI vv.* (Leningrad, 1964); A. I. Iakovlev, *Namestnich'i, gubnyia i zemskiia ustavnye gramoty Moskovskago gosudarstva* (Moscow, 1909); N. E. Nosov, *Ocherki po istorii mestnogo upravleniia russkogo gosudarstva pervoi poloviny XVI veka* (Moscow-Leningrad, 1957); idem, *Stanovlenie soslovno-predstavitel'nykh uchrezhde-*

nii v Rossii (Leningrad, 1969); Zimin, *Reformy,* especially pp. 418–437.
[79] Nosov, *Stanovlenie,* pp. 527–537.
[80] *AIu,* no. 23.
[81] *RIB,* 12, no. 4. A 1552 judgment charter refers to elected judges designated to try the case; Likhachev, *Sbornik,* no. 12. Unfortunately the first pages of the case are missing, but the conclusion of the case indicates that the designated judges sent the matter on *doklad* to the Nizhnii Novgorod *voevoda,* who in turn sent it to one of the Grand Prince's boiars.
[82] See generally Likhachev, *Razriadnye d'iaki;* S. O. Shmidt, "O d'iachestve v Rossii serediny XVI v.," *Problemy obshchestvenno-politicheskoi istorii Rossii i slavianskikh stran. Sbornik statei k 70-letiiu akademika M. N. Tikhomirova* (Moscow, 1963), pp. 181–190; Zimin, "O slozhenii prikaznoi sistemy"; idem, "D'iacheskii apparat v Rossii vtoroi poloviny XV–pervoi treti XVI v.," *Istoricheskie zapiski* 87 (1971): pp. 219–286.
[83] Veselovskii, *Issledovaniia po istorii oprichniny,* pp. 366–367. Not long before his execution in the summer of 1570, Visakovatyi "injured the honor" (*obeschestil*) of another leading *d'iak,* V. Ia. Shchelkalov. For other accounts of Viskovatyi's activities, see Vernadsky, *Tsardom* 1: pp. 37–38, 60–61, 67–70, 75–79, 87–88, 113–116, 127–129, and N. Andreev, "Interpolation in the Sixteenth-Century Muscovite Chronicles," *Slavonic and East European Review* 35, no. 84 (1956): pp. 95–115. Heinrich von Staden, who served in Ivan IV's *oprich-*

was taken by the secretary Vasilii Iakovlevich Shchel-kalov, who enjoyed the tsar's trust until the end of Ivan's life.[84] Shchelkalov's father had been an under-secretary in the Chancery for Banditry Affairs (Raz-boinyi Prikaz), his grandfather a priest, and his great-grandfather a dealer in horses.[85] In the latter part of the sixteenth century Vasilii Shchelkalov and his brother Andrei figured among the wealthiest and most powerful officials in Russia. The Shchelkalov brothers could hardly be considered as having been above inter-fering with due process of law in order to help their friends and injure their enemies.[86] Vasilii's name ap-pears in a judgment charter of 1584, the "case of the extorted deed," which records that he attempted to ob-tain a postponement in the proceedings on behalf of the co-defendants of Andrei Sherefedinov.[87] Defendant Sherefedinov was likewise a secretary and a powerful figure. He had been a so-called *oprichnyi d'iak*, a secretary of the *oprichnina*, who had been entrusted with many important commissions during the last twenty years of Ivan's reign.[88] Now, shortly after Ivan's death, he was accused of appropriating property belonging to a petty nobleman. With the sudden en-trance of the boiar Prince Vasilii Ivanovich Shuiskii as judge midway through the trial, the case took on polit-ical overtones, and it reflects the growing power strug-gle under Tsar Fedor Ivanovich.[89]

As noted above, the father of the Shchelkalov broth-ers had also been a Muscovite *d'iak*. Continuation of the profession within a family was not unusual. In some instances one member might follow the chancery tradition while another served the sovereign in a mili-tary capacity. The Moklokov family provides an illus-

tration. Three Moklokov brothers, Afanasii Semenov, Timofei Semenov, and Nikita Semenov, nicknamed Guba,[90] served as secretaries under Ivan III and Vasilii III. One of Guba (Nikita) Moklokov's sons, Fedor, who usually signed himself "Postnik Gubin," became a *d'iak*.[91] Guba's son Iakov, a petty nobleman (*syn boiarskii*), received lands on service-tenure, as did Bog-dan Fedorovich, the son of Postnik.[92] Iakov also appears as the tsar's deputy and judge in a 1547 judgment charter.[93] Vasilii Tret'iak Mikhailov Gubin Moklokov is mentioned as a petty nobleman under Vasilii III, for whom he performed diplomatic services.[94] There are numerous other examples of sons following their fa-thers into the bureaucracy.[95]

In addition to secretaries and undersecretaries, the court was staffed with constables (*pristavy*) and a variety of bailiffs (*dovodchiki, nedel'shchiki, praved-*

---

nina, reported that the seal-keeper Viskovatyi "was very proud, and one could be happy to get back the signed docu-ment from him within a month." Staden, *The Land and Government of Muscovy*, trans. and ed. Thomas Esper (Stan-ford, Cal., 1967), p. 16.

[84] Veselovskii, *Issledovaniia po istorii oprichniny*, p. 304.

[85] Shmidt, "O d'iachestve," p. 187.

[86] For accounts of their activities, see Likhachev, *Razria-dnye d'iaki*, pp. 124, 166–167, 191–217, 475–485; *Russkii bio-graficheskii slovar'* (25 v., St. Petersburg, 1896–1918) **24**: pp. 38–50. The Shchelkalovs were both state secretaries and were noted for their interference in matters of *mestnichestvo* and military administration. They were legendary for dis-torting genealogical lists and influencing the *mestnichestvo* order, compiling lists of administrative appointments; see Lik-hachev, *Razriadnye d'iaki*, p. 204; A. I. Markevich, *Istoriia mestnichestva v Moskovskom gosudarstve v XV–XVII v.* (Odessa, 1883), pp. 292–293. An outstanding example is a 1589 case, in which the Shchelkalovs altered documents because of their friendship with the Golitsyn princes; for the text of this case, see *Vremennik imperatorskogo obshchestva istorii i drevnostei Rossiiskikh* **14** (1852), Materialy, pp. 1–18.

[87] For the text of the judgment charter, see Iushkov, *Akty XIII–XVII vv.*, no. 220.

[88] Likhachev, *Razriadyne d'iaki*, p. 466, n. 2; Sadikov, *Ocherki po istorii oprichniny*, pp. 338–339.

[89] For an analysis of this case and its political implications, see H. W. Dewey, "Historical Drama in Muscovite Justice," *Canadian Slavonic Papers* **2** (1957); pp. 38–46.

[90] See *ASEI* 3, no. 390. On the Moklokov brothers, see Zimin, "D'iacheskii apparat," pp. 254–256.

[91] *ASEI* 3, no. 26. Tikhomirov believes that Postnik Gubin was probably the author of a chronicle account covering the years 1533 to 1547; M. N. Tikhomirov, "Zapiski o regentstve Eleny Glinskoi i boiarskom pravlenii 1533–1547 gg.," *Isto-richeskie zapiski* **46** (1954): p. 281. A judgment charter of 1551 records that the secretary Posnik [*sic*] Gubin testified concerning a judgment charter which he had issued previously to the defendant's father; Likhachev, *Sbornik*, no. 11. Posnik Gubin appears first in the list of *d'iaki* who remained in Moscow with Prince Iur'i Vasil'evich in the summer of 1557, while Ivan IV was in Kolomna on military matters; *Razriad-naia kniga*, p. 163.

[92] Likhachev, *Razriadnye d'iaki*, pp. 141–143. Bogdan Post-nikov syn Gubin appears in the service register under the year 1560, as the head of troops composed of Kazan' princes, Tatars, and newly baptized subjects of the tsar, in the right arm division of a force under Prince Ivan Fedorovich Mstislavskii sent from Pskov toward the Livonian border; *Razriadnaia kniga*, p. 184. A "Bogdan Gubin" is listed as a *d'iak* in the department of communications and transportation (Iamskoi prikaz) in 1613; *AFZKh*, 3, no. 54.

[93] *AIu*, no. 22. The case involved the return of a runaway indentured slave to Mikhailo Kolupaev, the son of another *d'iak*, Kolupai Priklonskii (Kolupai signed a judgment char-ter of 1528; *AFZKh*, 1, no. 222). Mikhailo and Petr, sons of Kolupai Priklonskii, had also brought suit in 1541 for the return of two runaway servant girls; *AIu*, no. 21. Mikhailo was a petty nobleman who served from Vladimir in the mid-sixteenth century; *Tysiachnaia kniga 1550 g. i dvorovaia tetrad' 50-kh godov XVI v.*, ed. A. A. Zimin (Moscow-Lenin-grad, 1950), p. 155.

[94] Zimin, "D'iacheskii apparat," p. 254. A Petrusha Moklo-kov also served as a *d'iak* in the first years of the sixteenth century (p. 255).

[95] The judge in a 1534 case was Fedor Gnevashov, son of Gnevash Stoginin; *AIu*, no. 20. His father, Mikhail Gnevash Mikulin Stoginin, had served as a judge in Beloozero at the turn of the century; *ASEI*, **2**, nos. 305, 309, 310, 336, 337, 338. Dmitrii Gorin, a secretary who testified in a 1551 case (Lik-hachev, *Sbornik*, no. 11), had been a treasury secretary in 1548 and was a secretary in Novgorod in 1550/1551–1554; see *AFZKh* 2, no. 230; Likhachev, *Razriadnye d'iaki*, pp. 249–250. He was probably the son of Maksim Gorin, a secretary of the Grand Prince at the end of the fifteenth and beginning of the sixteenth centuries; see *ASEI* 2, nos. 336, 337, 338, 421, 422, 429; *ASEI* 3, no. 50. For other examples, see Likhachev, *Razriadnye d'iaki*, pp. 162–166.

chiki), who handled such matters as arresting suspected criminals, summoning defendants and witnesses to court, arranging surety bonds, conducting investigations, and executing court orders and sentences.[96]

On the whole, one must beware of attributing too much order or system to the Muscovite administrative and judicial institutions, or of trying to apply modern concepts of procedure to their operations.[97] As N. P. Likhachev pointed out when discussing the workings of the chanceries,

". . . it is difficult to attribute concepts of bureaucracy or collegiality to the old patriarchal establishment of our *prikazy*." Practice and custom played a great role in the Muscovite government. No one thought about the systematic execution of a known juridical principle; they did the thing as was the custom, not being concerned that the principle of one-man administration was being mixed with the principle of collegiality, they knew the meaning and significance of the consultative-collegial principle not from a system of state law, but from a widespread maxim known to all: *"um khorosho, a dva—luchshe"* [two heads are better than one].[98]

Sometimes the government itself did not really know who was in charge of the court for a particular area. A charter sent to Novgorod in 1556 clearly illustrates this uncertainty. Directing the vicegerent and secretaries to carry out a trial between petitioners, the charter adds: "Your court will [be in charge of] that area, unless it (the area) is under someone else's jurisdiction (*budet tot pogost . . . sud vash, a ne v otkupu*)."[99] The judgment charters provide other examples, showing the uncertainty of the central courts about local conditions. One record includes among its final statements:

And after assessing [from the losers] the sum at issue the judge is to order fees taken from them in accordance with the Perevitsk administrative charter, and if there be no [such] charter, the judge is to take [fees] from them according to [the terms of] the Grand Prince's judicial [fee] list.[100]

Apparently confusion reigned, even in matters concerning the purse.

Yet much of the confusion, particularly concerning the court structure, may be the product of our sources. The men who worked within the system probably knew its operation very well and saw no necessity to record the obvious. Thus we are left with only a general impression—and many assumptions—about the court system in the fifteenth and sixteenth centuries. Apparently

it was possible in theory for almost any case to be handled by the Grand Prince in person. As judicial activity increased, however, the boiar judges and the *prikazy* took over more cases, with the Grand Prince's direct participation being limited primarily to trial over people who had been granted the privilege, and trial over the higher service classes. By the seventeenth century, however, the hierarchy had been established: legal punishment was decreed for anyone who turned to the court of the tsar and grand prince without knowledge of the courts of lower instance.[101]

III. LITIGANTS AND THEIR CLAIMS

The judgment charters are our best source of detailed information about Muscovite trial procedure. These documents show the court in action, providing concrete examples of the judicial process which supplement the fragmentary data in the Sudebniki. The trials recorded in the judgment charters illustrate several aspects of medieval Russian legal procedure: types of litigants and their use of representatives and substitutes, forms of proof (testimony, documents, several types of "God's justice"), and the respective roles of litigants and judges.

Who could bring suit in a Muscovite court? Apparently everyone—"neither sex, nor age, nor the legal position of the person would seem to have excluded him from this right."[1] Women and children could appear as plaintiffs, as could the clergy.[2] Priests and deacons, abbots and monks appeared in court not only as members and respresentatives of the ecclesiastical estate but also for themselves personally as private citizens.[3] Even bondsmen could bring suit, not only in the name of their masters,[4] but also in their own right.[5]

The judgment charters record trials between varied sets of litigants, from princes to peasants. Prince Danilo and Prince Davyd, sons of Prince Iurii Kemskii, brought suit against Princess Anna, wife of Prince Fedor Kemskii.[6] At the other end of the scale, the Grand Prince's beekeeper Fomka Tal'shanin sued Prince Fedor Davydovich Starodubskii-Pestryi.[7] There are trials between private landholders; for example,

[96] For a discussion of these officials and their duties, see *Russian Private Law*, pp. 28–32; M. V. Shakhmatov, *Ispolnitel'naia vlast' v Moskovskoi Rusi* (3 v., Prague, 1935–1937) 1: pp. 21–42. For English definitions, see *Dictionary of Russian Historical Terms*, pp. 13, 67, 101, 106.

[97] On this point, see Richard Wortman, "Peter the Great and Court Procedure," *Canadian-American Slavic Studies* 8, no. 2 (Summer, 1974): pp. 303–310.

[98] Likhachev, *Razriadnye d'iaki*, pp. 12–13.

[99] *Dopolneniia k aktam istoricheskim* 1, no. 51, sect. 11: p. 77.

[100] *ASEI* 3, no. 390.

[101] 1649 Ulozhenie, 10: art. 20; Vladimirskii-Budanov, *Obzor*, p. 628; S. V. Iushkov, *Istoriia gosudarstva i prava SSSR* (3d ed., Moscow, 1950), p. 302.

[1] Dmitriev, *Istoriia sudebnykh instantsii*, p. 167; see generally N. N. Debol'skii, *Grazhdanskaia deesposobnost' po russkomu pravu do kontsa XVII veka* (St. Petersburg, 1903).

[2] 1497 Sudebnik, articles 49, 52; 1550 Sudebnik, articles 17, 19.

[3] 1497 Sudebnik, article 59; 1550 Sudebnik, article 91.

[4] See, for example, *AIu*, nos. 21, 22.

[5] Iushkov, *Akty XIII–XVII vv.*, no. 128; *AIuB*, 1, no. 8. In these cases, the plaintiff is named as the "man" (*chelovek*) of his master. This term, "without an adjectival definition and with indication of a master, usually meant a bondsman"; *Dictionary of Russian Historical Terms*, p. 6.

[6] *AIu*, no. 13.

[7] *ASEI* 2, no. 496.

Matvei and Beket, sons of Grigorii Vel'iaminov, sued their brother Senia, claiming that he had sold their patrimony (*votchina*) to Semen Kuz'min.[8] Ivan Saraev, a private landholder, contested the claim of Efim Nikitin, a cantonal peasant, that the land in question was a part of Efim's hamlet and the Grand Prince's state taxpaying land.[9] Mikhalko Filatov brought complaint against the priest's sons Mitia and Sofonko.[10] Okish Oliunov and his comrades, peasants of the Vol'skaia canton, sued Gridia Teptiukov, the estate manager of Dmitrii Vasil'evich Shein (Morozov), for the hamlet Oleshinskaia.[11] The judgment charters also record suits between men from various levels of society which involved matters other than land. Khrap Oltuf'ev, for example, instigated proceedings against the servant boy (*parobok*) Sergeets, claiming that he had incited three of Oltuf'ev's slaves to flee across the border.[12] In yet another case, Ivanka, the "man" of Mikhailo Kaznakov, sued a certain Petrushka, Omel'ian's son, for recovery of money lent on a promissory note.[13]

The Grand Prince's courts also heard a few cases between ecclesiastical litigants. For example, the Suzdal' vicegerent presided in a trial between archimandrite Isaakii of the Spaso-Evfimiev Monastery and archimandrite Petr of the Rozhdestvenskii Monastery over the Vasil'kovo land.[14]

About three-fourths of the surviving judgment charters record litigation between laymen and churchmen.[15] Again we find varied combinations of litigants. Some cases involve secular landholders. Elder Isaiia of the Trinity-Sergius Monastery sued Prince Ivan Konstantinovich (Glupyi) Obolenskii, charging that he had crossed the boundary to plow the monastery's deserted village Zelenevo.[16] In suing the abbot of St. Cyril's Monastery, Leva, son of Aleksandr Zaitsov, claimed that the hamlet Shuklinskaia was his patrimony: "and, Sires, my grandfather Mikita and my father Aleksandr mortgaged that hamlet to Abbot Ignatei of [St.] Cyril's [Monastery] in [the amount of] three Novgorod rubles,

and for interest, Sires, they (the people of the monastery) were to plow that hamlet; and now, Sires, I [am trying to] redeem that hamlet from them, and, Sires, they will not return that hamlet to me, and they will not take the money."[17] Lev Ivanovich, his sister-in-law Ovdot'ia, wife of Gavrilo Ivanovich, and his brother Dmitrii Ivanovich brought complaint against Abbot Trifon of St. Cyril's Monastery and his brethren: "Sire, they are depriving us of judicial rights and tribute [in] the hamlet Mikhalevskaia Garkavoe in our patrimony Kistema."[18] Abbot Vasilii of the metropolitan's Prechistenskii Monastery was in litigation with Prince Boris Vasil'evich's petty boiars, Dmitrii Rozhov and his brothers Kriuk and Ostaf.[19] Other cases involve lawsuits between monastery authorities and townsmen.[20]

The largest number of these cases, however, involve peasants. Priest Grigorii of the Pokrovskii Monastery, for example, complained that two peasants of the Mikhailovskii borough, Rodiuka Onfukov and Nesterik Deshevkin, had erected a hut and storehouse illegally on his spring-crop field.[21] Priest Fedor and elders Iona and Vas'ian of the Pereiaslavl' Anton'ev Pokrovskii Monastery sued Tarasko Mamukhin and Kondratets, son of Danilko, peasants of the Argunovskaia canton, who had mowed the monastery's meadow.[22] Elders often went to court on behalf of the monastery. For example, elder Kas'ian of the Trinity-Kaliazin Monastery brought suit against the peasants Stepan and Aksen Shchelkov, who had moved into the monastery's new settlements without permission.[23] Elder Okul of the Spaso-Evfimiev Monastery's village Troitskoe sued Stepan Nora, a peasant of Prince Semen Borisovich Gorbatyi-Suzdal'skii.[24] Of course, litigation arose from both sides. The Grand Prince's peasants also brought suit against monastery elders and supervisors; for example, Ozarko Tregub and his brothers Gavrilko and Kharko, sons of Gridia, complained: "Sire, that is the forest of the Grand Prince's Pavlovskoe village and our new settlement; and, Sire, elder Nikon cut the forest, and, Sire, he erected an enclosure in our forest."[25] Other church representatives, in addition to monastery elders, also appeared in court. Iakush, the Chudov Monastery's estate manager, brought suit against cantonal peasants of the hamlet

[8] *ASEI* 1, no. 522; see also *RIB* 14, no. 17; *AIu,* no. 19.
[9] *ASEI* 3, no. 276.
[10] *ASEI* 3, no. 288.
[11] *ASEI* 1, no. 658.
[12] *ASEI* 3, no. 357.
[13] Iushkov, *Akty XIII XVII vv.,* no. 128; Senka, the "man" of Mikhailo and Petr, sons of Kolupai Priklonskii, representing his masters, brought suit against three "men" of Timofei Volynskii—the overseer (*prikashchik*) Shchetina, and Barych, and Mikitka the cook; *AIu,* no. 21.
[14] *ASEI* 2, no. 450; see also *AIu,* no. 1.
[15] Judgment charters were awarded to the victorious litigant, and many more documents have survived from monasterial archives, which were much more completely preserved. For comments on the survival of sources, see, *inter alia,* Ivina, "Sudebnye dokumenty," pp. 328–331; Samokvasov, *Russkie arkhivy.* A. A. Vvedenskii, "Monastyrskii striapchii," *Russkii istoricheskii zhurnal* 7 (1921): p. 49; Pokrovskii, *Aktovye istochniki,* pp. 24, 39.
[16] *ASEI* 1, no. 607.

[17] *AIu,* no. 15.
[18] M. F. Vladimirskii-Budanov, ed., *Khristomatiia po istorii russkago prava* (3 v., St. Petersburg, 1887–1889) 2: pp. 235–236; for some other examples, see *ASEI* 1, nos. 447, 557; *ASEI* 2, no. 411; *ASEI* 3, nos. 105, 477; *AFZKh* 1, nos. 204, 259; *AIu,* no. 16.
[19] *AFZKh* 1, no. 249; see also Likhachev, *Sbornik,* no. 9; *AIuB* 1, nos. 4, 7; *SGKE* 1, no. 76.
[20] *ASEI* 2, no. 332; *ASEI* 3, nos. 31, 56.
[21] *ASEI* 1, no. 582.
[22] *AFZKh* 1, no. 140; see also *AIu,* no. 20.
[23] *ASEI* 3, no. 173.
[24] *ASEI* 2, no. 458; for similar cases, see *ASEI* 2, nos. 229, 285, 334; *ASEI* 3, no. 223.
[25] *ASEI* 1, no. 581; for similar cases, see *ASEI* 2, nos. 285, 286, 288, 309, 310, 375.

Zubtsovo, Ivan and Fedor Soloninin,[26] while the peasant Andrei Pelepelkin contested rights to the deserted village Popkovo with Senka, the metropolitan's manager for the village Biserovo,[27] and Ivashko Pavlov, elder of the Lukovskii cantonal subdivision (*pogost*), sued Chebotai, estate manager of the Beloozero Resurrection Monastery, for a floodland meadow.[28]

Local officials likewise became parties to suits. For example, Sava, supervisor (*kelar'*) of the Trinity-Serguis Monastery, sued the Mishutino hundredman Malyga,[29] and Aristik Ivashkov and Kozlok, son of Vasilii, peasants of Metropolitan Gerontei, were in litigation with the Shakhovo hundredman Nekras Levonov.[30]

Peasants living under the jurisdiction of the church, as the previous example shows, became parties to suits in their own right. There are many other illustrations. Gavrilko, son of the priest Matvei, complained that the metropolitan's peasants Mikitka, and Andreiko, and Vlasko, and Gridka, would not get out of his hamlet Vasil'evskaia Goliamova.[31] The metropolitan's Miliatino peasants of the Boris and Gleb Monastery, Palka Krivoi and Maksimko and Ileiko, charged that the Grand Prince's Ivashov peasants, Semenko Zlobai and Ivashko Fedotov and Rodiuka Okulov, had erected homesteads in the monastery's deserted villages, on land which the plaintiffs had been plowing for thirty years.[32] In another case we find a direct one-to-one confrontation between Ivan Onisimov, a peasant of St. Cyril's Beloozero Monastery, and Martynko Kosiak, a peasant of the Siamskaia canton.[33] And in a slight variation, Palka Viatka and his son Vas'ka, peasants of the Moscow Archangel Cathedral's village Plotniche, challenged the right of Ofonasko, a peasant of the Grand Prince's Luzhskoe village, to plow a plot of land which he claimed was part of his Danilovskaia hamlet.[34]

Church people had disputes with still other members of society. A judgment charter of *ca.* 1463 records a trial between the Simonov monasterial supervisor Nikita and Misailo, the Bylovo estate manager, on one side, and the "counted men" (*chisliaki*) Efremko, and his son Ivasko, and Ruka.[35] When accused by elder Fegnast Batman of the Ferapontov Monastery, Fediunia Gavrilov, Ivashko Deev and Fediunia Stashov ex-

plained: "We, Sire, are newcomer peasants (*liudi prishlye*); and, Sire, Orel the [cantonal] elder and the cantonal people Semen Nefed'ev and Fediunia Troshin gave us this floodland meadow."[36] In 1525 three of the metropolitan's peasants sued the men and peasants of Chudin Okinfov for damages from robbery and assault.[37] A 1543 case records a suit brought by a village administrator of the Spasskii Monastery against two "men" of Prince Ivan Fedorovich Mstislavskii, charging that they had taken over several of the monastery's hamlets, ordering the residents not to pay any taxes, and had driven away the peasants from one of them. As soon as the monastery's administrator had presented his complaint, four peasants who had been driven out of the one hamlet also brought suit against the defendants, charging them with assault and theft of various items, including livestock, clothing (from a fur coat to underwear), household goods (towels, dishes, spoons, frying pans), agricultural implements (plows with moldboard, axes, scythes, sickles), jewelry, money, and grain. The defendants then declared that they had no knowledge whatever of all this, that the land in question belonged to their lord, Prince Mstislavskii. They in turn brought a countersuit against the monastery's administrator and peasants, claiming that the latter had placed nine new settlements on their lord's land.[38]

In most of the cases cited above, only a few people are named as litigants on either side. Other judgment charters show that many members of the community could participate in a legal action. A 1499 case lists the following men as plaintiffs: the metropolitan's estate managers of the Iur'ev villages, Mikhal' Vnukov and Mitia Konstiantinov, and the metropolitan's peasants—Davydko Viatchanin from the Stepanovskaia hamlet, and Matfeiko Onuchin from Krivdino, and Oleshko Vasilev from Pavletsovo, and Timokha Durniaga and Sysoiko Matfeev from the Bogoiavlenskoe village, and Mitia Ishchein from Manachiukovo, and Vasiuk Meshcherin and Ivashko Kolegaev from Andreevskoe, and Ivashko Fedorov and Kharka Efimov from Poelovo.[39] Another plaintiff alleged, "Sires, that hamlet Krokhinskaia has been taken away from us by the Beloozero hundredman Ivashko Obukhov, and the townspeople Eska Timofeev, and Ivashko Sunshutin, and Oliunka Iakovlev, and Gridka the tenman, and Emel'ian Gavrilov and Ivashko Tebikin, and Pakhom Kemlianin, and Matiuk Maliakhin."[40] One of the Kaliazin Monastery's village administrators brought suit in 1551 against Menshik Shusherin, Ivan Fedorovich Vorontsov's administrator of the village Ol'iavidovo, and fourteen peasants.[41]

[26] *ASEI* 3, no. 48.
[27] *AFZKh* 1, no. 114.
[28] *AFZKh* 1, no. 306.
[29] *ASEI* 1, no. 430.
[30] *AFZKh* 1, no. 261.
[31] *AFZKh* 1, no. 129.
[32] *AFZKh* 1, no. 125.
[33] *ASEI* 2, no. 287.
[34] *ASEI* 3, no. 50.
[35] *ASEI* 2, no. 374. *Chislenye liudi* or *chisliaki* were "counted men, thus those included in the census registers as a separate group. The term was a holdover from the Mongol period. Liudi chislenye were mentioned in the princely wills and interprincely treaties of the Moscow royal house from the fourteenth to the early sixteenth centuries," *Dictionary of Russian Historical Terms*, p. 53.

[36] *ASEI* 2, no. 336.
[37] *AIu*, no. 17; see also *AFZKh* 1, no. 222.
[38] Likhachev, *Sbornik*, no. 10.
[39] *AFZKh* 1, no. 157.
[40] *ASEI* 2, no. 332; for other examples, see *PRP* 2: pp. 325–327; *AFZKh* 1, no. 227; *ASEI* 2, no. 337; *ASEI* 3, no. 31.
[41] Likhachev, *Sbornik*, no. 11.

A few judgment charters record that all the peasants of a community or all the brethen of a monastery were named as one party to a suit. A very early document (first quarter of the fifteenth century) records only that "Ulaske Tupichin summoned Viacheslav and all the residents of Kniazh'ostrov to court."[42] In two cases of 1485–1490 "elder Andrei and all the peasants" of the Zalesskaia canton were plaintiffs.[43] A Pskov document of June 11, 1483, records in so many words that Abbot Tarasei and all the brethren of the Sneto-gorskii Monastery were present before the lord of Pskov, the city council elders and the hundredmen, to bring charges against Abbot Lavrentii and all the brethren of the Kuzmodem'ianskii Monastery, who were there with their fellow defendants, the hundredman Iurii, the Egor'ev elder, and Ortem and Il'ia.[44]

Much more frequently, however, we encounter a situation such as that found in a judgment charter of ca. 1501: "the Likurzskaia [sic; Likurzhskaia] canton peasants Martynko Larionov, and Ermolka Fedorov, and Ontsiforik Ontonov, [for themselves] and in place of all the peasants of the Likurzhskaia canton, were in litigation with Nekras and Drozd, sons of Vasilei Iur'ev, the metropolitan's petty noblemen."[45] Apparently it was a fairly widespread practice for litigants to ask someone else to speak for them in court. The judgment charters record several variations in litigants' use of representation and substitution.

One type occurred, as in the case cited above, when all the peasants of a community were named as parties to a suit. For example, the canton elder Filia appeared in place of all the peasants of the Shakhovskaia canton.[46] Four peasants of the Almeshskaia canton—Volodia Istomin from the hamlet Bogoroditskaia, and elder Ivashko Komel', Frol's son, from the Kniazhsel-skie hamlets, and Martynko from the Troitskie hamlets, and Ivashko Muroshka from the Rozhdestvenye ham-lets—brought suit on behalf of all the peasants of eight-een hamlets.[47] In another case, peasants of the Minskii borough sent their elder and one peasant.[48] Three "counted men" appeared for all the other "counted men."[49] The Pekhorka hundredman, along with the tenman, the beekeeper, and the smith, petitioned the

Grand Prince on behalf of the entire Pekhorka canton.[50] Monastic communities might likewise send agents. For example, elder Ignatii declared in court: "I, Sire, answer for Abbot Trifon and for all the brethen."[51]

Another type of representation took place when several individuals, rather than the whole community, made up one side to a lawsuit. Under such circum-stances one or more of those designated might answer for their relatives or comrades. In one case a land-holder who brought suit for himself, his sister-in-law and his brother, was the only one to appear in court.[52] Basalai Ragozin, one of the metropolitan's petty noble-men, brought suit on behalf of himself, his brother Ivashko, and his comrade Fedko, son of Foma Sakharu-sov.[53] A judgment charter of 1499 records that the defendants, Fedor and Kostiantin Kuchetskii, answered for themselves and for their brother, explaining that Ivan was at their service-tenure estate in Great Nov-gorod.[54] The defendant in a 1530 trial answered on behalf of his "comrades," the co-signers of a promissory note for two and a half rubles, who happened to be his parents and brother.[55] One of the Grand Prince's beekeepers brought suit for himself and for his brother.[56] These arrangements were not confined to members of a family. For example, a canton peasant answered charges brought against himself and another resident of the canton.[57]

When only some of those named as defendants showed up for trial, they did not have to answer for accused persons who were absent. In one case the bailiff explained that he had gone with a warrant and seized the defendants present, but their comrades were in flight. The judge then questioned the defendants, Chudin Okinfov's man Kozel, and the peasants On-driushka Kirilov and Nekrasko Ivanov, who was ap-pearing for himself and his stepson Kostia, and they re-plied: "Sire we answer for ourselves, and [as for] our

[42] PRP 2: p. 195.
[43] ASEI 1, nos. 524, 525.
[44] PRP 2: pp. 325–327.
[45] AFZKh 1, no. 254. This appears to be a primitive or embryonic form of advocacy, to the extent that representatives assist or plead for their principals; see Black's Law Dictionary (4th ed., St. Paul, Minn., 1951), p. 75.
[46] ASEI 3, no. 221. As another variation, the elder of the Dolgaia free settlement also answered in place of all his fellow peasants; ASEI 2, no. 416; see also ASEI 2, no. 307.
[47] AIuB 1, no. 6.
[48] AFZKh 1, no. 258. The peasants of the Arbuzhoves' can-ton were represented by their elder and seven other peasants; AFZKh 1, no. 309.
[49] ASEI 2, no. 374. Six beekeepers represented their com-rades in a 1530 case; Likhachev, Sbornik, no. 8.

[50] ASEI 2, no. 381.
[51] Vladimirskii-Budanov, Khristomatiia 2: pp. 235–237; see also AIu, no. 16; in another case, two elders, one of whom was a weir keeper, appeared for the archimandrite and all the brethren, ASEI 2, no. 416; another judgment charter records that the archimandrite appeared for the brethren, ASEI 2, no. 400; in yet another case, the monasterial supervisor and a priest appeared on behalf of the archimandrite, ASEI 2, no. 409; an elder appeared for an abbot, AIu, no. 15; a monasterial servitor represented the archimandrite and all the brethren, AIuB 1, no. 7; see also AIu, no. 23. Trial procedure in Muscovy was extremely formal, and success in court depended to a certain extent on the ability of the litigant to employ the prescribed phrases and actions. For a discussion of the use of "specialists" as agents in court, see Vvedenskii, "Monastyrskii striapchii," pp. 38–42.
[52] Vladimirskii-Budanov, Khristomatiia, 2: pp. 235–237.
[53] AFZKh 1, no. 222.
[54] AFZKh 1, no. 157.
[55] Iushkov, Akty XIII–XVII vv., no. 128.
[56] ASEI 2, no. 496.
[57] AFZKh 1, no. 140. In another case one peasant appeared in court to bring suit on behalf of himself and seven comrades; AFZKh 1, no. 1a.

comrades, Chudin Okinfov's men Sukhoi and Andreika Vakhromeev, and Chudin's peasants Kuzemka Trufanov and Mikitka Kipreanov, Sire, we know not where they are and we do not answer for them." [58] Another defendant agreed to answer on behalf of twenty co-defendants, but not for the twenty-first, a certain Malsha, claiming that his master had never had such a man. [59] Defendants in other cases refused to answer for some or all of their comrades, but gave no reason. [60] One of the defendants in another case not only refused to answer for anyone else but disclaimed any responsibility of his own: "Sires, I do not know that meadow on which ye are standing; Sires, I did not mow the hay, nor cart [it] off, I know nothing [about the matter]; my brother Selka knows, he mowed the hay and took [it]; and, Sires, I have no concern with that meadow." [61]

Yet another form of representation was simple substitution—the man who appeared in court did so strictly on behalf of someone else, and was not himself a party to the suit. Again there are variations in choice of agents. Sons took the place of their fathers. [62] One man sent his son-in-law. [63] The Bishop of Riazan' sent his boiar. [64] One archimandrite was represented in court by a monk, [65] another by an elder, [66] and yet another by both an abbot and an elder. [67] A long-time peasant resident also answered in place of an abbot. [68] Other litigants, both plaintiffs and defendants, dispatched their "men" to handle their legal matters. [69]

Apparently the arrangements for representation or substitution were worked out through private agreements. The fifteenth-century judgment charters, with their abbreviation of data and cryptic references, provide almost no information on this aspect of trial procedure. A judgment charter of 1532, however, gives a more complete explanation. When Vasiuk, one of the defendants, appeared in court, the judges asked him if he was answering for his father and brothers and why he had failed to present the other defendants as he had promised to do. Vasiuk then declared that he was appearing on behalf of his father and brothers, and

that the other defendants could not come; Grigorii Kologrivov was ill, and his sons had gone to Kargopol', but "Grigorei [has sent] his nephew Onikei, son of Ivan Kurtiaev, and Oleshko, son of Maksim Boran'a Golova, and here, Sires, are Onikei and Oleshko before you." The judges then questioned the two representatives, who stated that Grigorii had sent them in place of himself and his sons. After this the judges turned to the plaintiff Matfei, asking whether he consented to bring suit against Onikei and Oleshko, and Matfei replied: "If, Sires, they have come [here] to answer in place of Grigorei Kologrivov and his sons, then I, Sires, do bring suit against them." [70]

Litigants were not the only ones to make use of representation and substitution during a trial. One witness who gave testimony was also speaking for his mother and brother. [71] Ivan Vasil'evich Sheremetev, plaintiff in a 1547 case, presented a promissory note and boundary record in support of his claim to half of the village Gravoronovo. When the authenticity of the documents was challenged, the litigants called for the testimony of the witnesses named in them and the secretaries who had written them. The bailiff presented three of the four witnesses who had signed the boundary record "and in place of Ivan Gavrilov his man Remez, bearing a document with his signature." [72]

Litigants' use of representatives and substitutes was not limited to the original trial. They also sent such agents to the *doklad* proceedings. A 1498 judgment charter records that the plaintiffs, Fedko and Andreiko, appeared in the higher court for themselves "and in place of their brother Iakush and in place of their witnesses Palka Nazemov and Sysoiko Andreev," and the defendants, the metropolitan's estate manager Sukhoi, and Vashuta Petrishchev, and Grachko Pakhomov, and their witness Tarasko Vasilev, appeared for themselves "and in place of their comrades"—six other defendants and four other witnesses. [73]

As the 1498 case shows, some of the original litigants might represent the others in the upper court. [74] In other cases, however, the original litigants were represented by a third party who, according to the record, had not taken part in the original trial. For example, at one trial on *doklad*, the lower-court judge presented "Tret'iak, son of Vasilei Vnukov, in place of the plaintiffs, the metropolitan's estate managers of the Iur'ev villages and hamlets, Mikhal' Vnukov and Mitia Kostin, and in place of the metropolitan's peasants Davydko Viatchanin, and Matfeiko Onuchin, and Oleshko Vasilev, and Timokha Durniaga, and Sysoiko Matfeev,

58 *AIu*, no. 17; see also no. 19.
59 *AFZKh* 1, no. 222; see also Likhachev, *Sbornik*, no. 12.
60 See, for example, *AIu*, no. 21; Likhachev, *Sbornik*, no. 11.
61 *ASEI* 3, no. 223.
62 *ASEI* 2, no. 496; *ASEI* 3, no. 288.
63 *ASEI* 3, no. 35.
64 *ASEI* 3, no. 319.
65 *ASEI* 3, no. 31.
66 *ASEI* 3, no. 208.
67 *ASEI* 2, no. 411.
68 *ASEI* 3, no. 56.
69 *ASEI* 2, no. 493; *ASEI* 3, no. 276; *AIu*, nos. 13, 17, 22. Some cases seem to reflect a double substitution. Senka, the "man" of Mikhail and Petr Priklonskii, who brought suit in 1541 for the recovery of two runaway servant girls belonging to his masters, appeared in court "in place of his comrade Khripun"; *AIu*, no. 21. Iakush Mikhailov, the "man" of the boiar Ivan Vasil'evich Sheremetev senior, appeared in place of the plaintiff, "his master's man Selchuk"; *AIuB* 1, no. 8.

70 *AIu*, no. 19.
71 *ASEI* 1, no. 447. Another witness also testified for his brothers; *AIu*, no. 23. In another case a son appears as a witness in place of his father; *ASEI* 2, no. 404.
72 *AIuB* 1, no. 5.
73 *AFZKh* 1, no. 117.
74 See, for example, *ASEI* 1, no. 582; *ASEI* 2, nos. 332, 337; *ASEI* 3, no. 173; Anpilogov, *Novye dokumenty*, pp. 485–490.

and Mitia Ishchein, and Vasiuk Meshcherin, and Ivashko Kolegaev, and Ivashko Fedorov, and Kharka Efimov.[75] Occasionally we find more than one substistitute. To cite one example, elder Aleksandr appeared in place of the defendant, archimandrite Venedikt, in the lower court, and Matveiko, Mikula's son, took elder Aleksandr's place for the *doklad* proceedings.[76] Men of court occasionally sent substitutes.[77] Even the judge did not always appear in person for *doklad* proceedings, but sent his "man" to present the trial record and litigants in the higher court.[78] On one occasion, two of the three original judges performed their duties in the upper court "in place of" their absent colleague.[79]

A judgment charter of April, 1502, records what must be the ultimate in substitution at the *doklad* level. The charter indicates that not one of the men who appeared in the higher court had attended the original trial. Nikita Tarasov, in place of judge Gnevash Stoginin, presented the trial record and "brought both litigants—Kuzemka, son of Gridia, in the place of the plaintiff, elder Batman of the Ferapontov Monastery, and Minia, son of Nason, and Gridka, son of Mikita Brodovskoi, in the place of the defendants Fediunia Gavrilov, and Ivashko Deev, and Fediunia Ostashov, and elder Orel, and Senka Nefed'ev, and Fediunia Troshin."[80]

While use of representatives and substitutes was at times necessary in court proceedings, the informal nature of the relationship between principals and their agents could be detrimental to the principal's interests. The agent might not have adequate knowledge of the circumstances surrounding the dispute, and thus not be able to present his side of the matter to best advantage. In the absence of precise instructions, he might keep back information during the trial or speak to excess. Since no written agreement bound him, a representative might send some other substitute in his place, or even work in collusion with his principal's opponent. Yet, despite the dangers and disadvantages, many litigants found it necessary to make use of agents. Attending a trial in person might mean traveling long distances, particularly for hearings on *doklad*. Court procedure was time-consuming and expensive, a factor which undoubtedly prevented many litigants from pressing their suits at all. Because of other obligations and responsibilities, it might be impossible for a litigant or witness to appear in court at the proper time.[81] Thus

it apparently became common practice during the sixteenth century for "outsiders" to offer their paid services as court representatives. A decree of March 12, 1582, states that there were certain petty noblemen who, "fleeing from service, go back and forth to the courts for others." The document complains of these people as of the worst false accusers, indicating that they accepted bribes from the opposing parties and failed in various other ways to represent the interests of those who hired them. The decree prescribes severe punishment for those guilty of such behavior, as well as penalties for any court officials who assist them.[82] Thus there were later attempts to correct such abuses, but the Sudebniki in general looked at a trial as an almost completely private matter, and interfered little, except on the financial side and in certain procedural matters.[83]

Once a Muscovite plaintiff had decided upon legal action, his first problem was to get the defendant into court. In the earliest period of Russian history, summons to court was a purely private matter. The plaintiff himself asked the accused to come to court, and if he met opposition, brought the defendant in with his own hands. In actual practice this method continued in use for a long time, despite decrees about the use of a constable. Gradually, however, the law enabled officers of the court to take over the duty of summoning and presenting defendants. In the era of the Russkaia Pravda, the plaintiff gave a "public summons" (*zaklicha*) at the market place. The Pskov Sudnaia Gramota gave the plaintiff a constable; they went together to summon the defendant by "public summons" beside the church, where the defendant had to go to hear it. Only in cases when this was impossible did the plaintiff and his constable go to the defendant's residence.[84]

At the time of the Sudebniki, a court official often went after the accused; the Grand Prince's or boiars' court sent a *nedel'shchik* (central-court bailiff), while vicegerents sent a *dovodchik* (provincial-court bailiff) or *pristav* (constable). As a preliminary step, the plaintiff presented a petition to the court, stating the cause of action and requesting issuance of a warrant.[85] The court secretary then discussed this petition with the constable to see if the case was worth the court costs involved for summoning the defendant (the Sudebniki list the walking-distance fee (*khozhenoe*) and riding-distance fee (*ezd*) for summoning defendants from various places).[86] If the costs of summoning the defendant did not exceed the sum at issue in the case, the secretary signed the warrant, for which he

---

[75] *AFZKh* **1**, no. 157; for other examples of such substitution, see *ASEI* **1**, no. 523; *ASEI* **2**, nos. 286, 334; Likhachev, *Sbornik*, no. 12; *RIB* **12**, no. 4.

[76] *ASEI* **3**, no. 208.

[77] *ASEI* **2**, no. 458; *ASEI* **3**, no. 276.

[78] *ASEI* **3**, nos. 40, 276; Likhachev, *Sbornik*, no. 8; *AIu*, no. 20. Another judge sent his son; *ASEI* **2**, no. 422.

[79] *ASEI* **2**, no. 332; see also Likhachev, *Sbornik*, no. 9.

[80] *ASEI* **2**, no. 336.

[81] Such complaints were voiced frequently by members of the middle service class in their petitions for court reform during the years preceding issuance of the 1649 Ulozhenie; see Richard Hellie, *Enserfment and Military Change in Muscovy* (Chicago and London, 1971), pp. 61–65.

[82] *Akty istoricheskie* **1**, no. 154, sect. 20: pp. 271–272.

[83] See Dmitriev, *Istoriia sudebnykh instantsii*, p. 173; Vladimirskii-Budanov, *Obzor*, p. 635.

[84] M. V. Shakhmatov, *Kompetentsiia ispolnitel'noi vlasti v Moskovskoi Rusi* (2 v., Prague, 1936–1937) **1**: pp. 11–12.

[85] As far as we know, these petitions of plaintiffs remained unwritten in the fifteenth century; Meichik, *Gramoty XIV–XV vv.*, p. 27.

[86] 1497 Sudebnik, articles 28, 29, 30, 44; 1550 Sudebnik, articles 45, 46, 62.

received a set fee, and gave it to the constable; otherwise, a bailiff's warrant could not be issued and the court in effect rejected the action.[87] The constable, upon receiving a warrant, either went after the defendant himself or sent an assistant. If the defendant lived under the immediate jurisdiction of the court which had issued the warrant and summons, the bailiff went directly to the defendant's residence, notified him of the plaintiff's charges, and set a date for the defendant to appear in court. The procedure was somewhat more complicated if the defendant resided in another city or canton. Under such circumstances the bailiff, upon arriving in the town or canton named in the warrant, had to present the warrant to the resident vicegerent or his deputy, who arranged to bring the defendant to the bailiff.[88] The defendant received a summons designating the time for him to appear in court.[89] He was then placed on surety bond (*na poruki*) to ensure his appearance in court at the designated time.[90] Friends and neighbors of the defendant usually provided the surety bond. Acting as a surety did not involve the same responsibility in all cases, since one man might guarantee that a defendant would appear in court, another that a defendant not only would appear but would remain every day that the trial lasted. If the defendant failed to appear, the sureties paid a fine, the sum at issue, and all losses. When the accused was, for some reason, unable to find guarantors, he was placed in custody, taken in chains to the place where the court met, and held there until the date set for trial.[91]

Unfortunately for the health and well-being—both physical and mental—of the constables, summoning defendants to court was not a mere matter of serving them with papers. In the fourteenth and fifteenth centuries constables met resistance from semi-feudal boiars with their own armed forces, constables, and crowds of peasants and slaves ready to help their lord. This opposition continued through later years. Even members of "black" (state peasant) communes at times resisted being put on surety bond, "liberating themselves" from constables. Hardest of all to handle were gangs of thieves and brigands, huge armed bands. When confronting such obstacles, the constable might have to lay siege to a landholder-defendant on his estate, to enlist the aid of "community action" against brigands or runaway slaves, or, if such help was insufficient, even make use of military force.[92] Thus in medieval Russia the plaintiff might encounter several difficulties simply in the process of initiating his suit.

Most judgment charters begin with the trial itself, including none of the pre-trial material, and few of the documents refer to the presentation of the defendant. Of those judgment charters which do include a notation on the subject, some refer to presentation of the defendant by the plaintiff, others to the use of a constable. A very early document (first quarter of the fifteenth century) merely states that the plaintiff summoned the defendants;[93] there is no indication that he brought them by force, and, considering the time period and the fact that he summoned all the local residents, it seems likely that the defendants agreed to appear. The plaintiff in a case of January 30, 1492, personally presented the defendants, saying, "and here, Sire, that Kostia and Nekliud stand before thee."[94] In a 1532 case, one of the defendants had agreed to bring the others.[95]

There are also a few references to the work of constables, some of which are incidental information given in the course of the trial. In one instance, the plaintiff's witnesses said that the defendant, Oleksa, had mowed the meadow illegally for two years, "and last year was the third year, and, Sire, the estate manager Gridia (the plaintiff) brought the Grand Prince's constable for that Oleksa in that floodland meadow."[96] In another case the plaintiff Vania, estate manager for the metropolitan, was testifying about previous litigation over the same land. He presented a default judgment charter, explaining that when the Andronikov borough chief Iakush and his comrades Kostia and Eska had encroached upon the land, the metropolitan's estate manager Iakush sent the Grand Prince's constable Oleshka Chubarov after them. They did not appear in court at the designated time, so Iakush had been given the default judgment. The judge subsequently questioned Kostia and Eska, asking why they had failed to appear in court, and they explained: "Sire, the Grand Prince's constable Oleshka Chubarov came to us in that meadow, and, Sire, we sent our borough chief Iakush to answer in that matter at the designated time, and, Sire, death came upon our borough chief

[87] 1497 Sudebnik, article 28; 1550 Sudebnik, article 44; I. D. Beliaev, *Lektsii po istorii russkago zakonodatel'stva* (3d ed., Moscow, 1901), pp. 414–415. Apparently a plaintiff desiring to continue his suit could himself assume the responsibility for bringing the defendant to trial; see V. Sergeevich, *Lektsii i izsledovaniia po drevnei istorii russkago prava* (4th ed., St. Petersburg, 1910), p. 603.

[88] 1497 Sudebnik, articles 31, 37; 1550 Sudebnik, article 48. In criminal cases, the local authorities sent police agents with the bailiff to apprehend the accused criminal. The bailiff then took him into custody and brought him to court; for details, see Beliaev, "O vyzove v sud," p. 116.

[89] The summons (*srochnaia*) was a personal directive to the defendant, as opposed to the warrant (*pristavnaia pamiat'*), instructions to the constable, which might name several defendants residing in the same jurisdiction.

[90] 1497 Sudebnik, article 31; 1550 Sudebnik, articles 47, 49.

[91] For a more detailed discussion of surety bond and related procedures, see H. W. Dewey and A. M. Kleimola, "Suretyship and Collective Responsibility in Pre-Petrine Russia," *Jahrbücher für Geschichte Osteuropas,* N. F., **18** (September, 1970): pp. 337–354; Marc Szeftel, "The History of Suretyship in Old Russian Law," *Sûretés personnelles: Recueils de la Société Jean Bodin* **29** (1971): pp. 841–866.

[92] Shakhmatov, *Kompetentsiia* **1**: pp. 19–21. Muscovite bailiffs became notorious also for their corruption and abuse of power; see *Russian Private Law,* pp. 30–31.

[93] *Gramoty Velikogo Novgoroda i Pskova,* ed. S. N. Valk (Moscow-Leningrad, 1949), no. 92.

[94] *AFZKh* **1**, no. 204; see also *ASEI* **2**, nos. 410, 414.

[95] *AIu,* no. 19.

[96] *AFZKh* **1**, no. 248.

Iakush in Moscow, and, Sire, we had not heard of that default judgment until now." [97]

Two elders from the Simonov Monastery sent the Grand Prince's central-court bailiff after the defendant, elder Mikita of the Dolgaia free settlement. Learning that Mikita had gone to Moscow, they apparently followed: "And, Sire, we have given him over, here in Moscow, into the custody of that same constable Ivashko Tur; and here, Sire, are elder Mikita and the constable Ivashko Tur before thee!" [98]

One plaintiff summarized his pre-trial actions in later testimony. Charging that the defendant had been mowing the meadows for the four years that he, the plaintiff, had been the estate manager, he explained his previous attempts to bring suit:

Sire, since he mowed the meadows, I petitioned my lord Filip, Metropolitan of All Rus', and, Sire, he sent a document about that [matter] to Prince Danilo Dmitreevich, and then, Sire, God took him, and I, Sire, petitioned Gerontii, Metropolitan of All Rus', and he, Sire, sent [a document] to the Grand Prince and the Grand Prince, Sire, gave thee to us as a judge for those lands. [99]

A judgment charter issued between 1473 and 1489 contains a fairly detailed account of pre-trial procedure —perhaps because of the unusual manner of requesting the constable—although in other respects the document well illustrates the abbreviated nature of early judgment charters. On this occasion the plaintiff, Abbot Vasilii of the metropolitan's Prechistenskii Monastery, presented his petition before the court of Ivan Sukhoi on written instructions of the Grand Prince himself, saying, "Give me, Sire, a constable [to bring to court] the petty nobles of Prince Boris Vasil'evich, Dmitrei Rozhnov and his brothers Kriuk and Ostaf', and here, Sire, is a document of the Grand Prince [addressed] to thee." [100] This charter of the Grand Prince, which was incorporated in the text of the judgment charter, provides an example of a document authorizing the sending of a constable after defendants:

From Grand Prince Ivan Vasil'evich to Ivan Sukhoi. My father Gerontei, the Metropolitan of All Rus', has lodged a complaint with me against people of my brother Prince Boris, against Mitia Rozhnov and his brothers Kriuk and Ostas, alleging that there in Sota they ploughed and mowed the metropolitan's land. And thou shouldst go there and give [the monasterial representative] a constable for those people of Prince Boris, and try [the case between] them and the metropolitan's people, and having tried [the matter], tell me, the Grand Prince. And thou shouldst arrange to go there, so that my father the metropolitan will not pester me about this again.

Unfortunately the judgment charter does not tell us how or why the abbot received the benefit of the metropolitan's personal influence; he may have petitioned the metropolitan asking for help. At any rate, the Grand Prince did order one of his judges to go out and hear the case on the spot, and the abbot did get his constable. We might surmise, however, that the abbot had good reason to desire the Grand Prince's authorization in this particular matter. As was noted above, the constables themselves—not to mention individual plaintiffs—frequently had great difficulty in bringing defendants to court, and since the accused in this case were under the jurisdiction of the Grand Prince's brother, the abbot may well have feared that Prince Boris would intervene on their behalf.

A judgment charter of 1503 illustrates the activities of local officials who were enlisted by the plaintiffs to aid in identification of a thief. When Fedko and Kostia Poluev, Prilutskoe peasants of the Trinity-Sergius Monastery, brought suit against Gridia Tevelga, a peasant of the village Pavlovskoe, they explained that they had gone to the meadow one day to examine their hay, and found their thirty haystacks gone. Taking two Prilutskoe bailiffs and good men, the hundredman and seven other peasants, with them, they returned to the meadow, where the bailiffs and local representatives collected the rest of the plaintiffs' hay. All then set out along the track (sledom) where the hay had been carted off. It led to territory belonging to the village Pavlovskoe. The Prilutskoe officials sent one of their men to the Pavlovskoe village administrator (posel'skii), requesting a constable to continue the pursuit. He sent his son and four Pavlovskoe peasants. When they arrived, all continued along the track, which led to Gridia Tevelga's homestead, where they found two carts of hay in his log storage shed. The constables and local representatives then placed their sample of the plaintiffs' hay (seno sledovoe), which they had brought with them, beside the hay found in Gridia's shed, for comparison, and found it to be the same. The Prilutskoe men then placed their seals on the sample taken from the field and gave it into the custody of the Pavlovskoe men, while the officials from Pavlovskoe repeated the procedure in reverse with the hay found in the storage shed. All the hay, the alleged thief, the constables, and the local representatives were presented before the judge.

The constables, having affirmed the authenticity of their seals, unsealed the hay for comparison. The defendant thereupon claimed that they had placed that hay in his possession in secret. The Prilutskoe constables then confirmed the plaintiffs' account of their hot pursuit, explaining that they had followed the track of the hay dust and had entered Gridia's homestead in his presence. Gridia, they asserted, had declared that he had purchased the hay, but did not say from whom. The Prilutskoe local residents in turn confirmed the constables' report. The men from Pavlovskoe testified next, explaining that they had gone to the place where the Prilutskoe officials were standing on the track with their hay sample. They confirmed the account of the men from Prilutskoe, and agreed that

[97] AFZKh 1, no. 259; see also AIuB, 1, no. 4.
[98] ASEI 2, no. 416.
[99] AFZKh 1, no. 259.
[100] AFZKh 1, no. 249; see also ASEI 2, no. 409.

the hay found at Gridia's homestead was identical with the sample.

At this point the peasants from both villages testified concerning the general reputation of the defendant. Gridia, they said, was an evil man, a thief and a slanderer, and this was not his first theft. Other Pavlovskoe peasants had brought suit against him previously; after his conviction, the sum at issue had been collected from him and he had been beaten with the knout.

The judge then pointed out that Gridia's testimony in court, his claim that the hay had been placed in his homestead, conflicted with his statement to the constables that he had purchased it. From whom, the judge asked, had he bought the hay?

Gridia maintained that the hay had been placed in his possession, but admitted that he had been tried for theft earlier. The judge, he declared, "ordered me tortured in [the matter of] that theft and beaten with the knout, and, Sire, they beat me, and they did not find out anything."

Judgment was given for the plaintiffs. The judge declared Gridia a thief "and handed him over to the plaintiffs for punishment (na kazn') in accordance with the Sudebnik, and he ordered the [village] administrator to collect the sum at issue from his property." [101]

In addition to illustrating the procedure followed in cases of hot pursuit, this document reflects the provisions of the 1497 Sudebnik regarding theft. Article 10 of the code provided that a thief caught for the first time be flogged with the knout and made to pay the plaintiff's damages, while article 11 decreed that a thief caught for the second time be executed, the sum at issue to be paid from his property. [102] Interpretation of Gridia's reference to his being tortured in the earlier case depends upon whether he meant that he had been beaten during the trial, or whether he was referring to his flogging after conviction as torture. If he meant that he had been tortured during trial, this suggests that he may have been accused by another thief, since article 14 of the Sudebnik provided that one accused by a thief, who had been charged with theft in the past, be tortured, while the fact that he was not executed at the conclusion of that case would suggest that he had not been convicted of any earlier charge.

Testimony in a 1528 judgment charter indicates that apprehension of the defendants could be more difficult than it apparently was in the case of Gridia Tevelga. Basalai Ragozin brought suit against Andreiko Lapin, the man of Vasilii, son of Bund Neronov, and his comrades, two other men of Vasilii Neronov, eight men

of Aleksei Neronov, four men of Semen Neronov, and seven men of Mikhailo Neronov, charging them with assault and robbery—including the theft of currency, grain, salt, fishing nets, horses, clothing, fur coats, utensils, in all goods worth thirty-three and a quarter rubles—and with burning down the homestead. Only Andreiko Lapin appeared in court, and the judge asked the bailiff why he had not brought in the others as ordered. The bailiff explained that he and the local representatives had apprehended Andreiko, while his comrades, who were also named in the warrant, "ran away in my presence, and having gathered together, Sire, they wanted to take that comrade of theirs, Andreiko Lapin, away from me." Andreiko then declared that he would answer for all of the others except one ("our lords never had such a man"), denied the charges of assault and robbery as presented, but admitted to burning the plaintiff's homestead on orders of their masters and taking one axe, two loaves, a covered clay vessel, and a spoon. The plaintiff offered to support his charges by means of a judicial duel, which the defendant declared would be impossible for him and his comrades (nam ne moshchno). He also could not present his comrades, since they had run away. Judgment was given for the plaintiff, because the defendant had admitted to burning the homestead and stealing some items, had refused a judicial duel, and had answered for his comrades but could not present them. The defendant was to pay the sum at issue. The judge then ordered the bailiff to go again with a warrant for Andreiko's comrades, to seize them and bring them back. The judge also ordered that a document be sent to the Seneg canton, where the hamlets and people of the defendants' masters were located, "to the hundredmen, and tenmen, and all the peasants," ordering them to assist the bailiff in capturing the men and to hand over the defendants. Thirty-five days later the bailiff reported complete failure. He had gone with the local canton peasants to apprehend the defendants, but they were in flight, and Lapin could not pay the sum at issue. Lapin, appearing in court again, admitted that he could not pay and that there was no surety bond for him. So he was given over in bondage to the plaintiffs until redemption (do iskupa; until the debt was paid) and the judge condemned his comrades as fugitives—the plaintiffs were to seize them wherever they should encounter them, without being required to get a constable, and present them in court. [103]

Defendants in another case also sought to avoid the court's officials. In a 1541 document, three men of Timofei Volynskii were charged with talking two servant girls into stealing their masters' goods worth ten and a quarter rubles and running away. The girls had been located in one of Volynskii's villages, whereupon the plaintiffs petitioned for a bailiff to recover them and

---

[101] Kashtanov, Ocherki russkoi diplomatiki, no. 40, pp. 409–414.

[102] The sentence of execution also complies with articles 8 and 39, which decree that if evidence is brought against anyone of theft, and he is a known criminal, he is to be executed and the sum at issue taken from his property.

[103] AFZKh 1, no. 222; for a parallel situation in a 1525 case, see AIu, no. 17.

the goods. The bailiff seized them in the presence of local witnesses, and presented them before the proper authorities, where they admitted that they were the plaintiffs' slaves, that they had stolen the goods, and that the defendants had put them up to it. One defendant, the cook Mikitka, had brought them to the village, and he had married one of the slave women. The plaintiffs declared that when they had come with the bailiff, the defendants had gone into hiding and could not be found. The women had been returned to the plaintiffs in slavery, and now the plaintiffs had found Mikitka in Moscow, handed him over to a bailiff, and were bringing suit to recover the stolen goods and to have him declared a slave for having married their female slave.[104] Mikitka, refusing to answer for Volynskii's men, declared that he served Volynskii voluntarily, denied the charges, admitted marrying the girl, but claimed that there had been no reference to her being a slave. Both sides agreed to fight a judicial duel in support of their testimony, and the judge ordered each released on surety bond. Mikitka, when he was unable to get a surety bond, admitted his guilt and said that the stolen goods had been taken from them on the road by unknown persons. As a result, he was given to the plaintiffs in slavery because he had married their female slave, while the charges against Volynskii's other men were dismissed, because Mikitka, in admitting his complicity in the theft, had not named them as his accomplices.[105]

The complaint presented at the beginning of a 1584 case shows that a rather large force could be sent after one man. Timofei Shilovskii, claiming that the state secretary Andrei Sherefedinov had had him arrested on charges of being absent without leave in order to extort a deed to Shilovskii's estate, declared that Sherefedinov had first sent an undersecretary, who refused to show Shilovskii the order for his arrest, would not accept his offer of a surety bond, and had come without local witnesses and bailiffs. In the second attempt to execute the arrest, Sherefedinov had taken greater precautions. He sent a petty nobleman from the Office of Military Administration, accompanied by cannoneers, riflemen, local bailiffs, and local witnesses. After showing the arrest order to Shilovskii, they put him in irons and took him to Moscow. Shilovskii complained that Sherefedinov's actions were illegal, since the arrest had been made on false charges of desertion, for the purpose of extortion, and since he had been given into Sherefedinov's personal custody rather than taken to the Office of Military Administration. On the other hand, his complaint shows that Sherefedinov had eventually complied with procedural requirements in sending local officials.[106]

As we have seen, a plaintiff could encounter major difficulties simply in getting the defendant into court. Once both parties were present, however, the trial generally began with an exchange of statements between the litigants, starting with the plaintiff's complaint. In the majority of the surviving judgment charters, the complaint was presented orally: "I bring complaint, Sire, against (*zhaloba mi, gospodine, na*). . . ." Texts from the second half of the sixteenth century indicate a slight change in this procedure, as some trials began with the reading of a more formal written complaint.[107] In most cases, after hearing the complaint, the judge turned immediately to the defendant, ordering him to answer the plaintiff's charges, although on occasion the judge might examine the plaintiff's charges more closely before proceeding with the case.

Many of the surviving judgment charters record trials over land, and in these cases the nature of the dispute affected the court's attitude toward the complaint. One element which must be considered in land litigation is the principle of *davnost'*, the idea that there is a definite period of time during which certain claims may be presented (e.g., a plaintiff may demand the return of his land), or after the expiration of which some right is acquired or lost. In the fifteenth century there apparently was no fixed statute of limitations after which adverse possession became legal and the original holder lost his right to bring action against the man encroaching on his property. We find wide variations in the amount of time which elapsed between the original encroachment and the beginning of legal action. Some plaintiffs alleged very recent violations of their rights, like priest Grigorii, who claimed that the peasants Rodiuka and Nesterik "erected that hut and storehouse unlawfully on my rye and spring-crop field this spring on St. Athanasius' Day."[108] Other plaintiffs brought suit after two years,[109] six years,[110] and twelve years.[111] Still other litigants waited even longer. The peasants of the Zalesskaia canton, bringing suit for two floodland meadows, declared, "it is about twenty years since the Trinity [Monastery's] elders took those floodland meadows away from us."[112] Two landholders sued their brother for selling their patrimony without telling them—thirty years after the fact.[113] In 1492 the canton peasant Vasko complained:

"Sires, those hamlets Miasovo, and Medvedevo, and Khlamovo, and the deserted lands Parshina and Nikitino are the Grand Prince's lands of our Shukhtovskaia canton; and, Sires, the elders of St. Cyril's placed those ham-

[104] Article 66 of the 1497 Sudebnik reads in part: "Whoever marries a female slave becomes himself a slave."
[105] *AIu*, no. 21.
[106] Iushkov, *Akty XIII–XVII vv.*, no. 220.

[107] See, for example, *AIuB* 1, no. 8; *AIu*, no. 23; Iushkov, *Akty XIII–XVII vv.*, no. 220.
[108] *ASEI* 1, no. 582; for some other examples, see *AFZKh* 1, no. 249; *ASEI* 2, nos. 229, 285, 388a, 401, 402, 405, 483; *ASEI* 3, no. 208.
[109] *ASEI* 1, no. 557.
[110] *ASEI* 3, no. 56.
[111] *ASEI* 2, no. 287.
[112] *ASEI* 1, no. 524.
[113] *ASEI* 1, no. 522.

lets in [clearings made in] the Grand Prince's Shukhtov-skaia forests; and, Sires, they placed those hamlets [there] forty years ago, and they mow those deserted lands, encroaching beyond the river Chiulmosar on our side.[114]

All of the above cases were tried before Ivan III issued the 1497 Sudebnik. One of the code's provisions indicates that plaintiffs would be required to bring suit more promptly. Article 63 of the 1497 Sudebnik decrees that boiars, monasteries, *pomeshchiki* (holders of service-tenure estates), free peasants, and landlords' peasants must bring suit against each other within three years, while suit against a boiar or monastery for lands belonging to the Grand Prince must be brought within six years.[115]

Pre-Sudebnik judgment charters indicate that this limitation was not a matter of general practice earlier. After the code was issued, we might expect that the court officials would inform plaintiffs during the pre-trial procedure that the time within which they could bring suit had passed. Yet cases tried after 1497 indicate that the decree was not rigidly enforced. In 1501 the Shakhovskaia canton elder sued the Tolgskii Monastery for land of the hamlet Malaia Khinovka, declaring that the monastery had established the hamlet in the Grand Prince's forest, canton land, fourteen years earlier.[116] In 1505 a peasant of the Grand Prince complained that elders from St. Cyril's Monastery had been mowing meadowland of the Grand Prince's Mikhailovskaia hamlet illegally for fifteen years.[117] A judgment charter of *ca.* 1501 records that peasants of the Minskii borough sued the metropolitan's estate manager of the village Kulikovo, claiming that he was taking away tax-paying lands of the Grand Prince's Minskii borough:

Sire, those lands became depopulated because of the great plague, and, Sire, that Vania is holding those lands for the metropolitan's Kulikovo village, we know not why, and he is establishing hamlets; Sire, he established the Poddubnoe hamlet forty years ago, and he established a hamlet on the Katunino land ten years ago, and, Sire, he also began to plow and mow the deserted lands ten years ago, and, Sire, he calls them the metropolitan's lands.[118]

Another canton elder, bringing suit against an estate manager of the metropolitan in 1504, declared that the previous archimandrite had taken away their floodland meadow, black land of the Grand Prince, forty years earlier.[119] In a case tried at the end of the fifteenth century, the peasant Andrei Pelepelkin asserted: "That deserted village Popovskoe, Sire, is land of the Grand Prince, but the metropolitan's peasants, Sire, took possession of that deserted village fifty years ago."[120] Fedko Chevakin, bringing suit against Luka Proshchelykin in a 1530 document, charged that the defendant and his son had been living on land of the plaintiff's father for twenty years.[121]

In cases such as the above, however, both before and after issuance of the Sudebnik, the courts seemed more concerned with reasons for the plaintiff's long silence than with the number of years which had elapsed. The judge usually asked the plaintiff why he had failed to protest about the siutation for so long. Litigants gave various answers. In a 1501 case, for example, the judge asked the plaintiff why he had not spoken to the defendants about their actions in fourteen years, or sent a constable for them, or petitioned the Grand Prince or his boiar, and the plaintiff gave no answer whatsoever; he had simply done nothing.[122] Most litigants, however, gave some reason. Mikitka Lysoi, elder of the Dolgaia free settlement, explained that they had said nothing to the Simonov Monastery elders because "they told us, Sire, that they had a charter of grant for those hamlets, and for that reason, Sire, we were silent."[123] Others, for varied reasons, had not been concerned with the land earlier. A Zvenigorod resident offered an explanation which remains cryptic to the reader, since the rest of the document provides no clarification of his reasoning: "Sires, I did not bring suit against Ivashko for that land in that six years because we had no time, Sires—Sires, the Tatars were in our land, and, Sires, we were waiting for the heir of the patrimonial estate."[124] That fighting the Tatars could interfere with his plans for going to court is understandable, but the heir is not named, nor is his connection with the case stated. Perhaps the plaintiff was hoping to have the dispute resolved locally. Gavrilko, the priest's son, complained that the metropolitan's peasants had been living illegally in his hamlet for thirty years, and then declared: "Because of my sins, Sires, I was ill for eighteen years, and, Sires, I could not concern myself with that land."[125] He did not explain why he could not bring suit during the remaining twelve years.

[114] *ASEI* 2, no. 288. The nature of peasants' tenure on lands of the Grand Prince has long been a subject of controversy; for a review of the recent literature on the subject, see Gregory John Shesko, "'Black Lands' in Recent Soviet Historiography," *Kritika* 10, no. 3 (1974): pp. 121–147. What is obvious from this judgment charter and others is that peasants believed that they had a legal claim to the lands.

[115] For an historiographical survey of the question of *davnost'* in the Sudebnik, see *Sudebniki XV–XVI vekov*, pp. 100–104. The time limits were repeated in the 1550 Sudebnik, article 84. The editors of the *Dictionary of Russian Historical Terms* (p. 9) define *davnost' zemskaia* as "a law ruling that a landed estate, the possession of which was not contested in court within 10 years, became the legal property of the possessor." They give no source for the ten-year limit.

[116] *ASEI* 3, no. 221.
[117] *ASEI* 2, no. 309.
[118] *AFZKh* 1, no. 258.

[119] *AFZKh* 1, no. 306.
[120] *AFZKh* 1, no. 114.
[121] *RIB* 14, no. 17.
[122] *ASEI* 3, no. 221.
[123] *ASEI* 2, no. 416.
[124] *ASEI* 3, no. 56.
[125] *AFZKh* 1, no. 129.

There were, of course, lawful reasons for delay of legal action. The problem of essoins is not discussed in the Sudebniki, but the 1649 Ulozhenie does regulate the matter of appearance in court. If, for example, a litigant were ill, he was to send a trusted representative (*poverennyi*) in his place; if he claimed that he could not delegate anyone to handle the matter for him, a responsible undersecretary (*pod'iachii dobryi*) was to check on the situation, visiting the man to verify the fact of his illness and that he had no one to send in his place. If such were the case, the litigant was released from his court obligation until he recovered. A litigant might also be excused for reasons of state service (*gosudareva sluzhba*), military, diplomatic, or other matters especially entrusted to him by the tsar. This included, however, only non-voluntary service, in which the litigant was actually engaged at the time. To cite just one other category, men serving in administrative capacities (*sluzhba nepolkovaia*), such as military governors (*voevody*) and officials of the *prikazy*, were to send a representative. An exception was made for people serving in such places as Astrakhan' and Siberia; they were not required to answer in court before the end of their term of service.[126]

The judgment charters show, however, that some plaintiffs did not offer any excuse, such as illness or military service; they were more blunt about the situation. When one judge asked two brothers, who were suing the third, "How long ago did your brother Senia sell those lands? Are those lands far from you?" they replied that he had sold them more than twenty-five years earlier, and their lands were all in the same area. Why had they not protested? "We were silent, Sire, we did not need [the lands]."[127] Two peasants stated that elders from the monastery had come riding and began to plow the deserted lands in question about fifteen years before, and "we, Sire, were not [then] concerned with the land."[128] Leva Zaitsov claimed that he was trying to redeem patrimonial property mortgaged to St. Cyril's Monastery by his father and grandfather, and that the abbot would not accept the money. After Zaitsov admitted that the land had been mortgaged twenty years earlier, the scribe judges asked why he had done nothing about the situation. Zaitsov replied: "I did not speak to them [about it], Sires, because I was not able to redeem that hamlet from them; and now, Sires, I am able to redeem that hamlet from them."[129]

Over half of those questioned, however, claimed that they had indeed protested. Two peasants, speaking for the rest of the canton, declared: "Sire, we have petitioned the Grand Prince about those lands many times, and the Grand Prince does not listen, and it is impossible to gain access to the sovereign, and we, Sire, now bring suit before you."[130] Others had similar grievances:

We were not silent, Sires, we petitioned the sovereign Grand Prince more than once, and, Sires, the Grand Prince will not order anyone to give us an [official] boundary surveyor for that floodland meadow, and, Sires, they cross over [the boundary], and they will not give us an [official] boundary surveyor, on account of the metropolitan, and furthermore, Sires, we have not been able to gain access to the sovereign; and, Sires, when Iakov Kochergin wrote up [the land cadastres of] Poshekhon'e, Sires, we petitioned Iakov, and Iakov did not give us legal satisfaction.[131]

A 1463 case suggests that the best appoach was to keep petitioning until the desired result had been achieved. The judge asked the "counted men" why they had said nothing to the monastery elder who had been plowing their land "for fifteen years, while living with them in the same place, on the boundary strip." The men claimed that they had not remained silent:

When they began to plow [our land] unlawfully, Sire, we submitted a petition to Grand Prince Vasilei Vasil'evich. And the Grand Prince, Sire, sent out Mikhailo Karpov to [examine] the land. And Mikhailo, Sire, came riding out to this land and agreed, Sire, to tell the Grand Prince, but he did not tell the Grand Prince, and he obstructed justice for us and showed favor to them, and did nothing for us. And we, Sire, again petitioned Grand Prince Vasilei. And the Grand Prince, Sire, sent out Grigorei Vasil'evich Morozov. And Grigorei, Sire, also came riding out to this land, and likewise did not bring us before the Grand Prince, and gave us no justice.

The judge then asked them if they had petitioned the Grand Prince again, bringing complaint against either of the judges. When they stated that they had not submitted further petitions, the judge questioned the defendants, who reported that the second investigator had conducted a trial. Judgment was given for the defendants, partly because the plaintiffs had not lodged complaints against the Grand Prince's officials.[132]

In most cases there is no way of verifying such "protest" activity of the plaintiffs. Usually we have the word of one litigant against another. No one called upon the Grand Prince or his agents to verify the fact that a petition had been submitted. In one curious case, the plaintiff claimed that he had not remained silent, but had spoken to the hundredman

---

[126] For a more detailed discussion of essoins and notation of of the corresponding Ulozhenie articles, see Kavelin, *Osnovnyia nachala*, pp. 293–296.

[127] *ASEI* **1**, no. 522.

[128] *ASEI* **2**, no. 375.

[129] *AIu*, no. 15. The monastery then called for evidence from the Grand Prince's land cadastres to show that the hamlet was registered for the monastery. The plaintiff admitted that the books showed this, that he had not told the scribes that the monastery held the land on mortgage because he could not redeem it. He had no witnesses who could testify con-

cerning the mortgage. The court decided in favor of the defendant, because the plaintiff had brought suit after twenty years, had not called for evidence from the land cadastres, had admitted that the hamlet was registered for the monastery, and had no witnesses.

[130] *AFZKh* **1**, no. 258.

[131] *AFZKh* **1**, no. 306.

[132] *ASEI* **2**, no. 374. See also *ASEI* **2**, no. 414.

(rather than the defendant); the hundredman, he declared, had told him that the monastery held a charter for the disputed land. At this point the plaintiff himself seemed to admit that his case was questionable. Yet the hundredman, when questioned, testified that the plaintiff had never spoken to him about the matter.[133]

Some judgment charters record instances where the protest was successful. Gelaseia, a monasterial supervisor, explained that he had not remained silent when the canton peasants crossed the surveyed boundary and chopped down trees and boundary markers: "I petitioned the sovereign Grand Prince, Sires, and the sovereign Grand Prince, Sires, gave us [his official] Gnevash Stoginin [to hear our] case against them, and, Sires, Gnevash has not appeared on the land because of the Grand Prince's [other] matters." The scribes then questioned Stoginin, who verified Gelaseia's account. Testimony of the only surviving witness to the boundary establishment, as well as the official boundary record, supported the supervisor's claims, and the land was awarded to the monastery.[134] In another case, Elder Isaia emphasized the constant protest which had been carried on by the Trinity-Sergius Monastery:

Sire, we did speak to him, we protested to him every year; and, Sire, he plowed that deserted village of ours unlawfully over [our] protest. And, Sire, the sovereign Grand Prince's constable did not ride to him in Obolensk. And, Sire, the abbots and elders petitioned the sovereign Grand Prince more than once. And, Sire, the Grand Prince said: "Wait, I shall give you justice." And, Sire, Prince Ivan has been plowing that deserted village of ours, Zelenevo, unlawfully, over [our] protest, for ten years, and not twenty-five.

Prince Ivan eventually confessed that the land was not his.[135]

When both plaintiff and defendant were questioned on another occasion about their use of protest, the defendant admitted that he had mowed the land in question and built the mill, claiming the land was the Grand Prince's taxpaying land. He then affirmed that the metropolitan's peasants had been mowing the land "since olden times," while he, the chief steward, living there, had remained silent. On the other hand the plaintiff, who had claimed that the defendant was mowing the land illegally for the fourth year, declared:

Sire, I am the estate manager here for the fourth year, and, Sire, since he (the defendant) mowed the meadows, I petitioned my lord Filip, the Metropolitan of All Rus', and, Sire, he sent a document about that [matter] to Prince Danilo Dmitreevich, and then, Sire, God took him, and I, Sire, petitioned Gerontei, Metropolitan of All Rus', and he, Sire, sent [a document] to the Grand Prince, and the Grand Prince, Sire, gave thee to us as a judge for those lands.[136]

One protestor suddenly found that his opponent had seized the initiative. The Mishutino hundredman Malyga, the defendant, declared that the monastery's peasants had been plowing the Grand Prince's canton land for seven years: "Sire, we protested to them, and, Sire, they do not agree to the protests. And now, Sire, the [monastery's] supervisor sent a constable for us about our protests."[137] A few plaintiffs, however, seemed to realize the value of including a statement about such activity in the record, and made it a part of their original complaint. For example, the peasants Palka and his son Vas'ka brought suit against Ofonasko, charging: "Sire, he is plowing our land and mowing our meadow clearing, having crossed the border of the Bortnikova hamlet unlawfully, against our protest."[138] One protest was very successful. The defendants testified that after they heard it, "we [did] not have any document whatever for those new settlements; and, Sire, we moved out of those new settlements."[139] In other instances, however, the outcome was not as satisfactory. The brethren of the Trinity Makhrishchskii Monastery brought suit against Sharap Baskakov and his sons, claiming that they had sold property to the monastery for one hundred and fifty rubles. In the spring the Baskakovs had asked that payment of the last thirty rubles be postponed until Christmas, so that they could live in the village until then. At that time they had not surrendered the property. The brethren sent their servant Pyshko, whom the defendants allegedly had beaten and robbed. Next they sent a constable. When the defendants failed to appear in Moscow at the time designated in the summons, the court had awarded the monastery a default judgment. That had taken place a year ago; "and, Sire, two years have passed [since] St. George's Day in the spring, when that Sharap and his sons took our money, one hundred and twenty rubles, and a marten-fur coat in addition, and he will not get out of the village and he will not give the village and hamlet to the monastery." Despite Sharap's attempts to contest the monastery's documents, the brethren finally acquired the land.[140]

Failure to register a protest could lead to loss of a case. The defendants in a 1543 trial brought a countersuit, and among the reasons for the decision against them the judges mentioned that they had brought suit for the settlements "after nine years, and in that nine years they had remained silent, their lord Prince Fedor [Mstislavskii] had not petitioned the Grand Prince, and later his son Prince Ivan had not petitioned con-

---

[133] *ASEI* 2, no. 404.
[134] *ASEI* 2, no. 310.
[135] *ASEI* 1, no. 607.
[136] *AFZKh* 1, no. 259. In another case, the plaintiff explained that he had brought suit as soon as he had redeemed

his mortgaged land: "I petitioned the Grand Prince against the monastery and the Sovereign bestowed his favor on me, he gave thee to me as a judge for that land"; Likhachev, *Sbornik*, no. 9.
[137] *ASEI* 1, no. 430.
[138] *ASEI* 3, no. 50.
[139] *ASEI* 3, no. 173.
[140] *AIuB*, 1, no. 4.

cerning those disputed new settlements and had not asked for judges."[141]

After he had presented his claims, the most clear-cut way for a plaintiff to prove his case was to get a confession from the defendant. A few men did admit their guilt directly. The servant boy Sergeets, for example, when ordered to reply to the charges, immediately declared: "And what, Sire, can I answer? Sire, I did incite Khrap's three full slaves—Kazak and Eremeitsa and Senka—and I led them away beyond the border; and now, Sire, I know not where those slaves of his are living. I am guilty, Sire."[142] In another case, after the defendant had replied to the charges, the plaintiff admitted that he had no grounds for his action. When the judge asked why the land was the prince's, he replied: "Sire, I do not remember back many years, and the elders [who knew this] are gone; I have no means of proving my claims." The court awarded the land to the defendant.[143]

Other litigants, confessing indirectly, excused their actions by professing ignorance concerning rights to the land in question. The Kuchetskii brothers, charged with crossing the boundary, chopping down the forest, and taking over the metropolitan's land, explained: "Sire, we and our brother Ivan do not know the boundary between our Ezhov hamlet land and the metropolitan's lands." In the end, both sides agreed to accept the boundary indicated by the metropolitan's peasants.[144] A group of men accused of trespassing in the monastery's lake and river declared:

Until now, Sire, the archimandrite did not stand against us for that, nor did his estate manager, and we, Sire, were fishing in the lake and river; and now, Sire, the archimandrite orders us not to fish and we, Sire, do not fish [there any more] nor trespass in his lake nor in the Vashka river; and, Sire, we [now] know that the lake and the river Vashka are the church's property of the St. Mikhail Chudov [Monastery].

The court confirmed the monastery's possession.[145]

In other cases we find a type of "disguised confession." Defendants, while denying the charges brought against them, in effect admit that they have no rights to the land involved. A beekeeper of the Grand Prince claimed that Prince Fedor Davydovich Starodubskii-Pestryi had taken away the Grand Prince's lands and beekeepers' forests, sending in his own beekeepers; the plaintiff then presented his charter of grant from the Grand Prince. Prince Fedor's son, speaking for his father, answered:

Sire, my father, Prince Fedor Davydovich, and I have not taken those Grand Princely lands and beekeeping forests along the Ougot' river to the bank which remains above the spring floods from Fomka and his brother (the plaintiffs), nor have we sent our own beekeepers into those

beekeeping forests nor do we enter them; those, Sire, are the Grand Prince's beekeeping lands and forests along the Ougot' river to the bank which remains above the spring floods.[146]

Apparently the defendant here could present no counter-evidence to offset the plaintiff's complaint. He denied the charges, but in the process he gave up any claim to the land. Were these tactics designed to save face or to avoid paying damages for trespassing?

When litigation arose over lake Mukovo and adjacent land, the defendants first claimed that "those cleared areas came with our patrimony, as did the swamp." Later the judge asked about the precise location of their cleared area, if it was beyond the fence, and they replied: "Sire, our cleared area is not in Mukovo and the swamp, and we have called that swamp the prince's, and now, Sire, we do not bring suit for the swamp near the Mukovo lake."[147] Testimony in yet another case suggests that the defendant had encroached upon the plaintiff's land but did not want to admit it. Evidently he did not know the boundary (or pretended he did not know), and had simply extended his meadow to include meadowland which was not his: "Sire, up to now the boundary of my meadow [went] up to those points, but now, Sire, order [the plaintiff] Danilo's witnesses to show thee where the boundary is."[148]

A rather curious case involving a confession took place in 1547. The plaintiff, Princess Anna Shchenia-teva's man Il'ia, declared that the defendant Onisimko was a slave belonging to the princess, and had run away, stealing goods worth twelve rubles. Onisimko immediately confessed. At this point another man who was present in court declared that Onisimko was a runaway slave belonging to Mikhailo Kolupaev. Each claimant was then ordered to produce a document showing that Onisimko was his slave. Kolupaev's man Istomka, appearing in court on behalf of his master on the following day, declared that two of Kolupaev's men, Onisimko and his brother, had escaped from their irons and had stolen horses and clothing. He also presented a judgment charter issued to Kolupaev in a previous suit against the same slaves, which recorded Onisimko's confession that he served Kolupaev in accordance with the terms of a promissory note and that he had stolen goods from his master. After the document had been read, Onisimko denied that such a trial had taken place, but admitted that he and his brother had served out a term for Kolupaev in accordance with a promissory note, and that he had left Kolupaev's service without an accounting. Onisimko then called for the testimony of the judge and witnesses named in the judgment charter, but later changed his mind and confessed, adding, "I was falsely accused in

141 Likhachev, *Sbornik*, no. 10.
142 *ASEI* 3, no. 357.
143 *ASEI* 2, no. 465.
144 *AFZKh* 1, no. 157.
145 *ASEI* 3, no. 35; see also *ASEI* 3, no. 173; *AIu*, no. 15.

146 *ASEI* 2, no. 496.
147 *ASEI* 1, no. 485.
148 *ASEI* 3, no. 477. For other cases which eventually resulted in a confession, see *AIu*, no. 16; *AFZKh* 1, no. 222; Likhachev, *Sbornik*, no. 14; *AIuB* 1, no. 7.

the princess's suit, Sire, because they wanted to protect me from Mikhailo's claims and from the [terms of the] judgment charter." When the judge asked about the princess's man, who had promised to produce a document in court, the bailiff replied that the princess had left Moscow, taking her man with her. As a result of the trial, Onisimko was to pay the amount due from this suit and from the earlier trial, or be handed over in slavery to Kolupaev if he did not have the money. His brother was to be declared a runaway slave—Kolupaev could apprehend him wherever he found him. The suit of Princess Anna's man was rejected.[149] The court decreed no penalty for his action, and there is no further explanation of the princess's reasons for wanting to protect Onisimko. Perhaps it had been assumed that if Onisimko confessed the court would award him to the princess in slavery without any further investigation. She would have gained his services at no cost and he would have escaped from his obligations to Kolupaev. It is also possible that there had been an agreement on the length of time for which Onisimko would serve the princess.

Such confessions, however, direct or indirect, are found quite infrequently in the judgment charters. As a rule cases were not settled that easily. Most litigants continued to press their claims. In the process they could make use of several types of evidence. They might call for the testimony of witnesses, either directly or upon inquest. They might produce private documents of their own or request an examination of the Grand Prince's records. They might offer to resolve the dispute through various forms of "God's justice," such as marking off boundaries with an icon in hand, taking an oath, fighting a judicial duel, or drawing lots. In addition to presentation of proof, they might bring countersuits, make accusations of perjury or corruption, attempt to delay the trial, or contest the record in a higher court. Drawing upon any or all of these procedures, most litigants kept fighting to the end.

IV. TRIAL PROCEDURE: TESTIMONY OF WITNESSES

Testimony of witnesses was the form of evidence most frequently used in the trials recorded in the judgment charters. The majority of these documents dealt with land disputes, and here the witnesses called upon to testify most often belonged to the category known as *starozhil'tsy* (longtime residents of the area) or *dobrye liudi* ("good men," probably because they were reputable members of the community). The testimony of the longtime residents usually followed a standard pattern. Before stating the facts, the men indicated the period of years for which they had knowledge of local events, generally beginning with the eldest, al-

though a strict precedence based on age was not always followed.[1] A 1490 document provides a good illustration. The plaintiff, when asked why he called the land the monastery's, replied: "This is known, Sire, to [our] good men, the longtime residents Timokha Denisov, and Senka Veraksin, and Levon Nos, and Fedko Savelov, and Ivashko Medved', and Foka." All these men then appeared before the judge to testify. Timokha Denisov said: "I, Sire, remember seventy-five years that this Shishkinskoe deserted village is monasterial land of the Verznevskoe village." Senka Veraksin spoke next: "I, Sire, remember seventy years that it is monasterial land." Levon followed: "I, Sire, remember sixty-five years, and that deserted village is monasterial land." Fedko Savelov said: "I, Sire, remember sixty years, and that is monasterial land." Ivashko Medved' and Foka concluded the testimony: "And we, Sire, remember fifty years, [and] that deserted village Shishkinskoe is the Simonov Monastery's land and goes with their Verznevskoe village [for cadastral purposes]."[2]

Starozhil'tsy were usually peasants, but not always. In one case a longtime resident was an elder of a monastery, the monk Gerontii, who remembered for eighty years.[3] Another plaintiff presented the "longtime residents, good men—petty boiars—Zakhar'ia and Danilo Botvin'ev, and the peasants of the Ustenskoe village, Ofonia Korotkoi, and Ostash Ivakin, and Tiufei, son of Grigor', and Gridia Priazhinskoi, and the peasants of the Kapshin Monastery: Danilo Kasha, and Savka Cheshkov, and Oleshko Moskovkin, and Ortemko Sipin."[4]

The longtime residents served as "experts" on the land in question, testifying about its status (e.g., whether it was the Grand Prince's, a secular land-holder's, monastery's, or the metropolitan's), how long it had been in the holder's possession, or had been part of a particular village, hamlet, or canton, who had plowed or mowed it in which years, or what the boundaries were. The testimony of such longtime residents would carry greater weight than that of newcomers to the area, and a litigant's case undoubtedly appeared stronger if his witnesses were actually old. One plaintiff, in fact, challenged a witness for the other side on the basis of age: "Sire, [his] witnesses testified before thee that Prince Ivan (the defendant) has been plowing that land, the deserted village Zelenevo, for thirty years; and, Sire, his witness Gridka Alekseev is not thirty years old."[5] It must be kept in mind that the longtime residents, although called upon as experts, were not impartial; each litigant named his own

---

[1] The ages were frequently given in descending order, beginning with the eldest, but this order could be reversed, and occasionally the ages are randomly mixed.
[2] *ASEI* 2, no. 402.
[3] *AFZKh* 1, no. 249; see also Likhachev, *Sbornik,* no. 8.
[4] *ASEI* 3, no. 173.
[5] *ASEI* 1, no. 607.

witnesses, men he thought would support him, and he might include members of his own family.[6]

Memory was the basis for all testimony of longtime residents in land cases. As we have seen, these men usually testified that they remembered for a specific number of years. There are even some instances of witnesses claiming to remember for ninety or one hundred years. While one is inclined to doubt the precision of their figures, particularly in the case of witnesses claiming to remember for such long periods of time, their relative chronology may have been roughly accurate. Vasiuk, a longtime resident who declared that he remembered for one hundred years, was probably the oldest man around, while his comrades Karpik and Petiunia, who remembered for seventy-five years, knew they were about the same age, and the two younger witnesses, who remembered for sixty and forty years, knew they were of a completely different generation.[7] Witnesses tended to give their own ages in round numbers, yet would state that an event happened seventeen[8] or even forty-nine (*let s piat'desiat bez leta*)[9] years before. In no case is the year given by date. Usually there is just the simple statement that the witness remembers for so many years, or that the event occurred so many years before.

Occasionally winesses date their testimony from some important event which they remember, rather than by number of years. In a case dated 1499/1500, the longtime residents declared: "Sire, we remember for seventy years, from the plague (*ot moru*), that that is the Grand Prince's state taxpaying land of the Tartyshovskaia hamlet...."[10] Since the great plague occurred from 1410 through the 1420's, their chronology is roughly accurate, particularly if they are referring to the latter years of the plague. Another man's testimony, however, provides a striking example of inaccuracy. Abbot Elinarkh, during a trial which took place sometime between 1462 and 1505, declared: "Sire, two years before the great crop failure (*do velikie mezhaniny*—1410–1420's) I became a priest of [the Monastery of] Saints Boris and Gleb, and, Sire, I have been living at the Boris and Gleb [Monastery] as a priest for about twenty years, and, Sire, the Miliutino peasants have been plowing those deserted villages. . . ."[11] Such testimony would suggest that the trial took place in the 1430's or 1440's rather than after 1462. On the basis of data other than the priest's memory, Alekseev has suggested that the probable time limits for the trial are 1470/1471—1482/1483, the years during which one of the boiars present served in the Boiarskaia Duma. "Thus the trial was not later than the '80's, and the testimony of witnesses who remember Edigei's raid and the 'great crop failure' (i.e., the bad harvests which caused hunger and plague, 1410–1420's) is in accord with this."[12] Since the abbot's age is not given, he might well have remembered those events, but apparently his estimate of years was not very precise—by the time of the trial, he must have spent at least forty years in the monastery. In connection with very recent events, time is measured by church holidays: "It happened this year, in the week of Peter's Day (O.S. June 29); Sires, that Pronia summoned us [to go] with him to the land for a boundary division. . . ."[13]

Witnesses usually testified on the basis of their own knowledge. To cite just one example, Ivashko Ontonidin, testifying on behalf of the plaintiff in a case tried between 1496 and 1498, apparently felt that the defendant had in effect conceded that the disputed land was not his several years before:

Semen Beklemishev held that Pochap land; and, Sire, the barley of the Pochap peasants Gridka Poskrebin and his father-in-law Neznanko was sown in that deserted village Zelenevo; and, Sire, the livestock of Matfei, [the defendant] Prince Ivan Konstiantinovich's estate manager, broke into that deserted village Zelenevo; and, Sire, those peasants with the constable Semen and [his] men caught Matfei's livestock, cattle and sheep, in that deserted village in the barley; and, Sire, that Matfei, Prince Ivan's estate manager, paid those peasants, Gridka and his father-in-law Neznanko, damages for that barley.[14]

Other witnesses, less frequently, testified about what their fathers had told them. For example, Mitiuk Kostin said:

Sire, I heard from my father that that was the deserted village Popkovo, and Popko lived here, and he gave that deserted village to Biser, and Biser gave the village Biserovo and the deserted village Popkovo to the metro-

[6] See *ASEI* 1, no. 582, and 2, no. 309. In the legal documents, the term "starozhil'tsy" designates men who had lived in the area for a long time and thus might serve as valuable witnesses; for a discussion of the *starozhil'tsy*, see G. E. Kochin, *Sel'skoe khoziaistvo na Rusi v period obrazovaniia russkogo tsentralizovannogo gosudarstva konets XIII-nachalo XVI v.* (Moscow, 1965), pp. 395–427. Some scholars have claimed that the *starozhil'tsy* constituted a special social and economic group within the peasantry; for this view, see I. Smirnov, "K voprosu o starozhil'tsakh," *Voprosy istorii,* 1946, nos. 8–9; pp. 96–97; *idem,* "Prevrashchenie bobylia v starozhil'tsa," *Voprosy istorii,* 1947, no. 12: pp. 87–88; A. G. Man'kov, "Zapisi o starozhil'tsakh v prikhodnykh i raskhodnykh knigakh Iosifova-Volokolamskogo monastyria," *Nauchnyi biulleten' LGU,* 1947, no. 19; B. D. Grekov, *Krest'iane na Rusi s drevneishikh vremen do XVII veka* (2d ed., 2 v., Moscow, 1952–1954) 2: pp. 76–98.

[7] *AFZKh* 1, no. 306.

[8] *AFZKh* 1, no. 248.

[9] *AFZKh* 1, no. 259.

[10] *ASEI* 3, no. 276. In other judgment charters, men also remembered from the plague: *AFZKh* 1, nos. 254, 258, 259; *ASEI* 1, no. 658, and 2, nos. 368, 400, 414. Others based their chronology on military events: from the battle of the Shelon river (1471) (*ot Sholonskogo boiu*), *AFZKh* 1, no. 248; before Edigei's raid (1408) (*do Edigeevshchina*), *ASEI* 2, no. 229, (*do Edigeevy rati*) *ASEI* 2, no. 375; or before Prince Mamutek's great raid (1445) (*do Mamutiakovy rati*), *ASEI* 2, no. 492.

[11] *AFZKh* 1, no. 125.

[12] Alekseev, *Agrarnaia i sotsial'naia istoriia,* p. 19.

[13] *ASEI* 3, no. 288.

[14] *ASEI* 1, no. 607.

politan Fotei [to provide for prayers] for his soul, and [that was] about fifty years ago.[15]

In another case the witness Gridia testified:

Sire, my father Malakh lived in Pereboro, and, Sire, I went with my father to those deserted lands to gather mushrooms, and, Sire, my father told me that those deserted lands Mikhailovskoe and Bliznino [were] the metropolitan's lands, and it has been twenty-five years, Sire, since my father told me, and, Sire, it is thirty-five years since my birth.[16]

Frequently both litigants brought opposing sets of *starozhil'tsy.* In one case the plaintiffs, two peasants from the metropolitan's Viatskaia canton, presented two "good men, Viatskaia canton longtime residents," who testified: "Sire, we remember this for sixty years, Sire, Pavlik lived in that deserted village before the plague, and was registered with Viatets [for cadastral purposes], and the land is the metropolitan's." The defendant, the Shakhovskaia canton hundredman, also called for the testimony of two men, "good men, the canton longtime residents," who said: Sire, we remember for forty years that that is the Shakhovo land of the Grand Prince, and we have been mowing it for the canton." [17]

Sometimes the witnesses testified in much greater detail. One longtime resident, Elka S'ianov, recounted village history at length:

This village Korobovskoe, Sire, was in the possession of my father Grigorei S'ianov. And Fedor Nepliui brought the charter of Grand Prince Vasilei Vasil'evich to my father for that village Korobovskoe. And people had not settled on this land because of brigandage. And the Tatar envoys went along this road as well. And my father gave back that charter to the same Fedor Nepliui. And Fedor Nepliui gave this village Korobovskoe, with this meadowland, to Archimandrite Ivan and the brethren of the Simonov [Monastery] for the [house] of the Immaculate [Mother of God], in return for memorial services for his father Ivan Diadkov. And after Archimandrite Ivan my father-in-law Terentei Glodnev purchased the same village Korobovskoe from Archimandrite Gerontei of the Simonov Monastery, and with the same meadowland. And this land and meadowland have been [part] of the village Korobovskoe since olden times, and not Ondrei's.

His co-witnesses, Khariton Moklok, Vasil' Vlaznev, Ivashko Polozhi Sokha, Uvar Kirilov, and Iurka Elizarov likewise testified that the meadowland was part of the Korobovskoe village.[18] One of the witnesses in a 1463 trial over the deserted villages Kuzemkino and Dernkovo, recalling some seventy years, declared:

I, Sire, remember back fifteen years before Edigei's raid (1408): at that time Kuzemka Chechetka lived on this land, and on the other [land] lived Dernko—and these are the Grand Prince's regional deserted areas—and, Sire, [they] paid tribute [to the Grand Prince] and went with us in [the payment of] all levies. And, Sire, my father was then the fiftyman in these lands. And, Sire, when my father died, then, Sire, after Edigei's raid I was for eight years the fiftyman in these same lands.[19]

In some cases both parties claim the land in question, each declaring that he has been using it previously. When bringing suit against the Shakhovo hundredman Nekras Levonov, one of the metropolitan's peasants complained that Nekras "mowed the metropolitan's deserted village Pavletsovo unlawfully, and, Sire, he calls that deserted village land of the Grand Prince, but, Sire, I, Aristik, have mowed that deserted village for twenty years as the metropolitan's land." The hundredman in turn declared that Pavletsovo was the Grand Prince's land, which had been registered as part of the Shakhovo canton, "and, Sire, we have been mowing that deserted village for fifteen years." Both men then presented "longtime residents, good men" to testify in support of their claims. When the defendant eventually failed to appear for the trial on *doklad,* and in addition had taken the hay from the meadow against the court's order, decision was given for the plaintiff.[20] In a case of 1499/1500, the plaintiff, monk Efrem of the Ferapontov Monastery, declared: "Sires, we cleared this meadowland, and our elder Tikhon mowed [it] for twenty years. And we, Sires, have been mowing this meadowland, after Tikhon, for ten years. And, Sires, that Kurian has been illegally mowing these meadowlands of ours for the fourth year." The defendant, the peasant Kur'ian, answered: "Those, Sires, are the Grand Prince's meadowlands of the land named for Ivashko Rukin, [and they have] always been quitrent-paying [lands]; and no one cleared them for the monastery. And, Sires, I came to that tax-paying hamlet named for Ivashko Rukin, Sires, ten years ago. And I have been mowing the meadowlands along that river Sheleksha, up to the Porozobitsa river, on both sides." Again, both sides had longtime residents to present testimony. The defendant won, according to the decision because the plaintiff's witnesses would not fight a judicial duel.[21] But other elements in the case probably affected the outcome. The plaintiff was a newcomer who had no knowledge of the land and his two witnesses were only forty and thirty years old, whereas three of the defendant's longtime residents remembered for sixty years and another for forty.

Many of the judgment charters recorded cases which involved boundary questions. Each party might claim that the land lay within his territory, or one might accuse the other of crossing the boundary, or incorporating land which did not belong to him. Since more

---

[15] *AFZKh* 1, no. 114; see also *AFZKh* 1, nos. 249, 259; *ASEI* 1, no. 607, and 2, nos. 286, 287, 404, 407.

[16] *ASEI* 3, no. 105.

[17] *AFZKh* 1, no. 261; for a few other examples of cases in which litigants both presented longtime residents, see *ASEI* 1, nos. 523, 557, 582, 595, 607; *ASEI* 2, nos. 334, 336, 368, 375, 388a, 400, 401, 402, 404, 411; *ASEI* 3, nos. 48, 50, 105, 208, 221, 223, 276, 288; *AFZKh* 1, nos. 103, 114, 117, 125, 248, 249, 254, 258, 259, 306; Likhachev, *Sbornik,* nos. 8, 9, 10, 12; *AIu,* no. 20; *SGKE* 1, no. 76; *AIuB* 1, no. 6; Anpilogov, *Novye dokumenty,* pp. 485–490.

[18] *ASEI* 2, no. 411.

[19] *ASEI* 2, no. 375.

[20] *AFZKh* 1, no. 261.

[21] *ASEI* 2, no. 334.

effective surveying techniques had not come into use in Muscovy,[22] boundary demarcations consisted of marks (crosses or notches—*grani*) on trees, pits or holes (*iamy*) dug in the ground, and various physical features of the landscape—rivers, streams, swamps, lakes, sand bars, duck snares, weirs, gullies, ravines, fences, paths, roads, rocks, stumps, and all manner of trees, such as gnarled oaks, three birches growing from one root, three pines in a cluster, shrubs, and trees which were crooked, bent over, split, cracked, twisted, charred, dried out, or without tops.[23] Cases were tried on the disputed land, and often the judge was treated to an extensive tour of the neighborhood.

Bounday descriptions themselves were of two types, either very general or very specific. The land in question may be described as the area "where the plow has gone, where the axe has gone, where the scythe has gone,"[24] "where Vasilii's plow and scythe have gone, where the axe has gone."[25] The specific descriptions, on the other hand, are very specific indeed and vary from case to case. Testimony concerning boundary divisions often concluded with an offer from the litigant or his witnesses to lead the judge along the boundary: "and come, Sire, we shall show thee the boundary, up to what point the land of the Kozlovo manorial village [goes]."[26] "Sires, ride after us, we shall show you the boundaries between the Grand Prince's lands and the metropolitan's lands."[27] Sometimes first one litigant, and then the other, led the judge along the "true boundaries."[28] On other occasions, each litigant's witnesses acted as guides.[29] Some-

times one of the litigants led the judge, as did the witnesses for the opponent.[30] In yet other instances, each litigant, and then his witnesses, led the judge around the boundaries.[31] It was imperative in such situations that a litigant and his witnesses know the boundaries, and that witnesses point out exactly the same markers as their principal.

We do find some cases where a litigant or his witnesses did not know the boundaries. In one instance the defendants claimed that the land where they stood was not the Gorlovskaia land, but the Khotenovskaia land. When the judge ordered them to show him the boundaries of the Khotenovskaia land, they replied: "We, Sire, do not know the boundaries, but these are all the Grand prince's lands, and we are plowing them all alike."[32] During another trial the plaintiff's longtime residents led the judge

from the Bolon' stream to the hollow, and up the hollow to the enclosure, and along the enclosure, and from the enclosure up [another] hollow, and from the hollow to a little road, and along the little road, going a short distance, to a boundary strip, and along the boundary strip through the meadow to the gate, and from the gate along the old enclosure, and [where] the enclosure [was] newly torn down up to the fence, and along the fence as far as the sandbank, to the old enclosure, and along the old enclosure up to the Fominskaia land.

Reaching that point, they told the judge, "On the right, Sire, is the Simonov Monastery's land—[the land of] the Vatolinskoe village's Stepanovskaia hamlet, since olden times, and on the left, Sire, is the Grand Prince's Kobylinskaia hamlet land of Kuzemka and Timoshka." The defendants' longtime residents, on the other hand, could not match this performance: "Sire, the land on which thou art standing is the Grand Prince's; and this Kuzemka and Timonka have plowed this land from the Kobylinskaia hamlet—that is known to us; but we, Sire, do not know the boundaries of this land; all Usokh is the Grand Prince's."[33] The defendant's witnesses in another trial said: "We, Sire, do not know the land, and, Sire, we do not know the boundaries. And, Sire, our father Ustin will tell [thee]—he lived in Eremshino, beyond the ravine; but we, Sire, do not remember this, [for] we have lived up to this time with various boiar landlords."[34] The document provides no explanation for the failure of the defendant (or the judge) to call for Ustin's testimony.

When one side tried to bluff under such circumstances, the attempt could result in an embarrassing situation. On one occasion, after both sides had completed their testimony, the plaintiff's witnesses had led the judge along the boundary, straight along the Icheia river (which the plaintiff and his witnesses consistently claimed as the boundary), and declared

[22] See I. Beliaev, "O sovremennom sostoianii mezhevanii v Rossii," *Zhurnal ministerstva iustitsii,* 1860, 3, bk. 3, pt. 1: p. 56.

[23] In some instances, official establishment of a boundary was included as part of the court's final decision. After the decision had been given in a 1531 case, the lower-court judges were ordered to survey the land and establish the boundary. They cut boundary markers on the trees and dug boundary pits along the line pointed out by the longtime residents in the presence of eleven local witnesses; Likhachev, *Sbornik,* no. 9; see also Likhachev, *Sbornik,* no. 10; *AIu,* no. 20. A 1595 judgment charter mentions several different beekeepers' marks in use among various local residents, including "the sign of a pitchfork with a notch," "a hole in the middle of a notch," "scythes with a notch," "two lines," "horns with two notches." Some of the marks "fell into disuse after the plague"; Gorchakov, *O zemel'nykh vladeniiakh,* no. 6. On beekeeping in Russia, see Dorothy Galton, *Survey of a Thousand Years of Beekeeping in Russia* (London, 1971).

[24] *ASEI* 3, no. 105.
[25] *AFZKh* 1, no. 129. Litigants may explain that they mowed to the point "where scythe met scythe"; *ASEI* 2, no. 285; see also no. 287. This type of description appears with particular frequency in donation charters (*dannye*) and purchase deeds (*kupchie*) which are incorporated in the text of judgment charters.
[26] *ASEI* 1, no. 595.
[27] *AFZKh* 1, no. 258.
[28] *ASEI* 2, nos. 370, 405, and 3, no. 56.
[29] *ASEI* 1, nos. 595, 607; 2, no. 411; 3, no. 50; *AFZKh* 1, nos. 254, 258, 259; Likhachev, *Sbornik,* nos. 9, 10; *SGKE* 1, no. 76.

[30] *ASEI* 2, nos. 286, 288.
[31] *AFZKh* 1, no. 117; *ASEI* 3, no. 276.
[32] *ASEI* 2, no. 483.
[33] *ASEI* 2, no. 401.
[34] *ASEI* 2, no. 388a; see also *ASEI* 2, no. 406.

that the plaintiff's land lay on the right side of the river, and the defendant's on the left. The defendant's witnesses then set out, and led the judge "from the Icheia river to the right along the ravine slightly uphill, and from the slight rise to the left to the two aspen stumps across the grove through the enclosure, and from the two aspen stumps to the left along the little path; and having gone a short distance along the little path, they turned to the right through the grove straight to the dry oak." At this point, the plaintiff's witnesses claimed that the defendant's witnesses were lost, in the middle of the plaintiff's land. The judge then ordered the defendant's witnesses to continue on to the end of the boundary, and they replied: "Sire, we know the boundary up to this dry oak, but further, Sire, we do not know." After this the judge told the defendant to order his witnesses to lead the court to the boundary with other lands. And the defendant was forced to admit that his witnesses simply could go no further.[35]

The defendant in another case presented two sets of witnesses, longtime residents to testify about the land and other men who, he claimed, had been present at his boundary survey. After the alleged survey witnesses led the judge along the boundaries, the plaintiff and his witnesses pointed out that these men had followed the same boundary as the plaintiff's witnesses, along the new markers and pits, while the defendant claimed that the boundary had been set twenty years earlier. The defendant's position became even more ridiculous when his longtime residents led the judge along the boundary. They went along markers and paths, "from the oak to the ravine, and straight across the ravine uphill, going off quite a distance up the slope." At this point two men came up to the witnesses, a lay brother and an elder from the Nikolo-Ugreshskii Monastery, which was not involved in the suit but held lands contiguous to the territory in dispute. Protesting that the witnesses were trespassing on land belonging to one of the Ugreshskii villages, they threatened to bring suit against the defendant if he claimed this as part of his land.[36] The defendant's witnesses quickly retreated from the area—conduct which contributed to his loss of the the case.

When the defendants in another suit, Gridia Cherep and his comrades, canton peasants, presented their two longtime residents, the plaintiff pointed out that one of the witnesses, Tonkoi Gridin, had earlier appeared as a defendant in the case. The defendant-witness Tonkoi replied that the plaintiff had brought suit against him, but that his brother had appeared in his place. Despite this seeming irregularity, both sets of longtime residents proceeded to lead the judge along the boundaries. After the plaintiff's witnesses had taken their turn, the defendants' longtime residents started out from the Deriagina slash-burn clearing along the

moss marsh. Having proceeded half a verst, the canton's witness Ovdokim Dorofeev stopped and said: "Sire, I have not been on those boundaries, and, Sire, I do not know where to go." The judge pointed out that Ovdokim had claimed to know the boundaries earlier. Why did he not continue? "Art thou ill, or dost thou not see, or did someone pay thee? Go along the boundaries after thy comrade Tonkoi, Gridia's son." Ovdokim replied: "I am not ill, Sire, I [can] see, and, Sire, no one paid me; but, Sire, not knowing the boundaries, how can I proceed?" And he turned around. The judge then asked the defendants if they had other longtime residents who knew the boundaries. They had no one else, so Tonkoi proceeded alone to a point he claimed was Skochki, the end of the boundary. The plaintiff's longtime residents thereupon demanded a judicial duel with him, declaring, "Sire, that is not Skochki, in which thou art standing, that, Sire, is a nameless place, and, Sire, they led thee at all times along the monastery's plowed land, and, Sire, Skochki is that [place] that we showed thee on the boundary." Rather than agreeing to fight a judicial duel, Tonkoi called for evidence from the Grand Prince's land cadastres.[37] The poor performance of the defendants' longtime residents, contrasted to that of the plaintiff's six witnesses, who led the judge along a boundary which corresponded to the description given in a charter of grant presented by the plaintiff, undoubtedly contributed to the defendants' losing the case.

Another litigant took more forceful action when his witnesses came to a halt. Vasilii Obliaz Lodygin, plaintiff in a 1531 case, presented five longtime residents who offered to lead the judges to the boundary markers. They proceeded through forest land without boundary markers and then stopped. Obliaz, arriving on the scene, beat his longtime resident Ondronko, Ignat's son, about the ears with a lash, saying: "Why didst thou stop, peasant (*chego smerd stal*), lead [them], peasants, do not stop, straight to your boundaries." At this point the defendant intervened. "Sires judges! See for yourselves, Obliaz himself is instructing his own longtime residents!" The witnesses continued to lead the judges through the fields, but did not reach any boundary markers. The defendant's longtime residents then pointed out the boundaries, following markers. Obliaz lost the case, in part because he had refused to call for evidence from the land cadastres, admitting that he knew the land was registered for his opponent.[38]

A few judgment charters record suits which apparently were initiated only for the purpose of obtaining an official boundary establishment. The defendants admitted immediately that they did not know the boundary, and at the conclusion of the case boundaries were set.[39]

[35] *ASEI* 1, no. 607.
[36] *ASEI* 2, no. 411.

[37] *AIu*, no. 20.
[38] Likhachev, *Sbornik*, no. 9.
[39] *AFZKh* 1, no. 157; *ASEI* 3, no. 477.

Litigants called upon witnesses other than, and in addition to, longtime residents to settle their boundary problems. The defendant in one case explained that the boiar Vasilii Ivanovich Kokoshkin had previously been instructed, on orders from the Grand Prince, to mark off the land in question. The boiar had done so, and the defendant presented him in court. Kokoshkin then marked off the land again, as he had done before.[40] The defendants in another suit declared that they had purchased the disputed land from Pronka Iurkin and his brothers, and called for the testimony of Pronka, who had measured off the land for them. Pronka testified as follows:

Sires, that Sulinskaia land was our patrimony; and, Sires, I and my brothers sold that land to that Mitia and Sofonko (the defendants), and, Sires, we established the boundary of that land with Filat, [the plaintiff] Mikhal's father, according to the old boundary, and we placed new boundary markers. And, Sires, that cleared area has been since olden times [a part] of that Sulinskaia land, and, Sires, I measured off that Sulinskaia land with that cleared area for that Mitia and Sofonko.

The plaintiff thereupon denied that his father ever had any boundary division with Pronka. The judges then asked Pronka: "And whom dost thou have [as] longtime resident witnesses for that land, and whom did ye have as witnesses (lit. men) for that boundary division with Filatko?" Pronka named two longtime residents, and two men who had been present at the boundary division. The longtime residents, appearing in court, verified that the cleared area was part of Pronka's Sulinskaia land, and the boundary-division witnesses declared:

It happened this year in the week of Peter's Day (O.S. June 29); Sires, that Pronia [sic] summoned us [to go] with him to the land for a boundary division; and, Sires, we went with him; and, Sires, that Pronia sent for Filat, Mikhal's father, and, Sires, Filat came to him, and, Sires, that Pronia, with Filat, divided that Ukladnikovskaia land from the Sulinskaia land along the old boundaries; and they placed new boundary markers. And, Sires, that Pronia measured off that Sulinskaia land for those priest's sons Mitia and Sofonkoko [sic]. Sires, that was done in our presence, and we saw it.

The plaintiff offered no further evidence, and the defendants won.[41]

A judgment charter issued between 1495 and 1497 gives an even better account of boundary-setting procedure and its verification in land litigation. The plaintiffs, peasants of the Grand Prince, claimed that the Prilutskoe monasterial elder Nikon had chopped down the forest of the Grand Prince's Pavlovskoe village and their new settlement. Elder Nikon then declared that the forest was the monastery's, located near deserted lands which the monastery had purchased and upon which the monastery had erected homesteads. He then presented the monastery's purchase deed. The plaintiffs made their first partial retreat. They ad-

mitted that the forests, hamlets, and deserted lands were the monastery's, but asserted that they did not know the boundary between the monastery's lands and their new settlement, and asked the judge to show them the boundary. The judge questioned Nikon about the boundary, and he declared that Ivan Verkhogliadov, the Uglich chief steward of the Grand Prince, had been in the forest with good men, peasants from the Pavlovskoe village, Oleshko Kurap, Olfer, Ortem's son, and Oksenko Fedorov, and other good men, village residents.

And, Sire, Ivan conducted an inquest among the longtime residents concerning the boundary between the monastery's hamlets and that Ozarko's new settlement, and [then] he showed [me the boundary]; from the Kiiasovo deserted land to the fir stump, and from the fir to the maple, and they cut boundary markers on the maple, and from the maple to the oak, and from the oak straight to the Grebenevo enclosure. And, Sire, I cut down our forest up to that boundary.

The judge then questioned the plaintiffs, who retreated another step. They admitted that the chief steward had showed them the boundary, "but not there where Nikon says." At this point the judge took the initiative; he ordered that the men appear in court whom Nikon had named as being present with the chief steward. Oleshko, Olferko, and Oksenko testified that the chief steward had taken them to the forest, where he conducted an inquest among the longtime residents, peasants of the Grand Prince, concerning the boundary, "and, Sire, he showed that Ozarko and his brothers [their] boundary with the monastery's hamlets: from the Kiiasovo deserted land to the fir stump, and from the fir to the maple, and from the maple to the oak, and from the oak straight to the enclosure of the Grebenevo hamlet." The judge carried his investigation even further, questioning the Pavlovskoe estate manager Syta and other peasants of the village, Kliapik Kharitonov, Gridia Parfenov, and Vasiuk Dmitrov, asking whether they knew whose forest it was and who cut it down. Syta answered that a Pavlovskoe peasant had erected a homestead in the forest during the time of Prince Andrei, and the Prilutskoe elder Elisei had petitioned the prince about it. Prince Andrei sent Isak Dubrovin to investigate, and Isak told him that a new settlement had been erected in the cleared areas near the monastery's hamlets. "And, Sire, Prince Andrei sent me, and, Sire, he ordered me to dismantle that new settlement, and, Sire, I dismantled that new settlement. And since that time, Sire, the monastery's peasants have been cutting down that forest and they have been mowing their cleared areas up to this time." The Pavlovskoe peasants also testified that the monastery's peasants had been cutting down the trees. Through testimony elicited by Nikon and the judge, the plaintiffs were gradually pushed back, inch by inch, until they no longer had any ground to stand on.[42]

---

[40] ASEI 2, no. 450.

[41] ASEI 3, no. 288.

[42] ASEI 1, no. 581. The prince mentioned here is Prince Andrei Vasil'evich Bol'shoi of Uglich. The concluding section

Litigants presented various types of witnesses whose testimony was pertinent to their case. They called for testimony from the men who had sold them the disputed land [43] or had donated it to a monastery,[44] from former or current estate managers or officials,[45] or from priests.[46] In other instances men were asked to verify their handwriting on documents presented in evidence.[47] In one case Metropolitan Simon sent his secretary Levash to testify on behalf of the defendants, peasants living in one of the metropolitan's villages. The secretary brought a purchase deed showing that a priest had bought the disputed land from the plaintiff's grandfather.[48] The defendant in a 1493/1494 case stated that the disputed land was the Grand Prince's, that the peasants Ivashko Liapa, Ivashko Valov, and Ivashko Poryvka had mowed the meadow, and that, after them, he had been mowing it since the battle of the Shelon river (1471). He was unable to present these previous landholders, since two had died and one was in bondage, but he did have two other men who could testify that those peasants had mowed the meadow, and that he had been mowing it since the battle.[49] The defendant lost. Evidently the testimony of his witnesses was not enough to offset that of the plaintiff's seven longtime residents, who remembered the metropolitan's land exchange involving the disputed meadow seventeen years earlier.

A few judgment charters record that litigants asked the judge to investigate the matter further by questioning "outside" (oprichnye) people, that is, men with no interest in the case. During the course of one trial, after both sides had presented documents and called for the testimony of their longtime residents, the plaintiff suggested that the judge conduct a general inquest among the area residents: "And, Sire, besides the witnesses, ask the hundredman and all the peasants of the Korzenev canton [if] that deserted village has been since olden times the monastery's Kozlovo land." [50] In another case, after longtime residents for both sides had testified, one set of starozhil'tsy accused the other set of lying, and the witnesses agreed to fight a judicial duel. At this point the plaintiff stepped in:

And, moreover, Sire, I call for the testimony of three boroughs—the Mikhailovskii borough, and the Shuromskii borough, and the Verkhdubenskii borough, [including the testimony] of petty boiars—Iakov, Danilo's son, and Dmitrei, son of Mikhail Redrikov, [and] of the canton good men—Gridia Trofimov, and Onanii Nosar', and Mikhailo Ontsyforov, the chief steward of the Mikhailovskii borough, and of Gridia Zhukov, and Vasilei Vaganov, and Lagir' Loginov.[51]

In a case tried in 1499/1500, when longtime residents for both litigants had completed their testimony, the judge, apparently on his own initiative, questioned outside good men, neighbors who lived in the canton:

Tell [us], brothers, as is right before God, upon kissing the Grand Prince's cross, ye have been living here since olden times, whose is that land, [is it the land] of the Grand Prince's Tartashovskaia hamlet of the Toshinskaia canton or [land] of Ivan Saraev's Sergeevskaia hamlet? [52]

The sixteenth-century judgment charters record several instances in which litigants called for the testimony of additional witnesses on inquest (obysk) during land litigation, although the procedure was used more frequently to ascertain the general reputation and character of persons suspected of criminal activities.[53] Men questioned on inquest testified on the basis of common knowledge within the community. After each set of longtime residents had claimed a different boundary line during a 1530 trial, the judge asked the plaintiffs whether they had any other witnesses who could testify. They requested that two additional "good men" testify on inquest. These men, appearing in court, supported the plaintiffs' claims. The judge then turned to the defendants, who named twenty-one more "good men." After they had supported the defendants' claims, the defendants called for the testimony on inquest of two abbots and five priests. The clergymen appeared in court, affirmed that they had testimony to give, but declared that they would speak only to a church hierarch. The judges thereupon sent them to Archbishop Iona of Riazan', who sent back to the court a record of their testimony under seal.[54] The defendant in another case called for additional testimony on inquest from "the Grand Prince's peasants of three cantons," seven men in all.[55] Other plaintiffs called for

---

of this case also provides a good illustration of the abbreviated nature of statements by judges, giving their reasons for decisions, in the fifteenth century. The evidence outlined above is not spelled out as the reason for the decision: "he gave judgment against Ozarko and Gavrilko and Kharka, Gridia's sons, because they themselves had said: the monastery's peasants cut the forest near the monastery's villages." For the testimony of a witness in another case who had been present at the establishment of a boundary, see Kashtanov, Ocherki russkoi diplomatiki, no. 9: pp. 354–361.

[43] ASEI 1, no. 557; 2, no. 336; 3, no. 288; AIu, nos. 19, 23.
[44] Likhachev, Sbornik, nos. 10, 12; AIu, nos. 23, 24.
[45] AFZKh 1, nos. 103, 125; ASEI 1, no. 523.
[46] AFZKh 1, no. 103; ASEI 3, no. 276.
[47] Likhachev, Sbornik, no. 9; AIuB 1, nos. 4, 5; Iushkov, Akty XIII–XVII vv., no. 220.
[48] AFZKh 1, no. 129.
[49] AFZKh 1, no. 248.
[50] ASEI 1, no. 595.

[51] ASEI 1, no. 582.
[52] ASEI 3, no. 276.
[53] See Sudebniki XV–XVI vekov, p. 62; Vladimirskii-Budanov, Obzor, pp. 634–640. The Sudebniki had special provisions governing treatment of a "known criminal" (vedomoi likhoi chelovek); 1497 Sudebnik, articles 8, 39; 1550 Sudebnik, articles 59, 60. There are many references to such use of the inquest procedure in anti-brigandage documents from the mid-sixteenth century. See, for example, the anti-brigandage charters (gubnye gramoty or gubnye nakazy) in PRP 3: pp. 176–179; A. I. Iakovlev, Namestnichie, gubnye i zemskie gramoty moskovskago gosudarstva (Moscow, 1909), pp. 46–100; A. A. Zimin, "Gubnye gramoty XVI veka iz muzeinogo sobraniia," Zapiski otdela rukopisei G.B.L. 18 (1956): pp. 216–219; the Statute Book of the Banditry Office (Ustavnaia kniga razboinogo prikaza), PRP 4: pp. 356–360.
[54] Likhachev, Sbornik, no. 8.
[55] Likhachev, Sbornik, no. 9.

an inquest to obtain the testimony of two abbots, a priest, thirty-nine peasants, and the man Pribyloi of Prince Fedor Iukhotskii, who had served as the prince's estate manager when he donated the land in question to the monastery.[56]

A 1552 judgment charter provides a more detailed description of inquest procedure. Trial proceedings were apparently concluded in the court of first instance and the judges had agreed to refer the matter to the sovereign, when the record notes the introduction of a second complaint against the defendants. The plaintiff declared that the two judges who had just finished hearing their case had left the disputed land and gone to a nearby hamlet of the abbot. The defendants had come there "at noon when people were sleeping," and had beaten and robbed the monastery's elders, secretary, servitors, and peasants, and also the "longtime residents who were with the judges on the land." One of the judges and the petty noblemen with him had attempted to capture the defendants. After beating the judge and nobles, the defendants had proceeded to ravage another hamlet. "And the abbot, Sire, and the [other] judge Fedor Morozov, having locked themselves up, stayed in the first hamlet."

The defendants declared that they themselves had left the disputed land after the judges had heard their case, and they had no knowledge of all this.

The plaintiff offered to prove his case by a judicial duel, and then proceeded to call his witnesses: Fedor Morozov and Khomiak Chechenin, the two judges, "who happened to be in our hamlet," a peasant, and "outside" petty noblemen who were with them. "Sire, those petty noblemen saw that, and, Sire, I call on them [to testify]." The plaintiff had petitioned the sovereign in Moscow against the defendants and had brought the judge a trial and inquest charter. He called for an inquest to be conducted among the petty noblemen, the abbot, archpriests, priests, and all residents: "conduct an inquest, Sire, among all those people in accordance with the sovereign's decree."

The defendants agreed to fight a judicial duel and called for the testimony of those named by the plaintiff as eyewitnesses (v viden'e) and of those called on inquest.

Thereupon the judge ordered the constable to go after the witnesses, Fedor Morozov and his comrades, "and to proclaim in the market place that petty noblemen and abbots and priests and deacons and all residents should be present at Vasilei's (the judge's) in-

quest and give their testimony in accordance with the sovereign's charter."

The witnesses, the two judges, petty noblemen, and peasant, appeared before the judges, identified the litigants, and confirmed the plaintiff's account. At the inquest 81 petty noblemen, residents of Nizhnii Novgorod, and 164 other men, "local residents and wardens, best and middle and younger men," [57] testified on the basis of their general knowledge and supported the plaintiff's claims, although the local residents added that they knew about the beating but not about the robbery. Four groups of clergy also gave testimony. The Spasskii archpriest, archdeacon, three priests, and deacon reported that the plaintiff had made a deposition to them against the defendants, covering the events as noted. An abbot and priest testified that they and their brethren knew of the events by hearsay, and their reports of the matter confirmed the plaintiff's account. Another archpriest and four priests said that the defendants had come to the abbot in the hamlets and beaten the peasants, but they did not know about the robbery. Finally, thirty of the metropolitan's priests testified that they had heard an account of the beating but not of the robbery.[58] Not surprisingly, the testimony of all these men was one of the reasons given at the conclusion of the trial for the decision against the defendants.

Timofei Shilovskii, who brought suit against the state secretary Andrei Sherefedinov concerning the extorted deed to Shilovskii's estate, submitted a series of inquest applications during the course of the trial, each request extending the range of people to be questioned. First he called for the "testimony on inquest of Olenid, archbishop of Riazan' and Murom, to show, O Sovereign, that Andrei is in possession of our patrimonial estate, the village Shilovo, and that his overseers are living [there], and that I, Timoshka, was brought in chains to Moscow." The defendant agreed to accept the archbishop's testimony, but declared that the plaintiff had been brought to Moscow for being absent without leave. In his next inquest application, Shilovskii requested the testimony of the archimandrite of the Monastery of Our Saviour in Pereiaslavl' Riazanskii, of the abbots, the cathedral archpriest, the priests "in the city and outside the city," artillerymen, riflemen, musketeers, post-horse station masters, the metropolitan's peasants, the market guards, and all the townspeople of Pereiaslavl' Riazanskii "from gate to gate except those persons who are his sureties or relatives, to show that Andrei is in possession of our patrimonial estate, the village Shilovskoe, and that his managers are living [there], and that they brought me, Timoshka, to Moscow in chains." Sherefedinov also called for their testimony, and added that

[56] Likhachev, Sbornik, no. 10. See also a 1547 case, in which the defendants claimed that they had had no property division. The man who had divided the landholdings called for the testimony on inquest of petty boiars "for two or three versts on all sides of that village," abbots, priests, deacons, hundredmen, tenmen, and "all peasant good men there"; AIuB 1, no. 5. A 1538–1539 judgment charter likewise contains much inquest testimony; Materialy po istorii Karelii XII–XVI vv., ed. V. G. Geiman (Petrozavodsk, 1941), no. 53: pp. 131–140.

[57] Division of the community into three groups was made "according to economic status and did not create legal distinctions between the groups . . ."; Dictionary of Russian Historical Terms, p. 55.

[58] Likhachev, Sbornik, no. 12.

he was in possession of his son-in-law's patrimonial estate, and that the property did not belong to the plaintiff.

Shilovskii petitioned on the spot, calling for the testimony of witnesses in two cities, Kolomna and Riazan', "of all the people, on inquest." Sherefedinov agreed, and the plaintiff submitted another set of inquest applications. He asked for the testimony of the district elders of Pereiaslavl' Riazanskii, Mikhail Khvostov, and Kour Cheresov, and of the inhabitants of Khvostov's village Zheludevo, the priest, Khvostov's manager Erasim and Khvostov's peasants Moisei Zheludev and Nazar Artiukhin, and "all peasants of Zheludevo village from gate to gate." He called for the testimony of the abbot of the Terekhov Monastery, his brethren, and all inhabitants of his villages and hamlets, of the abbot of the Pustynskii Monastery and his brethren. He also called for the testimony of the inhabitants of the borough of Staraia Riazan' and the Glebovskii forest and Meshchera: "the petty noblemen, and their estate managers, and the priests, and [their] peasants, and, O Sovereign, of thy palace villages, and of [thy] beekeepers' villages, and of the monasterial [villages] from gate to gate, and of Staraia Rezan' [sic], [and] of Ustoron', and of Isady, and of Riasy, and of Zapol'e, and of Zadubrov'e, and of Bortniv'e, [and] of the village Osokina, [and] of the village Putiatino, and of all thy royal villages and cantons [and] of the petty noblemen around me for fifty and for one hundred versts, except for [members of] his (Andrei's) clan and tribe and group of sureties." Even this was not enough. "And, Sire, I call for the testimony of thy royal local bailiffs, who witnessed the guilty parties' actions," and the royal artillerymen and riflemen and their comrades who rode with them. The trial record itself does not report the testimony of these witnesses, but among the many reasons given for the decision in favor of the plaintiff there is a reference to an inquest conducted by Leontii Oksakov and the undersecretary Tret'iak Makeev. One hundred and seventy-six persons had given testimony, declaring that they had heard that many people had come to Shilovo, where they had seized Shilovskii and taken him to Moscow in chains, and that Sherefedinov's overseers had taken possession of the patrimonial estate.[59]

Judges might also ask for witnesses to verify information presented in testimony. Ivan III checked with the bishop of Kolomna about the bishop's life-estate sale deed which the defendants had presented before the Grand Prince.[60] Judge Vasilii Pushkin called in the local hundredman and tenman.[61] Another judge sent for witnesses who had been present at a boundary inquest, to confirm that it had taken place.[62] When a plaintiff presented two documents, a judgment charter and a default judgment charter, awarded to him in previous litigation over the disputed land, the judge called for the other parties to these suits to verify the records brought in by the plaintiff.[63] Yet another judge questioned one of the official boundary surveyors who, the witness declared, had established the boundary in question.[64]

On occasion the court also sent out investigators when witnesses were unable to appear in person. In 1490 Prince Ivan Iur'evich Patrikeev asked the plaintiff's witnesses whether they knew who had settled the defendants on the disputed land, and they replied: "Sire, Archimandrite Zosima of the Simonov Monastery, who is now the metropolitan, settled them in that deserted village, and it has been three years, Sire, that they have been living on that land." The judge then sent his son, Prince Ivan Ivanovich, to the metropolitan to ask him about it. Metropolitan Zosima sent Ivan Iur'evich the following answer:

That deserted village Shishkinskoe is the Simonov Monastery's land, and I settled those *muzhiks* on that land, and gave them a limited-exemption charter for three years, and they stayed out their time—this spring the three years had passed—and they came to our monastery [and] petitioned us to give them temporary exemption [from full-scale taxes and obligations] for two [more] years, and we did not give them the temporary exemption, and because of this they left [to work on] the Grand Prince's [lands].[65]

In 1508, when both sides called for the testimony of the witnesses named in a purchase deed presented as evidence, the judge ordered the central-court constable to summon the men and bring them before the court. The constable returned with the servant of one of the witnesses, who explained the absence of the witnesses: "Prince Ivan, Sire, is no longer alive, and Prince Afonasei, Sire, cannot [come] now; he is unable to come to thee; and he has sent thee, Sire, a deposition with his seal—his testimony."[66] In another case, when one of the witnesses was ill, the judge sent two court officials to see him and record his statement.[67] A plaintiff bringing charges of brigandage testified that the Grand Prince's secretary and his palace land secretary had been ordered to examine the victim, to find out what sort of wounds he had and who had beaten him.[68]

Some litigants charged that witnesses for the opposition were not testifying in good faith or were men of dubious character. The defendant in one case claimed

59 Iushkov, *Akty XIII–XVII vv.*, no. 220.

60 *ASEI* 2, no. 381. By the terms of this document, the bishop sold the land for the purchaser's lifetime only; upon the purchaser's death, the land reverted to the monastery. In another case where conflicting purchase deeds were presented, the judge called for the witnesses named in each document to determine which one was authentic; *AIu*, no. 1.

61 *ASEI* 2, no. 404.

62 *ASEI* 1, no. 581.

63 *AFZKh* 1, no. 259.

64 *ASEI* 2, no. 310.

65 *ASEI* 2, no. 402.

66 *AIu*, no. 13.

67 *AFZKh* 1, no. 259.

68 *AIu*, no. 17; see also *AFZKh* 1, no. 1a.

that he had been forced to write a purchase deed, selling his property to the plaintiff, against his will. The judge asked him whether he wished to call for the testimony of the witnesses named in the document. Had they signed the document after seeing that he was being forced to write it? The defendant replied that Timofei, the man who extorted the deed from him, had ordered the witnesses to sign in his absence (*za ochi*), and they were his own brothers: "Sire, how can I call for their testimony, they will not speak for me." The judge asked about the others named in the document, who were not Timofei's brothers, and the defendant likewise refused to call for them. "Sire, they are Timofei's relatives, and, Sire, they speak in everything in accordance with Timofei's [wishes]." Despite his claims, the defendant did not ask that Timofei be brought into court nor did he bring suit against him. Failure to take such action was one reason given for his loss of the case.[69]

Prince Iurii Tokmakov, one of the defendants in a 1547 case, claimed that his brother had redeemed the promissory note by which he had mortgaged land to the plaintiff. When Ivan IV, who was trying the case, asked him if there were any witnesses to this, he replied that Prince Andrei Dashkov and Andrei Diatlov had been present and counted off the money, while the *okol'nichii* Ivan Ivanovich Bezzubtsov and Prince Ivan Zvenigorodskii also knew about it. The plaintiff Ivan Sheremetev replied that he had petitioned the tsar against Bezzubtsov before the trial, declaring that "he does not wish us well." Bezzubtsov, he claimed, was trying to obtain his patrimonial property. Zvenigorodskii was a brother of the defendants, Dashkov their brother-in-law. Diatlov was an accomplice in their false charges, since it was at his residence that Sheremetev had seized an alleged forger and forged copy of the promissory note.[70]

The character of the men who signed as witnesses was one of the points raised by plaintiff Timofei Shilovskii in challenging the deed to his patrimonial estate which the defendant's son-in-law had produced. In addition to requesting an investigation of other aspects of the alleged sale (among other things, the fact that the deed covered the entire village Shilovo, including service-tenure land, not just his patrimony), Shilovskii asserted that the secretary named as having written the deed, Grisha Shilov, was a known forger who had fled from Riazan' to avoid prosecution and now lived with the defendant Sherefedinov's son-in-law. The deed also recorded that Shilovskii's spiritual father, priest Ivan of the village Zheludevo, had signed in his place, but Shilovskii declared this to be false: "And that priest, Sire, is a scoundrel; he is not my spiritual father, and he was being tortured on the 'righter' (*na

pravezhe)[71] in a brigandage case at Ondrei Sherefiadinov's [chancery] and left the central court bailiff's custody." Shilovskii declared that his real spiritual father was Semion, abbot of the Terekhov Monastery in Riazan'.

As part of his challenge to the authenticity of the document, the plaintiff called for the testimony of the secretary and witnesses named in it. Three witnesses appeared in court, but the bailiff reported that the others, including secretary Grisha and the priest Ivan, were in flight. Later in the trial the judges sent a memorandum to the Banditry Office requesting information about the Zheludevo priest. The Banditry Office sent back information excerpted from a brigandage case of the previous year involving men from Riazan'. One brigand had declared that their intentions had been known to the priest Ivan, and that they had divided up all the loot and gone to his residence. Bailiffs sent after the priest and other accused persons reported that Ivan was not there, and submitted an inquest record from the district elder, who had been told that the priest had been in prison in Pereiaslavl', and "had left the prison by unknown means." When the priest Ivan was located in Moscow and interrogated, he denied all charges. He declared that he had put up surety bond on his release from prison and petitioned that an inquest be conducted concerning him. The district elder, in a direct confrontation, said that Ivan had been released on bond. After the interrogation, Ivan was placed in the bailiff's custody for the duration of the inquest. Thus when the judges in Shilovskii's case asked about the priest, the bailiff was ordered to bring Ivan to the Banditry Office immediately. The bailiff reported that the priest had remained in his custody for over a year, being released on surety bond at Lent (this report was given in May) on condition that he not leave Moscow. Since then, however, Ivan had left the city. The bailiff explained that he had released him "because he had trusted him; he had hoped that the priest Ivan would not leave Moscow; God and the sovereign know that." The memorandum sent to the judges concluded with a note that a time had been designated for the bailiff to present the priest at the Banditry Office.

Apparently the priest Ivan was not apprehended before the conclusion of the case, but the plaintiff's comments concerning the man's character had the desired

---

[69] *AIuB* **1**, no. 4.
[70] *AIuB* **1**, no. 5.

[71] The method of torture known as *pravezh* was described in the following terms by Giles Fletcher, an Englishman who visited Russia in 1588–1589, only a few years after this trial took place: "This *Praueush* or Righter, is a place neare to the office where such as have sentence passed against them, and refuse to pay that which is adiudged, are beaten with great cudgels on the shinnes, and calves of their legges. Every forenoone from eight to eleven, they are set on the *Praueush*, and beate in this sort till the monie be payed." Giles Fletcher, *Of the Russe Commonwealth*, introd. Richard Pipes and glossary-index John V. A. Fine, Jr. (Cambridge, Mass., 1966). p. 51.

effect. One of the reasons given for the decision in favor of the plaintiff was that the Zheludevo priest had signed the deed in place of the plaintiff and his brothers, calling himself their spiritual father, whereas he was not only not their spiritual father but a brigand. Fines for his crime had been taken from his sureties, he had been in prison in Riazan' and in custody in Moscow, and the bailiff had let him leave. In addition, the Terekhov abbot had testified that he had been the spiritual father of the plaintiff and his brothers for twelve years.[72]

As Shilovskii's experience illustrates, witnesses could be a source of problems for the litigants as well as a source of support. Some men encountered difficulties because they were unable to present others to testify on their behalf. In the majority of cases, witnesses apparently accompanied the litigants to court; when a party named the men who would testify for him, he usually added, "and here, Sire, are those men before thee."[73] In other cases litigants had to send for their witnesses and place them before the judge.[74] On a few occasions, judges ordered the constable to bring in the witnesses.[75] One defendant lost the case because his witness would not appear. Stepan had explained that the land belonged to Prince Semen Borisovich, who had given it to him to mow. He asked for a postponement, since the prince was in Viatka; when the prince returned, the judges ordered the defendant to present him, and granted a week's extension. The judges set a second date, and yet a third, and still the prince would not come. On the third date the judges asked the defendant where the prince was, and Stepan replied: "Sires, he promised to appear, and, Sires, to my detriment he has not appeared." The court gave judgment for the plaintiffs.[76]

Other witnesses could not be presented in court because they had died. In response to the judge's question, one plaintiff declared that not one of the men of court named in his documents or the secretaries who wrote them was still alive, so he could not call for anyone to verify the documents.[77] A judgment charter of April 18, 1505, records that the plaintiffs were unable to present a longtime resident who could testify that the land belonged to the Grand Prince: "It was known, Sires, to our abbot German, and, Sires, he has died; and, Sires, it is ten years since he died; besides

that, Sires, it is not known to anyone of our [people]."[78] Since the plaintiffs claimed that the land had been theirs since the great plague (1410–1420's), it is hardly surprising that a witness who remembered those years had died.

Lack of witnesses also created a problem for the defendant in a 1552 document. The plaintiff, elder Tikhon, had presented the longtime residents Orefa and his comrades, who had ceded the disputed land to the monastery, along with the cession deeds. After confirming the elder's statements, Orefa had testified that there was a beekeeper named Sofron, "still older than I am," who could testify that the disputed land was the land named in the documents. Sofron declared that this was indeed the land of the hamlet Semikha, not of Vedishchevo as the defendant claimed. The defendant Il'ia could present no longtime residents: "Sires, the Tatars killed [some of] my longtime residents, and others died, and, Sires, I have one longtime resident, named Nefed, Matfei's son, Malysh's nephew, and that [Nefed] has gone to Kazan' on the service of the Tsar [and] Grand Prince." For reasons not given Il'ia did not request a postponement in order to present his witness, but rather agreed to accept the word of the plaintiff's witness as to where the boundary lay. Yet he made another attempt to claim the disputed land, presenting a document showing his title to the Vedishchevo hamlet. The question turned upon whether the stream flowing through the disputed area was the Semikha or the V'iunitsa. The defendant had documents which gave him title to the hamlet Vedishchevo and land along the V'iunitsa stream, but no longtime residents to support his contention as to the name of that stream. He lost the case. As the plaintiff pointed out, "Sires, the document [will] not go along the boundary itself without men."[79]

Considering the frequency with which we encounter opposing sets of longtime residents it might appear that a litigant called for men he was certain would support him. Yet this was not always the case. Some witnesses, at the crucial moment, admitted that they did not know. On one occasion the defendants claimed land because their great-grandfather built the church and it was their patrimony. The witnesses testified that to their knowledge the defendants' great-grandfather had indeed built the church, but, "Sire, we do not know whose land [it is]." The plaintiff's witnesses knew the history of the land, and he won.[80] Another defendant's witnesses admitted that they knew neither the land nor the boundaries.[81] Lack of knowledge also caused problems for a plaintiff, elder Efrem of the Ferapontov Monastery. He had presented a donation charter which did not specify the boundaries of land

[72] Iushkov, *Akty XIII–XVII vv.*, no. 220.

[73] See, for example, *AFZKh* 1, nos. 103, 117, 125, 261, 306; *ASEI* 1, nos. 447, 523, 524, 525, 557; *ASEI* 2, nos. 229, 287, 288, 336, 368, 401; *ASEI* 3, nos. 48, 50, 105, 173, 208, 221, 223, 477.

[74] *ASEI* 2, nos. 332, 375, 402, 411, 458; *ASEI* 3, nos. 221, 288; *AFZKh* 1, nos. 117, 140, 254, 258.

[75] *AFZKh* 1, no. 254; *AIu*, nos. 13, 19; *ASEI* 2, no. 402; Likhachev, *Sbornik*, no. 14; *AIuB* 1, no. 5. Witnesses could also present witnesses of their own: *ASEI* 1, no. 523; 3, no. 288; *AFZKh* 1, no. 125.

[76] *ASEI* 2, no. 458.

[77] *ASEI* 2, no. 229.

[78] *ASEI* 1, no. 658; for some other examples, see *ASEI* 1, no. 557; 2, no. 309; 3, no. 173; *AIu*, no. 13.

[79] Likhachev, *Sbornik*, no. 12.

[80] *AFZKh* 1, no. 249.

[81] *ASEI* 2, no. 388a.

given to the monastery. When the judge asked him to show the court around the monastery's land, he declared that he was a "newcomer elder" and presented two witnesses. These men—who hardly seem longtime residents, since one was forty years old and the other only thirty—testified that the monastery's peasants were mowing the meadow, but "more than that, Sires, we cannot recall."[82] The plaintiff in another case confidently called for the testimony of a "good man of the Grand Prince, the longtime resident Leva Kolosov," only to hear his witness respond: "Sire judge, I do not know the name of that place where we stand, what that place is called; Sire, I am not a longtime resident of that place."[83]

Some litigants found that their own witnesses were in effect testifying against them. The defendant's witnesses in one case testified that the plaintiff's peasants had been plowing the land in question for ten years; the defendant's longtime residents, who claimed to remember for seventy years, could not recall who had plowed the land before the plaintiff.[84] Peasants of the Arbuzhoves' canton, in litigation with the metropolitan's manager, elder Iakim of the Novinskii Monastery, declared that a certain peasant named Guba Polutov had lived in the disputed hamlet, which was the Grand Prince's taxpaying land, and had been registered with the rest of the canton residents. When Guba appeared in court, he supported their opponent: "I lived in that hamlet for the metropolitan for ten years, and, Sires, I went away from that hamlet of the metropolitan's, and, Sires, [that was] three years ago, and, Sires, the scribe Vasilei Naumov registered me [as living] in that hamlet for the metropolitan." Examination of Naumov's land cadastres revealed that Guba had indeed been registered as a resident of the disputed hamlet, which was property of the metropolitan's Novinskii Monastery.[85] Witnesses called by the defendants in another case, apparently outraged at having to appear in court at all, supported the monasterial plaintiff completely: "Sire, that Okulik and [that] Olferko (the defendants) have senselessly called for us [to testify]; we, Sire, remember fifty years, and this is the Simonov Monastery's land, and it goes with that Verznevskoe village [for cadastral purposes]."[86]

A few judgment charters record both litigants calling for testimony of the same witnesses, each man seemingly expecting that the witnesses would support his claims. Apparently such witnesses were the only men possessing knowledge of the matter; otherwise it is difficult to believe that a litigant would ask a man to testify, when the man had already appeared on behalf of the opposition. In one instance, the plaintiff presented two men, Mikhailo and Ondrei, from whom the

land was purchased. The defendant called on the same witnesses—they were his brothers-in-law, and together with his aunt, who had since died, had given him the land in question. They pointed out the boundary, declaring that the defendant had been given the land up to that point. The court awarded the land on the other side of the line to the plaintiff.[87] In another case the plaintiff presented a donation charter from a mother and two sons, along with one of the sons to confirm it; the defendant presented a purchase deed naming the same people as vendors, and called upon the same son to testify about his document. The witness testified in favor of the plaintiff, who won his case.[88] In yet another judgment charter both sides called for the same longtime resident, who testified that he was the only man still alive who had been present at the official boundary survey.[89]

As we have seen, litigants called upon witnesses for support whenever possible. In many respects medieval Russian society relied to a much greater extent upon the memory of men than it did upon written records, and litigants frequently could prove their claims in no other way than by testimony of witnesses. Thus a litigant could encounter difficulties if his witnesses could not or would not appear in court. It was very important at all times that the witnesses' testimony corroborate exactly the statements made by the principal. With regard to longtime residents, their number and age played a significant role, as did their ability to demonstrate actual knowledge of the disputed land and its boundaries. The court or an opponent might demand confirmation of a document's authenticity by those who had signed it. Litigants might request that a general inquest be conducted in the area, in order to obtain support for their claims from the community as a whole. Even judges might on their own initiative ask witnesses to substantiate evidence presented in court. And when one party questioned the character of his opponent's witnesses, the investigation was carried out by obtaining the testimony of still other men. Testimony of witnesses, in all its variations, was the form of proof most commonly presented in Muscovite courts. The second most frequently encountered form, which litigants used increasingly in the sixteenth century, was documentary evidence.

V. TRIAL PROCEDURE:
DOCUMENTARY EVIDENCE

As we have seen, the judgment charters record that litigants presented witnesses of various kinds to testify on their behalf. Such testimony was the form of proof most commonly used. Written records took second

[82] *ASEI* **2**, no. 334.
[83] *ASEI* **3**, no. 208.
[84] *ASEI* **3**, no. 276.
[85] *AFZKh* **1**, no. 309.
[86] *ASEI* **2**, no. 402.
[87] *ASEI* **4**, no. 557.
[88] *ASEI* **1**, no. 447.
[89] *ASEI* **2**, no. 310; see also *PRP* **2**: p. 325.

place. Litigants presented several different types of documents to support their claims: many had charters of grant, usually from the Grand Prince but occasionally from another landholder;[1] some offered title-confirming charters;[2] others presented purchase deeds.[3] Still other documents could help prove title to disputed land: a purchase deed reported to higher authorities,[4] life-estate sale deed,[5] cession deed,[6] land-exchange charter,[7] property-division charter,[8] marriage settlement conveying land,[9] promissory note,[10] redemption charter,[11] injunction charter,[12] or reconciliation agreement.[13] One party in a 1532 case even had a rent receipt for his land.[14] Litigants might claim the land by right of a last will and testament.[15] Monasteries frequently had donation charters for lands given to them.[16] Other litigants had charters recording the boundaries of their land.[17] On occasion, when a witness could not appear in court, he sent a deposition containing his testimony.[18] One deposition recorded a pre-trial agreement concluded by the litigants.[19] In some cases litigants called for evidence from the land-cadastre books compiled by the Grand Prince's officials to prove that the disputed territory had been registered as their land.[20] A few parties even presented default judgments[21] or judgment charters from previous trials as proof of their claims.[22]

One man had both a judgment charter and a default judgment.[23]

Most litigants could present only one or two documents supporting their claims to land. In a case tried between 1465 and 1469, however, the defendant managed to place six documents before Ivan III, who was trying the case: a land-exchange charter (combined with a charter of grant) of the Grand Prince's great-grandfather, two life-estate sale deeds, a purchase deed, a purchase deed referred to the metropolitan for confirmation, and a donation charter.[24] The judgment charter itself is a curious document. Apparently it later served as a charter of grant; after the usual concluding formulae, we find several notations, reconfirmations of the "charter of grant" by Vasilii III and Ivan IV.

On occasion we find only a partial text, a summary of a document's contents, or even a brief statement that the judge had examined a document and found that it did (or did not) support the litigant's claims.[25] Usually, however, the judgment charters incorporate the complete texts of such documentary proof, word for word, apparently in just the way that the record was read aloud in court. One 1529 record[26] includes, as part of the evidence presented, the text of an earlier judgment charter from sometime between 1470 and 1485,[27] and a 1529 copy of a judgment charter originally issued between 1485 and 1490, included in a trial record which formed part of an original 1529 boundary-description charter.

In some of the judgment charters—although not as frequently as we would expect—we find instances where verification of a document's authenticity was required. This could be done in several ways. The man who originally granted the charter might be summoned to testify. In a case tried between 1495 and 1497, the defendant, an elder of the Spaso-Iaroslavl' Monastery, presented a donation charter which named the disputed land as one of fifteen meadows given to the monastery. Although the plaintiff never questioned that the donation charter was genuine, the judge later asked the donor to affirm that he had given that meadow to the monastery. Only after this did the court award the land to the defendant.[28] The plaintiff in another case produced a donation charter and brought one of the donors

[1] For some examples of such charters, see *ASEI* 1, nos. 595, 658; *ASEI* 2, nos. 286, 307, 332, 374, 381, 400, 404, 406, 410, 411, 416, 496; *ASEI* 3, no. 223; *AFZKh* 1, no. 254; *AIu*, no. 20; Likhachev, *Sbornik,* nos. 10, 11.

[2] *ASEI* 2, nos. 286, 332, 404; *AIuB* 1, no. 5.

[3] For sample texts, see *ASEI* 1, nos. 430, 447, 524, 525, 581, 658; *ASEI* 2, nos. 229, 285, 307, 381, 387, 410; *ASEI* 3, no. 105; *AFZKh* 1, no. 129; Anpilogov, *Novye dokumenty,* pp. 485–490; *AIu*, nos. 13, 23; *AIuB* 1, nos. 4, 5; *SGKE* 1, no. 76; Iushkov, *Akty XIII–XVII vv.*, no. 220; *RIB* 14, no. 17.

[4] *ASEI* 2, no. 381.

[5] *ASEI* 2, no. 381.

[6] *AIu*, no. 23; Likhachev, *Sbornik,* no. 12; *AIuB* 1, no. 5.

[7] *ASEI* 2, nos. 381, 411; *SGKE* 1, no. 76.

[8] *AIu*, nos. 13, 23; *SGKE* 1, no. 76.

[9] *AFZKh* 1, no. 117.

[10] Likhachev, *Sbornik,* nos. 9, 14; *AIuB* 1, nos. 4, 5, 8.

[11] *ASEI* 3, no. 105; *AIuB* 1, no. 5.

[12] *ASEI* 2, no. 493.

[13] *ASEI* 2, no. 411; *SGKE* 1, no. 76.

[14] *AIu*, no. 19.

[15] *ASEI* 1, no. 523; 2, no. 387; 3, no. 105; Likhachev, *Sbornik,* no. 9; *AIuB* 1, no. 4.

[16] For sample texts, see *ASEI* 1, nos. 447, 595; *ASEI* 2, nos. 309, 334, 337, 375, 381, 401, 464, 492, 493; *ASEI* 3, no. 208; *AFZKh* 1, no. 103; *AIu*, nos. 1, 23; Likhachev, *Sbornik,* no. 10.

[17] *ASEI* 2, nos. 188, 229, 310; *AFZKh* 1, no. 309; *AIu,* no. 16; *AIuB* 1, no. 5.

[18] See, for example, *AIu,* no. 1; *ASEI* 2, no. 402; Likhachev, *Sbornik,* no. 11.

[19] *ASEI* 2, no. 409.

[20] *AFZKh* 1, nos. 204, 258, 259, 309; Anpilogov, *Novye dokumenty,* pp. 485–490; *ASEI* 2, no. 310.

[21] *AIuB* 1, no. 4.

[22] For some examples, see *ASEI* 2, nos. 336, 405, 411, 422, 483; *ASEI* 3, no. 32; *AFZKh* 1, nos. 259, 309; *AIu,* nos. 17, 22; *AIuB* 1, nos. 5, 8.

[23] *AFZKh* 1, no. 259.

[24] *ASEI* 2, no. 381. For other cases in which several documents were introduced, see *AIuB* 1, nos. 4, 5; *AIu*, no. 23.

[25] One unusual instance occurs in a judgment charter issued between 1490 and 1500/1501. When litigants presented an earlier judgment charter as part of their evidence, the text was usually incorporated in full (see sources cited above, note 22). In this case, however, we find only an extract, recording the decision, of a judgment charter produced by the defendants; *ASEI* 2, no. 406. For the text of the entire document, see *ASEI* 2, no. 338.

[26] *ASEI* 2, no. 483.

[27] This judgment charter text is also published as a separate document; *ASEI* 2, no. 465.

[28] *ASEI* 3, no. 208.

to verify it. The defendant then claimed that he had bought the land from the same people named as donors in the plaintiff's document; he presented his purchase deed, and called upon the same witness. The judge examined the defendant's document, "and the [purchase] deed [was so] damaged (*likha*), [that] it was impossible to read it." The witness supported the plaintiff, and he won the case.[29]

In a judgment charter of 1475/1476, the judge's questions about documents destroyed the plaintiff's case. An elder of St. Cyril's Monastery brought suit against peasants of the Grand Prince, charging that they were mowing the monastery's meadowland and had destroyed the boundary markers. The elder then produced a purchase deed and boundary-setting charter. The purchase deed, written by the Grand Prince's secretary Iarlyk, named several witnesses: Koz'ma Glebovich, Ivan, son of Amin, Volodia Ushakov, Ivashko Narmachskoi, and Kostia Stepanov. The boundary-setting charter, written by Il'ia Petrov, named as witnesses Vasilii Ivanov Peresvet, Nestor Karpov, Kosta Stepanov, the hundredman Ivashko, and Olferko. The plaintiff declared that not one of these men was still alive, and he had no additional witnesses for the land. Besides, he himself was not a local resident, and the abbot had only recently sent him to oversee this territory; "Apart from the documents, I have no one as a witness for [our title to] that meadowland." The defendants, on the other hand, had longtime residents to support them. After these men had testified, the judge returned to his examination of the plaintiff, asking why he had not presented his documents earlier or protested about the situation. The elder replied: "I said nothing to them, Sire, because these documents were in the possession of Nastas'ia, wife of Fedor Andreevich (the purchaser of the land), and [only] when leaving this world did she give us those documents." The judge, however, was not yet satisfied with the explanation, and asked which of the plaintiff's predecessors had been in charge of the area when Nastas'ia died, and who had mowed the meadow at that time. The plaintiff declared that the peasants had mowed it then, "because, Sire, we did not find the documents until now."[30] No further evidence was presented, and judgment was given in favor of the Grand Prince's peasants. The judgment charter has no section listing the judge's reasons for his decision. Perhaps the testimony of the defendants' longtime residents, who remembered for more than seventy years, outweighed documents which could not be authenticated. Yet one is tempted to put greater emphasis on the doubtful character of the documents themselves. Apparently the judge's suspicions were aroused—he certainly questioned the plaintiff in greater depth than was usual when such evidence was produced. We must note also that there is no

reference to a donation charter by which the monastery acquired the land. Nastas'ia's husband is named in the purchase deed and boundary charter, but the monastery is not. Apparently some time had passed—we do not know how much—between Nastas'ia's death and the trial. Even if the documents were genuine, where had they been? How did the monastery happen to "find" them?

Occasionally when one party presented a document as proof, his opponent challenged the evidence, alleging that it was fraudulent in some way. In one instance the plaintiff, after referring to his charter of grant, continued: "And, Sires, I call for the [land cadastre] books [to show] that I [was] granted the Kondusha [lands], with whatever went with them [for cadastral purposes], as of old." After the plaintiff's longtime residents had testified, the defendants produced a purchase deed for portions of several lands. The plaintiff immediately declared that their charter was false (*lzhivaia*) and again called for evidence from the Grand Prince's records. When the judges asked him why he questioned the document's authenticity, he replied: "He (one of the defendants) owns [land] in Chimkinichi by the terms of that charter, but elsewhere, Sires, he holds nothing. And those lands of theirs, Sires, are not registered [in his name] in the books, nor are the meadowlands which are described (lit. written) in his charter." After all this, the judges turned to an examination of the defendants' longtime residents, and the judgment charter records no further reference to, or inspection of, the Grand Prince's record books. Apparently the charge of forgery was not investigated, and the judges eventually decreed that the matter be decided by drawing lots.[31]

Testimony given in a 1492 case, however, does provide an illustration of authentication methods. The plaintiffs, peasants of the Grand Prince, charged that boundary surveyors from St. Cyril's Monastery had measured off part of the Grand Prince's lands for the monastery. The surveyors answered that they and their fathers had been mowing the Kochevinskaia land for fifty years, that they had measured off the land as of old, and that Savka, one of the plaintiffs, had begun to erect his homestead on Kochevinskaia land that autumn. An elder from the monastery then testified that the abbot had purchased Kochevinskaia sixty years earlier, and he produced a purchase deed. Further testimony by the elder shows us one method by which documents could be proven fraudulent. He declared that Savka, one of the plaintiffs, had formerly lived in one of the monastery's hamlets but had transferred that autumn to the Grand Prince's canton, after which he had sowed the Kochevinskaia clearing with oats. Savka had then gone to Beloozero, where "he fraudulently obtained from [the vicegerent] Timofei Mikhailovich [Iurlo-Pleshcheev] an exemption charter

[29] *ASEI* 1, no. 447.
[30] *ASEI* 2, no. 229.

[31] Anpilogov, *Novye dokumenty,* pp. 485–490.

(charter of temporary exemption from fiscal and service obligations) for that clearing, and said, Sires, that that was the Grand Prince's forest, and, Sires, he began to haul planks to that clearing, [and] to erect dwellings." Monastery authorities had then petitioned the vicegerent Timofei Mikhailovich for justice. Timofei ordered the cantonal good men to appear before him, and learned by questioning the good men of the whole canton that Savka had put the monastery's Kochevinskaia land under cultivation. Following the inquest, Timofei took back his exemption charter and gave the land to the monastery, with the seed grain which Savka had planted. The elder concluded: "And we, Sires, taking pity on that Savka, gave him back the seed grain. And this autumn, Sires, he disobeyed your surveyors, and he, Sires, began to erect that cottage against Timofei's instructions." The elder then presented two good men, who had testified before Timofei, to substantiate his account of Savka's fraudulently acquired exemption charter. These men declared: "Not only we two, Sires, appeared before Timofei; many cantonal peasants, Sires, appeared [with us before him], and we told Timofei, Sires, that that Savka was cultivating [the land] in the monastery's Kochevinskaia clearing and had begun to erect a homestead." The judges ordered Savka to produce Timofei's charter, since possession of the document would explain why he was erecting the homestead, but Savka could not do so: "Timofei, Sires, did take from me that charter, by which he had bestowed his favor on me." The plaintiff Savka lost, in part because he had erected his hut on land belonging to the monastery.[32]

After the defendant in a case tried between 1494 and 1499 had presented an earlier judgment charter as part of his evidence, the plaintiffs declared: "Sire, that is not written in [judge] Zinovei's [authentic] charter; Zinovei was not on that land; neither witnesses nor a boundary demarcation are written in that charter. Sire, place those charters before the Grand Prince [for verification]."[33] This did not become necessary, since the defendant and his witnesses later destroyed their credibility when they were unable to show the judge the boundaries of their land and, in the process, trespassed on the territory of a third party.

A judgment charter of 1508, however, records a case in which the court did verify the authenticity of documentary evidence.[34] The plaintiffs, Prince Danilo and Prince Davyd, sons of Prince Iurii Kemskii, declared that they had purchased their uncle's patrimonial estate, a manorial village with hamlets and deserted lands, with the condition that their uncle Prince Fedor should remain in possession until his death. He had died two years before, and, they charged, the defendant—their uncle's widow Princess Anna Kemskaia—refused to relinquish the estate and was living on it illegally. The plaintiffs then produced their purchase deed, which, they claimed, had been written by their uncle. Princess Anna's slave Timoshka, who was representing her in court, immediately denied that the sale had ever taken place. Nor had his master ever given the plaintiffs a purchase deed: "That, Sire, is a forged deed; [that] is not [their uncle] Prince Fedor's handwriting." Timoshka then presented a note (*zapis'*) written in the prince's hand, and called for the testimony of the two witnesses named in the plaintiff's purchase deed. One witness, Prince Ivan, had died, and the other, Prince Afonasii, could not come, but Afonasii sent a deposition containing his testimony, and included a purchase deed written by Prince Ivan, and a property-division charter written by Prince Fedor, the plaintiffs' uncle, for comparison of handwriting. In his deposition, Afonasii stated that the plaintiffs had purchased the estate, and Fedor had written the purchase deed to which Afonasii and his deceased brother had been witnesses. Then the judge proceeded to a comparison of the handwriting in the various documents. He assembled the plaintiffs' purchase deed, in Prince Fedor's writing, and the property-division charter, also in Fedor's writing, which Afonasii had sent, and the sample of Fedor's writing brought in by the defendant's slave, and placed all these documents, plus the others produced in court, before all the secretaries of the Grand Prince. The secretaries declared that the purchase deed and property-division charter were written in the same hand as the sample brought by the defendant's slave. The handwriting of Prince Ivan, who had signed the purchase deed as a witness, was the same as that in one of Ivan's other documents which Afonasii had sent. This comparison by the Grand Prince's secretaries—who were the most expert handwriting analysts available—apparently decided the case. The widowed defendant lost, for, instead of proving the

[32] *ASEI* 2, no. 285.

[33] *ASEI* 2, no. 411.

[34] Forgery was a serious problem and often very difficult to detect, as recent critical studies have shown; for analysis of a variety of texts which appear to be forgeries, see, *inter alia,* A. I. Andreev, "O podlozhnosti zhalovannoi gramoty Pechengskomu monastyriu 1556 g." *Russkii istoricheskii zhurnal* 6 (1920): pp. 132–157; N. Kalistratov, "Zamechanie o dvukh podlozhnykh gramotakh," *Trudy Mariiskogo gos. ped. instituta* 5 (1946): pp. 63–68; V. I. Koretskii, "Pravaia gramota ot 30 noiabria 1618 g. Troitse-Sergievu monastyriu," *Zapiski otdela rukopisei G.B.L.* 21 (1959): pp. 173–187; Likhachev, *Razriad-nye d'iaki,* pp. 431–433; M. N. Tikhomirov, "O chastnykh aktakh v drevnei Rusi," *Istoricheskie zapiski* 17 (1945): pp. 225–244; S. N. Valk, "Nachal'naia istoriia drevnerusskogo chastnogo akta," *Vspomogatel'nye istoricheskie distsipliny* (Moscow-Leningrad, 1937), pp. 285–318; A. A. Vvedenskii, "Fal'sifikatsiia dokumentov v Moskovskom gosudarstve XVI–XVII vv.," *Problemy istochnikovedeniia* 1 (1933): pp. 85–109; A. A. Zimin, "Aktovye poddelki Troitse-Sergieva monastyria 80-kh godov XVI v.," *Voprosy sotsial'no-ekonomicheskoi istorii i istochnikovedeniia perioda feodalizma v Rossii* (Moscow, 1961), pp. 247–251; idem, "K izucheniiu fal'sifikatsii aktovykh materialov v russkom gosudarstve XVI–XVII vv.," *Trudy moskovskogo gosudarstvennogo istoriko-arkhivnogo instituta* 17 (1963): pp. 399–428.

purchase deed a forgery, her man had presented a sample of Prince Fedor's writing which turned out to be in the same handwriting as the purchase deed and the property-division charter which Afonasii sent as samples of Fedor's writing.[35]

Forgery was a main question in the dispute over half of the village Gravoronovo, mortgaged by Prince Andrei Nozdrovatyi to Ivan Sheremetev. The record begins with Sheremetev's petition for justice, requesting a bailiff. Andrei Nozdrovatyi, he charged, had mortgaged half the village to him for a loan of two hundred and fifty rubles. Now, he claimed, Princes Iurii and Vasilii Tokmakov, in their abode, were drawing up false mortgage-redemption notes with the help of forgers, to show that they had redeemed the village. He asked for a bailiff to help him apprehend the forger and seize the forged documents. The Tsar ordered the town commissioner (gorodovoi prikazchik) and three central-court bailiffs to go with the plaintiff's man Olesha to search the Tokmakov dwelling. The officials reported later that day. They had gone, taking seven "good men" along as local witnesses, and had questioned Prince Iurii in the presence of the witnesses. Iuri declared that his brother was in the village, and asserted that no outsiders or forgers or forgeries were in his dwelling: all the people there were his own. The officials then ordered the plaintiff's man Olesha, in the presence of the witnesses and Iurii, to conduct a thorough search. Before Olesha began, however, "Prince Iurii, Sire, himself conducted a search of Olesha and felt around [with his fingers] in his mouth," to make sure Olesha was not smuggling anything in. When Olesha came to a locked room, the officials ordered it opened, and Olesha cried out, "Here, Sires, are the forger and the forgeries!" The officials continued:

And we, Sire, together with the local witnesses [and] good men, entered the room and there, in the room, lay a man on Prince Iurii's bed, and [that man] said his name was Vlasko, son of Ivan, and he was dressed in the short cotton-print kaftan which Prince Iurii [himself] is now wearing in your presence, and at his head lay a piece of writing, we know not what kind, and at his feet stood ink and a flask of wine.

After taking Vlasko into custody, they sealed "that piece of writing" and gave it to the local witnesses for safekeeping. They then presented Olesha, Prince Iurii, Vlasko, and the local witnesses, with the document, before the Grand Prince. After the local witnesses had confirmed the preceding account, Prince Iurii charged collusion between the tsar's officials and

35 AIu, no. 13. For the history of the Kemskii patrimonial lands, see A. I. Kopanev, Istoriia zemlevladeniia Belozerskogo kraia XV–XVI v. (Moscow-Leningrad, 1951), pp. 157–165. A fragmentary judgment charter of 1521 records another instance of handwriting comparison and requests by the judge that witnesses be presented to authenticate documents produced in evidence; Kashtanov, Ocherki, no. 74, pp. 467–477.

the others, claiming that they had planted "that muzhik and document" on his premises, and he demanded a judicial duel.

The tsar next questioned Vlasko. At first he denied all knowledge of the affair, claiming to be a humble man who supported himself with his pen: "I go, Sire, among good people, here a day, there a night." He had gone to visit a servant of Andrei Diatlov's at the Tokmakov residence, where, for his sins, he had gone to sleep in the prince's room. Sheremetev then charged that Vlasko had been caught in a previous act of forgery, and Vlasko admitted it when confronted with the testimony of the state treasurer Ivan Ivanovich Tret'iakov, who had heard the earlier case.

The promissory note seized at Tokmakov's residence was read aloud, and Sheremetev declared it a forgery. Tokmakov claimed that Nozdrovatyi had redeemed the note, and that the Tokmakov brothers had then purchased the estate. Each litigant was ordered to present his promissory note in court, while the forger Vlasko was to be tortured. After torture, Vlasko declared that Iurii Tokmakov had given him a paper containing various signatures and asked him to draw up a promissory note, claiming that the original had been lost. The defendants presented their promissory note, which was compared with that seized earlier and found to be identical. Then the plaintiff produced his promissory note, which the defendants declared false. Sheremetev countered by referring to a previous suit which he had brought against Prince Andrei, in which the defendant had admitted that he had given Sheremetev the note. They had become reconciled in the matter, but the boiar judges had ordered copies of Sheremetev's documents incorporated into the record. Next the plaintiff presented a land-partition charter, which he declared the defendant had given him as a boundary record. Andrei claimed that this document was also false, that no property-division had taken place.

The next step was interrogation of the witnesses and secretaries named in all the documents and of the land surveyor alleged to have carried out the property division. The men named as witnesses in the defendant's promissory note immediately declared the signatures to be forgeries, as did the secretary, who demanded a confrontation with Vlasko the forger. Vlasko repeated his previous testimony. One of the witnesses then added that he had signed another purchase deed for the Tokmakovs, which they had used in preparing the forgery. The witnesses to Sheremetev's document, on the other hand, affirmed that the signatures on the promissory note were theirs, as did the men named in the boundary record. The land surveyor declared that he had indeed conducted the land partition. The Grand Prince's secretary subsequently presented the record of the previous trial between the litigants, which incorporated the plaintiff's documents word for word. Needless to say, all this testimony and checking of documents against each other figured prominently among the reasons for the decision in favor of the plaintiff.[36]

Thus some litigants contested the authenticity of documentary evidence on the basis of forgery. Others protested that their opponent had extorted the documents from them by force. In challenging the "extorted deed" to his property produced by the defendant Sherefedinov's son-in-law in a 1584 case, Timofei Shilovskii not only attacked the character of the witnesses and secretary named in it [37] but also pointed out other questionable elements. The vendors named in the deed were Timofei and Vasilii, sons of Dmitrii Shilovskii; Pervyi and Dmitrii, sons of Stepan, son of Volk Shilovskii; Iev and Nenash, sons of Mikhail Zapol'skii; Elisei and Luka and Grigorii and Boris, sons of Grigorii Shilovskii; and Karp and Fedor, sons of Ivan Shilovskii. Signatures on the back of the document indicated that Denisei, son of Fedor Mozharov, had signed in place of Grigorii Shilovskii. Aleksandr, son of Petr Liapunov, had signed for Iev and Nenash Zapol'skii. And the Zheludevo priest Ivan had signed on behalf of his spiritual sons Timofei, Elisei, Grigorii, Luka, Boris, Pervyi, Mitka, Karp, and Fedor Shilovskii.

When challenging this document, the plaintiff Timofei declared that Sherefedinov had extorted the deed to his portion of the estate. Elisei said that he had been "subjected to the 'righter' (na pravezhe) at Ondrei Sherefedinov's [chancery] for unpaid taxes," and that the defendant had extorted a deed for Elisei's portion. They explained that Pervusha was not in Moscow at the time—hearing that Timofei and Elisei were being tortured for the estate, he had fled. Sherefedinov had thus obtained deeds to two portions of the estate, but his son-in-law's document included the village Shilovskoe and the entire hamlet Vyrkovo. The plaintiff declared that only half the land there belonged to their patrimonial property, the remainder being service-tenure land. Vasilii Shilovskii, named as a vendor, had died six years earlier. Luka, also named, had been in the Don area for four years. Karp and Fedor had not been in Moscow; they too had fled. "And why did Denis Mozharov affix his hand in place of Grigorii Shilovskii? Is this not obvious skullduggery?" Grigorii Shilovskii had two sons who were literate—he would have asked them to sign in his place.

Subsequently the plaintiffs presented a petition, in which they declared that the defendants had ordered their relatives to sign the deed. The Shilovskiis pointed out that, if they had really sold their estate, they would have asked their own relatives or spiritual father to sign, and listed seven members of their family, in addition to their spiritual father, who were literate.

After conducting investigations concerning the status of the land and character of the witnesses, and ordering the property placed under court protection until further order, the judges examined Chetvertyi Shilovskii, one of the literate relatives. They ordered that he write in their presence, and he did so, submitting a petition in which he declared that his signature had not been on the deed.

Among the reasons for decision in favor of the plaintiff, the court noted that the witnesses who signed Sherefedinov's deed had done so despite being aware that Shilovskii had literate nephews, who would have signed had the deed not been extorted. With regard to the plaintiff's statements that his "co-vendors" could not have participated in the sale, the court noted that Sherefedinov had denied this "but offered no evidence whatever that Vasilii Shilovskii had been alive when Rodion (the defendant's son-in-law) bought the patrimonial estate from them, or that Luka and the others had been in Moscow at that time." [38] Thus Shilovskii successfully challenged the document presented by his opponent. The case illustrates that documentary evidence in itself was not enough. The court's attitude also reveals another feature of Muscovite justice—under such circumstances, the litigant was expected to counter the challenge with further evidence.

Sharap Baskakov, defendant in another suit, tried to claim that a whole series of documents had been extorted from him. The plaintiff, Abbot Iona of the Trinity-Makhrishchskii Monastery, declared that Sharap and his sons had sold their property two years before, but refused to collect the remainder of the money and surrender the village. The abbot presented a purchase deed. Sharap affirmed that the document was written in his hand, but declared that he had written it under duress (u nevoli). He had borrowed forty rubles on a promissory note and gone to Moscow. The treasurer had sent a constable after him, and he borrowed another twenty rubles. When the constable came again, he claimed, the secretary Timofei Klobukov, "showing favor to the abbot," had ordered all the money collected without allowing a postponement. Thus Sharap had been forced to write the purchase deed. Timofei, he alleged, had ordered Sharap's son brought to his residence by force and had compelled him to sign the deed. All the other witnesses were Timofei's relatives. The bailiff whom Sharap had named as bringing his son to Timofei's residence appeared in court and denied the charges. Sharap took no action against him or Timofei, and stated that no one had witnessed the use of force. As noted above, Sharap claimed that he had received only sixty rubles; the abbot, on the other hand, declared that Sharap had taken one hundred and twenty rubles and a marten-fur coat in addition. He

---

[36] *AIuB* **1**, no. 5. A 1567 judgment charter records further litigation over this half-hamlet, in which the 1547 decision served as evidence. Apparently Andrei Nozdrovatyi had not paid off the mortgage twenty years later. For the text of this judgment charter, see *AIuB* **1**, no. 8.

[37] See above pp. 44–45.

[38] Iushkov, *Akty XIII–XVII vv.*, no. 220.

produced Sharap's document to that effect. Again Sharap admitted that it was in his handwriting, but he had written this too under duress, "so that they would not order me tortured for the purchase deed." Abbot Iona then presented Sharap's promissory note, written before the other two documents. Sharap admitted that he had written the note, "because I needed the money in a hurry." The abbot declared: "Sire, Sharap says that he wrote everything under duress"— and Iona produced another document, written before the purchase deed, in which Sharap had promised not to sell the property without the monastery's consent. Once more, Sharap admitted that he had written the document: "I needed the money urgently." Next the abbot presented a default judgment against Sharap and his sons, issued to the monastery when the Baskakovs had failed to appear in a previous suit. The monastery had brought complaint because they refused to surrender the property and had beaten and robbed the monastery's agent sent to them in the matter. Sharap declared the default judgment false. He had never been served with a summons. One of his men had, however, and he had sent the man to Moscow. There two petty boiars had secured his release on surety bond, but Sharap did not remember the sureties' names. Nevertheless he asserted that the monastery had obtained the default judgment by deceit. Once again, he produced no proof for his allegations. Next the abbot presented other documents showing title to the land, which, he declared, Sharap had turned over to the monastery in accordance with their agreement, upon receiving the one hundred and twenty rubles. This time Sharap declared that he had taken the documents to the monastery to have them copied, and that the abbot had not returned them.

Suddenly Sharap's brother Levontii appeared in court and petitioned the judge. Sharap, he complained, had sold their patrimonial property without his knowledge. He asked that he be allowed to redeem it. The abbot pointed out that Levontii had been named as a witness in Sharap's original promissory note. Levontii stated that Sharap had written his name, but he had not been present, and Sharap admitted that this was true.[39]

The judge ordered that Levontii be allowed to redeem the property by paying his brother's debt of one hundred and twenty rubles, plus five rubles for the marten-fur coat and interest for two years, because Sharap had caused delay for that time and had had the use of the property. Six days later the bailiff reported,

and Levontii confirmed, that he could not obtain the money to redeem the property and was ceding possession to the monastery. In the end, the court gave judgment for the plaintiff, awarding the land to the monastery upon payment of the remaining thirty rubles to the defendant. Interestingly enough, Sharap's signing of his brother's name is not mentioned among the reasons for the decision against him, perhaps because the brother had been given an opportunity to redeem the property. But the court did stress Sharap's claim that the documents had been extorted and his failure to produce any evidence of this, to take any action against the alleged extorters, or to call for the witnesses.[40]

Presentation of written proof gave rise to other problems. Some litigants, for various reasons, could not produce documents which would have supported their case. For example, in a trial which took place between 1462 and 1470 the defendant, monk Semen of the Simonov Monastery, explained that the monastery had formerly possessed such proof of title: "Sire, we had purchase deeds and donation charters for those lands and deserted areas, but they burned up in the Suzdal' fire."[41] Fire was the reason most commonly cited in explaining loss of documents.[42] The defendant in a mid-fifteenth-century trial declared that he had his father's purchase deed for the land, and offered to produce it if the judge would give him a postponement. When he returned to the land on the designated date, however, he did not bring the document: "Sire, my purchase deed has burned up."[43] The judgment charter is abbreviated, and there is no more information. Perhaps the defendant had been trying to bluff, hoping that no one would ask to see his purchase deed, and then fell back upon loss of the document in a fire to explain his failure to bring it. On the other hand, he could easily have been telling the truth; fires were not an uncommon event in Muscovite Russia.

Ivan Fedorovich Vorontsov, defendant in a 1551 suit tried by Ivan IV, declared that his family had previously held documents giving them title to the disputed land, "and, Sovereign, for our sins thy sovereign disgrace fell upon my father." His documents had been confiscated and taken to the tsar's treasury, where they had been destroyed by "'the great fire" while in the sovereign's possession.[44] In response to the tsar's ques-

---

[39] In general, the right of redemption (*vykup*) of patrimonial property was granted to other members of a clan within a forty-year period. The signature of relatives as witnesses to purchase deeds, land-exchange charters, and other such documents was considered an indication of their acquiescence in alienation of the property; 1550 Sudebnik, article 85; 1649 Ulozhenie, **17**: art. 30. On the right of redemption, see Veselovskii, *Feodal'noe zemlevladenie*, pp. 17–39.

[40] *AIuB* 1, no. 4. Three years earlier, Sharap Baskakov had served as a judge in a case in which the plaintiff declared the record from the lower court false and presented an "authentic draft trial record" which he claimed was in Sharap's handwriting. For a discussion of this case, see below, pp. 70–71.

[41] *ASEI* 2, no. 368.

[42] See, for example, *ASEI* 2, nos. 374, 381, 400, 404, 406, 410, 411; *ASEI* 3, no. 221; *AIu*, nos. 16, 24.

[43] *ASEI* 2, no. 358.

[44] Fedor Vorontsov fell into disgrace briefly in the fall of 1545 and again in the summer of 1546 when he was executed; *Polnoe sobranie russkikh letopisei*, **13**, pt. 1: pp. 147, 149; pt. 2: pp. 446–449; *Razriadnaia kniga*, p. 109. Some of the

tions, Vorontsov replied that he did not remember which secretary had given his father the charter for two meadows or know whether there had been one for the third. He requested a postponement until the following day, so that he could ask his mother about the documents.

Vorontsov subsequently reported that the secretary Posnik Gubin had issued a judgment charter to his father for the land, while another secretary had given them a document clearing the title: "and, Sovereign, those documents burned in thy treasury in the great fire; and, Sovereign, the secertary Grigorei Zakharov is no longer alive." Posnik Gubin testified next. He affirmed that he had given Fedor Vorontsov a judgment charter for the village but did not remember whether the document named the disputed meadows; "and, Sovereign, my draft [judgment] charter burned in the great fire." Another secretary sent a memorandum containing his testimony, in which he claimed that Fedor Vorontsov had taken one of the meadows, Vysokoe, away from him by force. To complicate matters, he added that there were two meadows of that name on the same river.

The defendant did not know whether there were two: "I have spent little time in that village." The plaintiff, on the other hand, explained that there was another Vysokoe meadow downstream from theirs. Judgment was given for the plaintiff in accordance with his charter of grant for the land. The defendant lost, partly because he could produce no documents to support his claims. In this instance witnesses were hardly a substitute. The testimony of one secretary did not help him, since the man could not remember what had been recorded in the document, while the second secretary had contradicted the defendant's report. And once again, the court stressed Vorontsov's failure to challenge the second man's testimony.[45]

Fires were not the only reason which prevented litigants from bringing their evidence to court. One man said that the Grand Prince had given him the land and a charter, but he could not place it before the judge because his documents were with Mikhal' Ofonin, who had left for Tver'.[46] A 1471 judgment charter records an interesting variation of the problem. The defendants, the Simonov Monastery estate manager and his peasants, had presented a purchase deed for the land. The plaintiffs, explaining why the land was their patrimony, declared: "Sire, we had the last will and testament of our father, Ivan Lopot, and, Sire, that Malechkino land is given to us in that will; and now, Sire, that will is in the Simonov Monastery's archive." The defendant then placed the plaintiff's documentary evidence before the judge. After hearing the will, the judge addressed the plaintiffs as follows:

Ye call the Malechkino land your patrimony, and ye said that that land was given to you in the will of your father, Yvan Lopot; yet the Malechkino land is not [mentioned] in your father's will, and in the Simonov Monastery's purchase deed for the Verznevskoe village that Malechkino land is mentioned; [the deed states] that it was purchased along with the Verznevskoe village from Princess Ofrosin'ia, Prince Petr Dmitreevich's [widow].[47]

The plaintiffs apparently had no suitable response, and the judge proceeded to give his decision in favor of their opponents.

A 1504 case provides yet another variation. The document which the judge wanted to examine could not be presented, not because it had been lost, but because it had never been granted. The defendants, accused of moving illegally into new settlements in Krutets and into the deserted village of Krasnoe, declared: "Sire, Tropynia, the chief steward of the Zhabenskaia canton, settled [us] contractually in those new settlements." The judge then asked them for their exemption charters, but they had none.

Sire, the chief steward Tropynia settled us in those new settlements, and, Sire, he did not give us exemption charters for those new settlements; and, Sire, we rode to the chief steward, and, Sire, the chief steward [was] ill; and, Sire, we petitioned him to bestow favor—to give us exemption charters for those new settlements.

Their effort, however, proved unsuccessful. "And the chief steward, Sire, told us: 'When, God willing, I recover, I will be with you and give you exemption charters.' And, Sire, after that the chief steward Tropynia died."[48] Thus the defendants remained unchartered, and had no papers to help them retain their settlement.

Some litigants had copies, not original documents. One man presented a copy of his land-exchange charter, since the original had been destroyed by fire.[49] The plaintiff in an August, 1502, judgment charter, elder Fegnast Batman of the Ferapontov Monastery, declared: "Sire, we have, in the Grand Prince's archives, a donation charter for that forest from Prince Mikhailo Ondreevich; and Vasilei Dolmatov took [the original charter] from us; and Mikhailo Shapkin and Ivan Golova have a copy of that [donation] charter, signed by Vasilei Dolmatov; and the copy of that charter, Sire, is before thee." Later, on instructions of the Grand Prince, the judge "searched out Prince Mikhailo Ondreevich's charter of grant in the archives, and he examined the charter; and in the charter that forest was recorded [as belonging] to the Ferapontov Mon-

---

Vorontsov property was confiscated; see Zimin, *Reformy Ivana Groznogo*, p. 269. The "great fire" mentioned by Vorontsov was undoubtedly the Moscow fire of 1547.

[45] Likhachev, *Sbornik*, no. 11.
[46] *AFZKh* 1, no. 259.

[47] *ASEI* 2, no. 387. The defendant in a 1494 case, who had lost his copy of the deposition presented by the plaintiff, verified the authenticity of his opponent's document; *ASEI* 2, no. 409.
[48] *ASEI* 3, no. 173.
[49] *ASEI* 2, no. 381.

astery with the same boundary description as was written in this [trial] record," that is, in the incorporated text of the copy.[50]

Another plaintiff, the metropolitan's estate manager Vania, said: "Before this, Sire, there was a trial in these same meadows and in Ikonniche before the Grand Prince's judge Ivan Golova, between the land administrator Korovai and our estate manager of the metropolitan, Malga, and, Sire, Ivan Golova gave judgment in favor of our estate manager of the metropolitan, Malga, for that land, and for those meadows, and for the bank of that land, and, Sire, Ivan Golova gave our estate manager Malga a judgment charter for that land and for those meadows, and here, Sire, is a copy of that judgment charter before thee, and the charter, Sire, is in the metropolitan's archives; and, Sire, I will place that judgment charter before the Grand Prince." Before deciding in favor of the plaintiff, the judge verified the document by questioning Korovai, who had lost the earlier case, and also ordered Vania to present the original charter at the trial on *doklad*.[51]

Under other circumstances litigants could not present their evidence on the spot because their documents were located elsewhere. The defendants in a judgment charter of April, 1505, two elders from St. Cyril's Monastery, said that the donation charter for the floodland meadow was in the Grand Prince's archives. After hearing testimony and going around the boundaries, the judges found the donation charter in the archives.[52] Elder Isaiia of the Trinity-Sergius Monastery likewise stated that its donation charter, from Princess Nastas'ia, wife of Prince Aleksandr of Kiev, and her sons Prince Semen and Prince Mikhail, was in the Grand Prince's archives.[53] In another 1505 judgment charter, the defendant, Dmitrii Vasil'evich Shein's estate manager Gridia Teptiukov, declared: "Sires, my master Dmitrei has documents for that village; and, Sires, my master Dmitrei will place the documents before you in Moscow." He gave no explanation for his inability to produce these records—perhaps Dmitrii Vasil'evich himself was in Moscow or kept his records there. At any rate the judges did not object to changing the location of the trial, and Shein placed a purchase deed and a charter of grant before them in Moscow.[54]

When a party called for evidence from the Grand Prince's land cadastres, naturally he himself could not show the books to the judges. In a 1498/1499 case, the metropolitan's estate manager Mitia Sarykhozin called for evidence "from the three books of the Grand Prince's scribes [to show], Sire, that those are lands of the metropolitan." After his opponents, the secular landholders Andrei and Ivan Koriakin, had presented their evidence, Mitia repeated his demand:

Sire, Andreika and Ivashka Koriakin have placed before thee the last will and testament and purchase deeds of their father Stepan, and, Sire, I do not contest the last will and testament and purchase deed; but, Sire, I call for [evidence] from the [land] record books [to show], Sire, that those hamlets Mikhailovskoe and Bliznino are recorded [as belonging] to the metropolitan's manorial village Vorok; and, Sire, I do not remember the names of the scribes, Sire, [I do not remember] which scirbes wrote [the records].

The Koriakins' documents, in addition to the testimony of their longtime residents, supported their claim to the land. Their father had left his purchases to them. Besides, Mitia, by his refusal to challenge the documents, apparently acknowledged the strength of their evidence. Yet he persisted in his demand for the record books, despite his evident uncertainty as to who had compiled them. Perhaps he hoped that something damaging to his opponents' case would turn up. If so, he was disappointed. The judge did as Mitia requested, and examined the land cadastre books of Aleksei Poluekhtov. "And in the books [was] written: 'The metropolitan's manorial village Vorok,' and those hamlets Mikhailovskoe and Bliznino [were] not recorded in the books [as going with] the manorial village Vorok." The judge awarded the hamlets to the Koriakin brothers.[55]

Other litigants, however, had greater success with this tactic. In some instances, merely calling for evidence from the land cadastres proved sufficient to make the point. The opponent declined to request that the records be examined, admitting that the land was registered for the first party.[56] Other situations, however, required that the books be examined. Vania, estate manager of the Kulikovo village, called for the land cadastres of Mikhailo Volynskii to show that the disputed hamlets were the metropolitan's lands. After hearing all testimony, the judge examined Volynskii's books, found that the hamlets were recorded as lands of the metropolitan, and gave judgment for Vania.[57] In a 1505 case the land cadastres were used to check

[50] *ASEI* 2, no. 337. A judgment charter of 1505/1506, incorporated in a 1511 text, records that the plaintiff presented a copy of a purchase deed as evidence. He explained that there had been a previous trial over the land, in which the original deed had been presented. They had reached no conclusion in the case, and the secretary Tishko Moklokov was in possession of the documents. The judges heard the copy read aloud, and later compared it with the original, which they took from Moklokov. The plaintiff won the disputed meadows, but the settlement in question was awarded to the defendants because it was not recorded by name in the purchase deed; *AFZKh* 1, no. 309. The plaintiff in another case said that the original charter of grant from the sovereign was in Riazan' and asked for a postponement to get it. In the meantime, he presented a copy of the document as evidence. The judges ordered the copy attached to the trial record. When the plaintiff brought the original, the judges had it compared with the copy; *AIu*, no. 24.

[51] *AFZKh* 1, no. 259.
[52] *ASEI* 2, no. 310.
[53] *ASEI* 1, no. 607.

[54] *ASEI* 1, no. 658.
[55] *ASEI* 3, no. 105.
[56] *AIu*, no. 15; Likhachev, *Sbornik*, no. 9.
[57] *AFZKh* 1, no. 258.

a boundary. After the defendant had led the judges around the land, he presented a longtime resident who had been present at the official boundary survey. "And in addition, Sires, that boundary is recorded in Mikhailo Shapkin's books; and the books, Sires, are in the Grand Prince's archives; and I, Sires, call for the books [as evidence]." When the judges later found the boundary-demarcation record of Mikhailo Shapkin and Ivan Golova in the archives, the boundary was recorded as the defendant and his witness had shown. They gave judgment for the defendant.[58] The defendants in another case called for land cadastres, in addition to longtime residents, when the judge pointed out, "in your charter of grant those lands are not recorded by name." There was no further reference to these records until the conclusion of the case, when verification of their claim in the land cadastres was given as one reason for the decision in their favor.[59] Apparently the judge consulted the books, although his examination of them was not recorded in the trial record.

As we have just seen, documentary evidence could easily be questioned when the wording was imprecise. After records had been lost, particularly in fires, landholders on occasion received documents, referred to in court as charters of grant or title-confirming charters, which were intended to replace the records which had been destroyed. Elders of the Simonov Monastery, defendants in a 1463 case, could not present a donation charter when the judge asked for it. "Sire, we had charters but they burned up in the fire during Archimandrite Gerontei's tenure; and the donation charters for those lands and other monasterial lands, and the purchase deeds and [other] donation charters were lost in the fire." However, they continued,

[our] lord the Grand Prince Vasilei Vasil'evich bestowed his favor on us—he gave us his charter of grant for all those lands without naming them: whatever lands went with the monastery during the tenures of Archimandrite Iona and Archimandrite Ivan—all those lands are the monastery's; and in accordance with that charter did Grand Prince Ivan [Vasil'evich], after his father's death, grant us his own charter.[60]

Fortunately for them, the plaintiffs did not contest their documents; in fact, the plaintiffs admitted that the monastery had been in possession of the land for fifteen years, and the court gave judgment for the defendants.

In 1492 Fedko Efunin brought suit against the elders of St. Cyril's Monastery for seventeen hamlets and the Sysoevskoe land, which, he claimed, were part of the Grand Prince's village Iarogomzh. Elder Martem'ian of the monastery replied that Roman Ivanovich had given the settlement Vasil'evskaia to the monastery, and the hamlets and deserted land were a part of that settlement. As Prince Mikhailo Ondreevich had later conducted an investigation, the elder could present a charter of grant and a confirmation of title, but the land was described only as "the settlement Vasil'evskaia, with all that has gone with that settlement [for cadastral purposes], whither the plow and scythe and axe have gone." After examining the charters, the judges asked Martem'ian: "In the copy of the charter of grant and in the confirmation of title it is written [that] Roman gave you the settlement Vasil'evskaia, but the hamlets and deserted lands are not written by name; do ye have Roman's donation charter for that settlement and the hamlets?" The elder could not produce it: "Sires, we did have Roman's donation charter, but for our sins we lost that charter, and, Sires, we hold that settlement and those deserted lands by those documents." After this the judges asked for witnesses and inspected boundaries. They finally decided in favor of the monastery, in accordance with the documents and because the plaintiff had said that the elders had established the hamlets forty years earlier.[61]

Documents other than charters of grant also contained such vague wording. The plaintiffs in a 1498 case had a marriage settlement, which read in part: "I, Fedor Struna Sukherin, have given to my son-in-law Ivan for my daughter Oksineia the deserted village Fedorovskoe [in] the Zaretskoe [land], [part] of my patrimony, as far as our plow and axe and scythe have gone." The judge immediately asked them to present witnesses, since the document did not contain a description of the actual boundaries.[62] Purchase deeds and donation charters frequently described the limits of the

<hr/>

[58] *ASEI* 2, no. 310.

[59] *AFZKh* 1, no. 254.

[60] Their first charter read as follows: "For the mercy of the holy Mother of God, [and for] her pious dormition, I, Grand Prince Vasilei Vasil'evich, have bestowed my favor upon Archimandrite Gerontii and the brethren of the Simonov Monastery, for the house of the holy Mother of God. They had charters of grant for the monastery from my grandfather, Grand Prince Dmitrei Ivanovich, and from my father, Grand Prince Vasilei Dmitreevich, and from me, Grand Prince Vasilei Vasil'evich—and those charters of theirs burned up in the city. Likewise whoever gave lands to the monastery, and [gave bodies of] water, and meadows, and forests, and any appurtenances whatever, and whatever they themselves (the monasterial authorities) purchased from anyone—all those charters of purchase and donation perished in the fire. And whatever went with the monastery prior to that fire, during the tenure of Archimandrite Iona and Archimandrite Ivan—whatever lands, and bodies of water, and meadows and any other

appurtenances whatever—all that shall go with the monastery in the same way as it went before. And no one shall trespass on their [lands] in any matter. And [this] charter was given in the year six thousand nine hundred and fifty-six (1448) on the fourth day of January." The second charter was incorporated by reference, rather than being copied in its entirety: "And in Grand Prince Ivan Vasil'evich's charter the same was written, word for word"; *ASEI*, 2, no. 374. Fires were not the only reason for loss of documents and the issuance of such blanket charters of grant to replace the originals. Sometime between 1461 and 1485 Grand Prince Mikhail Borisovich of Tver' issued a charter of grant to Efim Dobrynia, noting that Dobrynia's original purchase deeds and land-exchange documents for his patrimony had been stolen by brigands; *ASEI* 3, no. 154.

[61] *ASEI* 2, no. 286.

[62] *AFZKh* 1, no. 117.

land as "wherever the plow and scythe and axe have gone." Usually, however, such documentary evidence was not challenged for this reason. Litigants presented longtime residents to testify when the case involved a boundary problem, or the judge brought up the matter.

On a few occasions presentation of documentary evidence was connected with a curious courtroom maneuver. The litigant flatly refused to present his records before the judge who was hearing the case, declaring that he would show a document only to the Grand Prince. For example, one defendant, claiming that the land belonged to the Grand Prince, presented a copy of his charter from the Grand Prince's palace-land administrator. After examining the document, the judge asked him where the original charter was, and he replied: "Sire, my charter is with Semen Plemian-nikov in Tver'; and I will place it before the Grand Prince, Sire, but I will not place it before thee." As the plaintiff had already presented his documentary evidence, the judge proceeded to the testimony of witnesses for both sides. The case was then sent to a higher court on *doklad*. After the trial record had been read, the defendant, rather than presenting his charter, declared that the trial had not been as the record said. The upper-court judge therefore sent for the men of court, but when they appeared in court, the defendant, who had been placed on bond, had already run away with his sureties.[63] Two peasants, defendants in another case, claimed that the borough chiefs had given them a charter for the land which they had plowed and mowed. The judge asked: "Who gave you that charter? Place that charter before me." The peasants replied: "That, Sire, we do not remember, who is recorded in the charter, and we will not place the charter before thee, but, Sire, we will present that charter in Moscow before the Grand Prince." Again the judge heard the remaining evidence and then referred the matter to his superiors. This time both sides agreed that the trial had been as recorded, but the defendants did not produce their charter, and they lost the case.[64]

In yet another suit one of the defendants' witnesses took this approach. Declaring that he himself did not know the boundaries, he added: "But, Sire, I have a boundary [description] charter, and it is in Mitia Ma-loi's keeping, and now Mitia is in Kholopii." The judge asked the witness when he could present the charter in court. Would he like a postponement? But the man replied: "Sire, I will not place that charter before thee, but I shall place it, Sire, before the Grand Prince [at the trial] on *doklad*." At the *doklad* proceedings, the upper-court judge ordered that the charter be read, but it did not contain a boundary description. The defendants lost, because their other witnesses had upheld

the plaintiff's claims and this one did not know the boundaries.[65]

The purpose of this maneuver is far from clear. The parties seemingly had no fear of anything resembling a fine for contempt of court, and, at least according to the record, none of the judges reacted adversely to this tactic. The statement was noted in the record, and the court proceeded to an examination of the remaining evidence. Apparently these litigants wanted to force the original judge to refer the matter to his superiors for decision. If, at the *doklad* proceedings, they had presented the evidence which they had claimed to have, we might attribute their actions to suspicion of the original judge's impartiality or to a belief that the Grand Prince's court would be more likely to decide in their favor. Yet in the first example the defendant tacitly admitted his guilt by flight. In the second, the defendants did not know who gave them the charter which they claimed to have, and then failed to produce it. One is tempted to assume that they had no charter at all. In the third example, the defendants called upon four witnesses, two of whom had testified for the plaintiff, a third whom they could not bring to court, and the fourth, who produced a document which did nothing to help their cause. Refusal to present documents seems to have been a delaying tactic. Perhaps litigants hoped that during the remainder of the trial an opponent would somehow compromise his own case by lack of knowledge or by presenting witnesses who did not support him. Perhaps such litigants thought that a superior judge, assessing the sum total of evidence for both sides, might find a flaw of equal weight in the opponent's proof, thus improving the chances for a favorable outcome. Or perhaps these men simply took a chance—if they managed to delay the proceedings long enough, the court might overlook their failure to produce the document.

If such litigants hoped that the court would not ask for their documents, they certainly used the wrong approach. Refusal to produce evidence and an offer to present it before the Grand Prince would be recorded and read aloud in the upper court, raising obvious questions. Other litigants had a much more successful method: they simply mentioned—without emphasizing the fact—that they had a purchase deed or donation charter or some other document, and then proceeded immediately to presenting their other evidence. To cite just one example, an elder of the Trinity-Sergius Monastery stated, as part of his complaint, that the donation charter was in the Grand Prince's archives. The judge then turned to the defendant, Prince Ivan, who claimed that his father had given him the land, but who had no documents of any kind. Returning to his questioning of the plaintiff, the judge asked whether he had witnesses. Witnesses for both sides then testified, and the defendant's men got lost while leading

[63] *ASEI* **1**, no. 595.
[64] *ASEI* **1**, no. 582.

[65] *ASEI* **3**, no. 48.

the judge around the land. The judgment charter records no further reference to the plaintiff's donation charter.[66] The defendant had lost his case during the court proceedings, and the plaintiff was never asked to produce his document. No one checked in the archives. We do not know whether such a donation charter really existed. But, of course, the judge could have demanded it at any point. On the whole, if a litigant, for one reason or another, wanted to support his case by claiming documentary proof but did not want to (or could not) produce the evidence, this method would seem to involve less risk.

Vasilii Petlin, defendant in a 1561 case, adopted a number of these tactics, finally admitting that he had hoped the plaintiff would not be able to produce his evidence. Litigation arose over property which the defendant had mortgaged on a promissory note. The plaintiff claimed that Vasilii had not paid the money and was holding the property. He presented Vasilii's document clearing title to the land, which repeated the mortgage terms but did not record the disputed hamlets by name. Vasilii demanded that he produce the note itself. The plaintiff said that he did not have it, that it had been stolen, and Vasilii immediately declared that he had redeemed his property, paying the money in full. This had been done in private, with no witnesses, and he had not taken back the disencumbering note because the plaintiff had claimed that it had been lost. He did have the redeemed promissory note, however, but had left it with Fedor Baskakov when he was called away suddenly by the boiars to receive a service-tenure estate. After a postponement, the plaintiff produced the promissory note, which had been located among the belongings of a member of the family. The defendant admitted borrowing the money, acknowledged that the handwriting in the note was his, but submitted a petition claiming that the property, while in the plaintiff's possession, had been ruined—peasants had been driven away, structures sold off or burned—and that he could not pay because of this destruction. The plaintiff asserted that the property was in the same condition as it had been earlier. Apparently there was an interruption in the trial at this point. The next thing noted in the record was a petition submitted by the plaintiff, stating that the defendant was about to leave on military service and had not yet paid the money. He should either redeem his property or cede possession. When Vasilii appeared the next day, the judge referred to the redeemed promissory note which the defendant had claimed to have, and asked him to present it. At this point Vasilii admitted that he had not paid the money: "I do not have the redeemed promissory note and I have nothing to place before thee." He had claimed to have it because the plaintiff had said that the document had been lost, "and I hoped that in the future that

promissory note would not be [found]." Vasilii had tried to recover his property without paying off the mortgage, and had failed. Five weeks later the court bailiff reported that he had been unable to collect the money. Vasilii declared that he was unable to redeem the property, that he could get no sureties, and that there was no need to give him a postponement in the matter. The land was awarded to the plaintiff.[67]

Very curious circumstances surrounding use of a document arose in a judgment charter of April, 1502. The defendants, three newcomer peasants of the Volokoslavinskaia canton, declared that the canton elder Orel and two of his men had given them the floodland meadow in question. Orel and his comrades then testified: "Sire, we did [indeed] give this floodland meadow to that Fediunia and his comrades to mow; and, Sire, it is the Grand Prince's floodland meadow. And, Sire, we had a trial over this floodland meadow with the elder of the Ferapontov Monastery. And here, Sire, is the charter before thee." The document placed before the court was a judgment charter of 1499/1500,[68] issued to the peasant Kur'ian of Volochok Slovenskii, for meadowlands along the left side of the Sheleksha river. As the plaintiff, elder Fegnast Batman of the Ferapontov Monastery, pointed out, the judgment charter had no bearing on the case:

Sire, they have presented a document for the left side, for unnamed meadowlands. And, Sire, those meadowlands on which the trial took place are about four versts from here. And we, Sire, are not encroaching on them. And thou, Sire, art standing on the right side of the Sheleksha, at the Porozobitsa [river], on the Krestnoi floodland meadow.

The elder then presented longtime residents who declared that this land was the Krestnoi floodland meadow and had been the monastery's land for seventy years. Turning to Orel and his comrades, the judge pointed out that they were standing in a meadow on the right side of the river, and asked them if they had any evidence and how long they had been in possession. The canton elder and his men answered: "Sire, we have been in possession of this floodland meadow for two years [now], since they gave us this charter." The defendants lost the case, "because they had placed before the judge a judgment charter of a trial by Mikhailo Shapkin and Ivan, son of Semen Golova, for unnamed meadowlands down the Sheleksha stream, on the left side, and not for the Krestnoi floodland meadow; and besides that judgment charter they produced no other evidence whatever for that [Krestnoi] floodland meadow."[69] Why did the canton peasants base their claim on this judgment charter? Two possible explanations come to mind. Perhaps the peasants were illiterate, and not knowing what the judgment

---

[66] *ASEI* 1, no. 607.

[67] *AIuB* 1, no. 7.

[68] This judgment charter text is also published as a separate document; *ASEI* 2, no. 334.

[69] *ASEI* 2, no. 336.

charter said, thought that it was a document for the Krestnoi floodland meadow. According to their own testimony, they had mowed the land only since they had received the charter. On the other hand, they may have simply appropriated the land, knowing that they had a document for "meadowlands" on the Sheleksha. The key figure in the case is missing—Kur'ian, the peasant to whom the judgment charter had been awarded originally. Was he still in possession of his meadows, or had he moved away or died, leaving his document to the canton?

One additional point should be noted with regard to documentary evidence—the attitude of the litigants themselves toward the written word as a form of proof. We learn incidentally from one judgment charter that some illiterate members of society apparently had great faith in the power of anything written, regardless of what it said. In explaining their presentation of a redemption charter, litigants declared that their father had had a purchase deed for part of the land in question, but "the bondsmen Levsha Tregub and Maksimko ran away from our father, and, Sire, those bondsmen stole that purchase deed for Bliznino, thinking [it was] their bondage document." [70] These men apparently believed that removing the written record would aid them in attaining liberty. Others, however, upon being confronted with documents disproving their claims, expressed complete skepticism as to the accuracy of the evidence. When defendants in one case produced a judgment charter previously issued against the plaintiffs' father in an earlier trial over the disputed lands, the judge asked the plaintiffs whether they accepted the document. They replied: "Why should we accept [that]? Whatever they wanted for themselves, they wrote down." [71] In this instance, one might suspect that the plaintiffs' attitude bore a direct relationship to the effect which the judgment charter might have in negating their claims.

As we have seen, litigants ran into various problems when presenting documents as evidence. Boundary descriptions might be vague or non-existent. Witnesses might be unavailable, dead, or not recorded in the document. Charters might have been destroyed or lost. The opposition might raise the question of forgery or other fraud. Yet the importance of such evidence is shown by the emphasis which the litigants placed upon their documents and the lengths to which they would go—even so far as claiming to have non-existent documents themselves—in order to counteract written materials presented by the other side. Testimony of witnesses and documentary evidence were the two main forms of proof used in Muscovite courts. In addition to these, however, litigants might request to support their claims through some type of "God's justice."

VI. TRIAL PROCEDURE: "GOD'S JUSTICE"

In addition to the evidence presented in witnesses' testimony and documents, cases could be decided upon the basis of other forms of proof. These methods of settling the issue, which could be suggested by the litigants or their witnesses, or decreed by the judge, can be termed collectively "God's justice."

The pagan custom of swearing by the earth continued to be used occasionally up to the nineteenth century. During boundary demarcations men walked around the borders of land which they claimed, and throughout the procedure carried a piece of turf (*dern*) on their heads. In theory, if they did not show the true boundaries, the earth would strike them dead. The church, however, opposed this heathen survival, demanding that an icon be substituted, so that the symbol of the Mother of God would replace that of Mother Earth. [1] A judgment charter issued between 1494 and 1499 refers to use of this procedure, walking with an icon to mark off the "true" boundaries, during an earlier boundary division. The defendant's witnesses, in the course of the trial, led the judge along the same markings and pits where "the Simonov [Monastery's] witnesses, with icon, had measured off [the land] for Ivan Bitiagovskoi" several years before. [2]

Most judgment charters do not record the use of either icons or turf during boundary inspections conducted in the course of the trial. Occasionally there are references to the carrying of an icon in previous boundary divisions. For example, in one boundary-division charter incorporated as part of a judgment charter, elder Fofan declared: "We, Sire, shall take the icon of the Immaculate [Mother of God] and shall mark off the boundaries of our land." He then took the icon, and, accompanied by the brethren, led the judge along the boundary. [3] In other instances, the judgment charters mention the use of icons in connection with the decision and final setting of boundaries. After *doklad* proceedings, the judge in a 1534 trial awarded the land to the plaintiffs; their longtime resident witnesses were to measure off the boundary with an icon along the same line which they had shown the judge during the trial on the land. The lower-court judge was ordered to place boundary markers and then give the litigants boundary charters. [4] The defendant in a 1552 case, unable to produce any witnesses, agreed to accept the word of the plaintiff's longtime resident Orefa as to where the boundary lay: "go, Orefa, along the boundary with God's image (*obraz;* an icon); where

[70] *ASEI* 3, no. 105.
[71] *ASEI* 2, no. 406.

[1] For a discussion of this type of "God's justice," see N. P. Pavlov-Sil'vanskii, *Feodalizm v udel'noi Rusi* (St. Petersburg, 1910), pp. 427–433.
[2] *ASEI* 2, no. 411.
[3] *AIu*, no. 16; for other examples, see *ASEI* 2, no. 409; *AIu*, nos. 18, 20.
[4] *AIu*, no. 20.

Orefa shall go with the image, Sires, that shall be my boundary and I shall be guilty in everything." Orefa agreed to do so, stressing that he knew the land was theirs. In the end, judgment was given against the defendant, one reason being that he had placed the burden of proof "on Orefa's soul." The court ordered Orefa to measure off the disputed land with an icon in order to establish the official boundary line. The hamlets of the litigants, however, were to be confiscated for the tsar and given on quitrent to the beekeepers or others, whoever "would increase the quitrent most," because "both litigants were in dispute about quitrent-paying hamlets of the tsar and Grand Prince" and the Nizhnii Novgorod stewards had given the hamlets to the litigants on quitrent "without the knowledge of the tsar and Grand Prince." A boundary memorandum subsequently submitted by the lower-court judge recorded that Orefa had measured off the land with an icon. The judge also reported that the plaintiffs' hamlet had been granted to them anew by the tsar, while the defendant's property had been conferred upon a newly baptized Mordvinian.[5]

Pososhkov, writing at the time of Peter the Great, expressed complete confidence in this form of "God's justice." Certain people, he noted, "having forgotten the fear of God, measure off the land, having taken the holy icon in hand and placed a bit of turf on their heads." According to Pososhkov, such action could be fatal. It happened many times, he declared, that men who had sworn to abide by God's justice, while going around the land, pointed out false property lines and died right there on the boundary.[6]

In Muscovite Russia another form of "God's justice" was an oath taken upon kissing the cross (*krestnoe tselovanie*); it was used for religious, political-administrative, and judicial purposes.[7] Some judgment charters record instances where witnesses were asked to testify "after kissing the Grand Prince's cross." In a 1499 case, the defendants admitted that they did not know the boundaries of their land and agreed to accept whatever dividing line the plaintiff's longtime residents would point out. The judge then ordered the peasant witnesses to carry out their task: "Upon kissing the Grand Prince's cross, lead [us], brothers, in God's truth, where ye know that the boundary of the metropolitan's land with the Ezhov land has been since olden times, since both litigants have placed themselves on your souls."[8] Apparently the plaintiff's witnesses in a 1503 case were also required to take an oath, since the judge instructed them: "Tell [us] in God's truth, after kissing the Grand Prince's cross, whose are these

hamlets, at which we are standing?"[9] In another early sixteenth-century judgment charter, the judges did not refer to cross-kissing in their questioning, but longtime resident witnesses for both sides began their testimony with the phrase "upon kissing the cross."[10] A judgment charter of 1499/1500 records that "outside" longtime residents were asked to kiss the cross, although there had been no reference to the oath when longtime residents for both sides had testified.[11] We find the same situation in a judgment charter of 1504/1505.[12]

Thus a few of the earlier judgment charters mention cross-kissing in connection with testimony, but the majority do not. Considering in addition that the documents cited above all date from the end of the fifteenth century, or the beginning of the sixteenth, it seems possible that swearing an oath before giving testimony was not standard procedure in the fifteenth century. Of course, the possibility remains that fifteenth-century scribes did not consider it necessary to record oath-taking, and that this detail was one of the many finer points which later scribes included as record-keeping became more complete. References to witnesses' kissing the cross become more frequent, however, later in the sixteenth century. According to the judgment charters, individual witnesses[13] as well as groups of longtime residents[14] gave their testimony "upon kissing the Grand Prince's cross," as did men questioned on inquest.[15] Rather than kissing the cross, clergymen testified "upon their holy calling" (*po sviashchenstvu*).[16]

Thus cross-kissing could be used as a preliminary step to the giving of testimony. In addition, it could

[5] Likhachev, *Sbornik*, no. 12.

[6] I. T. Pososhkov, *Kniga o skudosti i bogatstve,* ed. B. B. Kafengauz (Moscow, 1951), pp. 185–186.

[7] For a discussion of this form of "God's justice," see H. W. Dewey and A. M. Kleimola, "Promise and Perfidy in Old Russian Cross-Kissing," *Canadian Slavic Studies* 2, no. 3 (Fall, 1968): pp. 327–341.

[8] *AFZKh* 1, no. 157.

[9] *ASEI* 2, no. 307; see also *ASEI* 2, no. 493.

[10] Anpilogov, *Novye dokumenty*, pp. 485–490.

[11] *ASEI* 3, no. 276.

[12] *ASEI* 3, no. 223.

[13] See, for example, *AFZKh* 1, no. 309; Likhachev, *Sbornik*, no. 12; *AIu*, nos. 19, 23. The continuing inconsistency of use or recording of the formula is shown in a document of 1551. When one secretary of the grand prince testified in court, there was no reference to his having kissed the cross. Another secretary sent a written memorandum containing his testimony, the first line of which declared that he was testifying "upon kissing the cross of the tsar and grand prince"; Likhachev, *Sbornik*, no. 11.

[14] See Likhachev, *Sbornik*, nos. 8, 9, 10; *AIu*, no. 20; *SGKE* 1, no. 76; *AIuB* 1, no. 6.

[15] See Likhachev, *Sbornik*, nos. 8, 9, 10, 12; Iushkov, *Akty XIII–XVII vv.*, no. 220. The decree ordering an inquest in a 1595 judgment charter made special arrangements for non-Orthodox residents. The court ordered that an inquest be conducted "among all the Russian people for five and six and ten and twenty versts and more, petty boiars, and their estate managers, and beekeepers, and Mordvinians, and Cheremis, and among the Russian people upon kissing the cross, and among the Mordvinians and Cheremis upon oath [given] according to their faith"; Gorchakov, *O zemel'nykh vladeniiakh*, no. 6, pp. 65–73. "Men of court" who testified during *doklad* proceedings also kissed the cross; Likhachev, *Sbornik*, no. 9.

[16] See Likhachev, *Sbornik*, nos. 8, 10, 12; *RIB*, 12, no. 4; Iushkov, *Akty XIII–XVII vv.*, no. 220.

serve as an independent means of proof.[17] A judgment charter of 1567 records a rather curious case in which both litigants were willing to settle the dispute by cross-kissing, but the judge apparently was not satisfied with this method. The plaintiff, appearing on behalf of a "man" of Prince Ivan Vasil'evich Sheremetev senior, claimed that Sheremetev's man had gone to a meadow to mow his master's hay, and that Prince Andrei Nozdrovatyi, declaring the meadow was his, had driven the man from the land and taken his horse. Nozdrovatyi denied the charges. Ivan IV, who was trying the case, asked the plaintiff what evidence he had. He replied that Sheremetev's man was willing to kiss the cross, and would believe Nozdrovatyi if he would do so. When the tsar questioned the defendant, he declared: "Sire, let Ivan Vasil'evich's man Selchuk kiss the cross, and I shall pay the sum he seeks." In other words, if Selchuk dared to kiss the cross, Nozdrovatyi would pay for the horse. The plaintiff affirmed that Selchuk was willing to do so.

At this point one might assume that the matter could be resolved without further investigation. Yet the tsar continued to question the litigants, asking the plaintiff to produce the mortgage note by which his master held the land. The plaintiff declared that the note was recorded in a judgment charter from an earlier trial between his master and Nozdrovatyi, a case which the sovereign himself had tried.[18] Only after the plaintiff had produced the document and the defendant had acknowledged its authenticity did the tsar award the land to the plaintiff, ordering that Sheremetev be allowed to make use of the land according to the terms of the earlier judgment charter and promissory note. The litigants reached an amicable settlement in Selchuk's suit for damages, and each agreed to pay half of the court costs.[19] It would appear that the land, rather than the stolen horse, was the real object of litigation.

In this instance, as noted above, Ivan IV continued to press for further evidence after the parties had indicated their willingness to resolve the matter through kissing the cross. Perhaps his thoroughness arose from concern for justice and a conviction that cross-kissing was not the best form of evidence. Yet one might suspect that his attitude was connected more closely with the identity of the plaintiff's master. Ivan Vasil'evich Sheremetev had been close to the tsar's former advisor Aleksei Adashev[20] and a surety bond had been taken for his good behavior in 1564.[21] By June, 1571, Sheremetev had been forced to enter a monastery.[22]

While cross-kissing could be used as an independent form of proof, the judgment charters mention it most frequently in connection with a third form of "God's justice," the judicial duel (*pole*). Litigants (or more often their witnesses) could offer to fight a duel with the opposition in an attempt to counter the other side's evidence. Some requested a judicial duel after declaring that the opponents had not pointed out the true boundaries. In a judgment charter of 1499/1500, after witnesses for both sides had testified and each group had shown the judge the boundaries, the plaintiff's longtime residents declared:

Sire, those longtime residents of the Grand Prince, Petrushka Koshelev and his comrades, led thee incorrectly about the Archangel [Cathedral's] land of the Plotniche village; and, Sire, that deserted village Opraksino is Archangel [Cathedral land], that deserted village across [which] they led thee. Sire, give us God's justice with them, and, having kissed the cross, we shall go to the [dueling] field to fight.[23]

In other cases, one side asserted that the opposition's witnesses had lied. For example, longtime residents testifying on behalf of the peasant Kur'ian, defendant in a 1499/1500 case, declared: "Sires, the monastery's witnesses Kuzemka and Kondratik have given false testimony; give us God's justice with them: after a week's fast and after kissing the cross, we shall go with them to the field to fight."[24] At other times one party offered a judicial duel not to challenge evidence presented by the other side but to add support to its own claims: "Sire, we shall support [our statements] by this, having kissed the cross, we shall go to the field to fight [a judicial duel] about that deserted village Pavletsovo."[25]

The suggestion that a judicial duel be ordered usually appears to have been a voluntary step taken by one of the parties,[26] although occasionally the judge seems to

---

[17] 1497 Sudebnik, articles 46, 47, 58; 1550 Sudebnik, articles 25, 27. A memorandum from the Chelobitnyi Prikaz of May 20, 1625, included regulations for administration of the oath by cross-kissing in the courts. In an attempt to combat false witness, slaves were forbidden to take oaths on behalf of their masters more than three times, and such slaves had to be more than twenty years old. Litigants below twenty years of age could kiss the cross themselves if they had no slaves to represent them. Russians took the oath in the church of St. Nicholas Gostynskii in the Kremlin, not far from the prikaz buildings. A Russian sued by a foreigner might kiss the cross, but had to do so in the prikazy, since foreigners could not be taken to the cross in the church. A foreigner sued by a Russian could also take an oath, which would be administered in the prikazy according to the foreigner's faith; *PRP* 5: pp. 336–337, 396.

[18] For the text of this judgment charter, see *AIuB* 1, no. 5.

[19] *AIuB* 1, no. 8.

[20] Zimin, *Reformy Ivana Groznogo*, p. 317.

[21] *Sobranie gosudarstvennykh gramot i dogovorov* 1, no. 180.

[22] Zimin, "Sostav boiarskoi dumy," p. 61. Nozdrovatyi may have been connected with the *oprichnina*, but his name does not appear in Kobrin's list; V. B. Kobrin, "Sostav oprichnogo dvora Ivana Groznogo," *Arkheograficheskii ezhegodnik za 1959 god* (Moscow, 1960), pp. 16–91.

[23] *ASEI* 3, no. 50. For other examples, see *AFZKh* 1, no. 117; *ASEI* 2, no. 411.

[24] *ASEI* 2, no. 334. For other examples, see *ASEI* 1, no. 582; 3, nos. 223, 364; *AFZKh* 1, no. 259.

[25] *AFZKh* 1, no. 261; see also *ASEI* 2, no. 375; *AFZKh* 1, nos. 1a, 222; Likhachev, *Sbornik*, no. 9; *AIu*, nos. 17, 21, 22.

[26] *ASEI* 1, no. 582; *ASEI* 2, nos. 334, 407, 411; *ASEI* 3, nos. 50, 223, 364; *AFZKh* 1, nos. 117, 259; *AIu*, no. 14.

have prompted the action.[27]   It was, of course, possible to decline a duel. In one case, after the plaintiff's longtime residents had accused the defendant's witnesses of lying and had challenged them to a duel, the defendant stepped in: "Sires, why should my longtime residents go to the field to fight for the Grand Prince's land?" He then suggested an alternative procedure: "Sires, question the Grand Prince's cantonal peasants, outstanding citizens, by inquest upon cross-kissing, not as witnesses [in adversary proceedings]."[28] Perhaps he should have agreed to combat—the outstanding citizens supported the plaintiff's claims, and failure to agree to the duel was given as one of the reasons for the court's decision against the defendant. Monk Efrem of the Ferapontov Monastery, plaintiff in another action, also refused to let his longtime residents participate in a duel: "We, Sires, do not allow our witnesses to go to the [dueling] field to fight."[29] Again, failure to support his claims through a duel cost the litigant his case. There was, however, other evidence against him: he did not know the boundary, and his witnesses knew nothing about the land.

It was possible, however, even if infrequently, to refuse a judicial duel and still win the case. In one instance, after longtime residents for both sides had testified and the plaintiff's men had offered to fight, the defendants replied:

Sire, the house of the Immaculate [Mother of God]—the Simonov Monastery—is [on] the sovereign Grand Prince's [land], and, Sire, the lands are both the monastery's [and] God's and the Grand Prince's. And to the [dueling] field, Sires, we shall not let our witnesses go. And thou hast thyself heard, Sire, that which Kornilko and Ivashko (the plaintiffs) are saying before thee: that we have plowed this land for fifteen years. And, Sire, we have plowed this land for almost thirty years. And these lands have all been cleared [of conflicting claims] by Grand Prince Vasilei Vasil'evich's charter of grant. And these lands were given [to the monastery] in the tenure of Archimandrite Iona and Archimandrite Ivan. And here, Sire, is that charter.

In addition the defendants had a charter from Grand Prince Ivan Vasil'evich and a donation charter, while the plaintiffs admitted that they had not brought suit for over fifteen years because they had not been concerned with the land.[30] Despite the defendants' refusal to allow their witnesses to participate in a judicial duel, they won the suit.

As we have seen, declining a judicial duel could contribute to losing a case. On the other hand, as was noted in the concluding sections of a few judgment charters, failure to request a duel could lead to the same result.[31] For example, one defendant lost "be-

cause he did not speak to the metropolitan's [peasants] (i.e. protest) about that land for fifty years, and he did not petition the Grand Prince about that land, and his longtime residents did not ask for a judicial duel [with the opposing witnesses]."[32]

Requests for cross-kissing and judicial duel would appear to have been made more as a form of supplementary evidence, a procedural step taken to counterbalance or offset the opponent's proof, than as a serious suggestion that the court should order the dispute to be resolved in this fashion. An outline of the actions taken by the parties in a 1543 suit will illustrate the underlying pattern. One plaintiff charged the defendants with taking over hamlets by force and ordering peasants not to pay taxes, while peasants from one of the hamlets charged the same men with robbery and assault as well as with driving them away. The defendants denied the charges and brought a countersuit, claiming that the plaintiff had established settlements on their land. The plaintiffs asked to go to the dueling field in the matter of the assault and robbery, and called for the testimony of longtime residents concerning the disputed land. The defendants agreed to the judicial duel and named their own longtime residents. The witnesses for the plaintiffs supported their claims, and the defendants asked for a judicial duel with the longtime residents. The witnesses agreed. Next the longtime residents for the defendants supported their claims, and the plaintiffs requested to go to the dueling field with these men. They also agreed. Then each set of longtime residents led the judges along the boundaries. After the plaintiffs' witnesses had taken their turn, the defendants' longtime residents declared that they had not pointed out the correct boundary and requested a duel—the other side agreed. The defendants' witnesses set out next, and when they had finished their tour, the plaintiffs' longtime residents charged that they had not shown the true boundaries. Again a judicial duel was offered and accepted. The plaintiffs then called for the testimony of abbots, priests, and peasants on inquest, and presented a donation charter supporting their title to the land. More than forty men testified on inquest, all of whom supported the plaintiffs. The defendants requested a judicial duel with all these witnesses. Finally both parties called for evidence from the Grand Prince's land records; this information also supported the plaintiffs, who won the case. Despite their numerous offers to fight a judicial duel, one reason for the court's decision against the defendants was their failure to contest the donation charter

[27] *ASEI* 2, no. 375; *AFZKh* 1, no. 261.
[28] *ASEI* 3, no. 223.
[29] *ASEI* 2, no. 334; see also *AFZKh* 1, no. 222.
[30] *ASEI* 2, no. 375.
[31] The Sudebniki indicate that such procedure was expected from the defendant if a witness testified against him: he could either go to the dueling field with the witness or produce the

sum asked in damages or the litigated property; 1497 Sudebnik, article 48; 1550 Sudebnik, article 16. Witnesses were expected to support their principals to the extent of fighting a duel; see commentary to article 48 of the 1497 Sudebnik and article 15 of the 1550 Sudebnik in *Sudebniki XV–XVI vekov,* pp. 82–85, 204–209.
[32] *AFZKh* 1, no. 114; see also *ASEI* 3, no. 223; *AFZKh* 1, no. 306; Likhachev, *Sbornik,* no. 9; *AIu,* no. 23; *AIuB* 1, nos. 5, 6.

presented by the plaintiffs.[33] There were positive reasons for the decision as well, such as the inquest testimony in favor of the plaintiffs and the fact that their longtime residents had proceeded along the same natural boundaries recorded in the document which they had presented. Yet the court's conclusion indicates that a litigant was expected to contest all the evidence produced by his opponent.

In many of the judgment charters which record trials including a request for a judicial duel as part of the procedure, the offer is made by one side, agreed to by the other, and the case is then referred to a court of higher instance. Thus, in these cases, the judicial duel offer and response appear to be a preliminary ritual to *doklad*.[34] In addition, the exchange served as a part of an elimination process; if a litigant or his witnesses refused the duel, this might be interpreted as proof that his claims were unfounded or that his witnesses' testimony was false, since they were unwilling to support their statements.

Various scholars have written detailed descriptions of judicial duel procedure, drawing upon sources ranging from tenth- and eleventh-century Arab accounts (Ibn-Dasta and Muqaddesi) and the 1229 Smolensk-German treaty to the 1589 Sudebnik and the so-called Svodnyi Sudebnik (1606?).[35] The Sudebniki of 1497 and 1550 contained several provisions to regulate duel procedure. For cases tried in the central courts, the codes gave separate fee lists for combat, depending on the circumstances: in case of reconciliation before the duel[36] or on the field before fighting;[37] for duels in the question of a loan or physical violence,[38] or in matters of arson, murder, brigandage or theft,[39] or in cases tried on *doklad*.[40] In addition, the 1497 code declared that the loser forfeited his armor, and was handed over to the boiar and secretary for punishment and fine.[41] In 1550 the loser paid three rubles instead of forfeiting his armor and was placed on bond.[42] Fees

in the vicegerents' courts were listed separately.[43] Choice of the judicial duel was left to the defendant.[44] The provisions of the Sudebniki regulated use of hired fighters by litigants and witnesses.[45] The codes also outlined the responsibilities of court officials, who were to keep order on the field. After ascertaining the identity of the litigants' backers and sureties, the officials were to keep these men on the sidelines, making sure that they had no armor, oak clubs, or sticks in their possession, and outsiders were to be sent away.[46]

Although the Sudebniki devoted much attention to the problem, relatively few of the surviving judgment charters record cases in which references to the judicial duel occurred, and only in a few of these instances did the judges actually decree that combat should take place. Since the texts of all court records are not extant, it is possible that trial by combat was more common than our documents indicate. It should also be noted that most of the judgment charters record land litigation, and the Sudebniki contain no specific reference to the use of the judicial duel in such cases. On the whole, however, it would appear that this form of "God's justice" was little used by 1497. A recent Soviet study provides one explanation, suggesting that "the judicial duel, which still existed in the early feudal period, did not answer the needs of the developed feudal state, since the formal right was granted to any free member of society to challenge another free [man] regardless of his social position."[47] On the other hand, one might suggest that by the fifteenth century both litigants and judges recognized that this form of procedure was archaic and of questionable value as a method of decision.

In the fifteenth-century judgment charters, the judicial duel seems to be a matter of much talk and very little action. In fact, our only descriptions of duels which were carried out come from the sixteenth-century accounts of two foreign visitors. One of these men, Baron Sigismund von Herberstein, who served as an ambassador of the German Emperor Maximilian, visited Russia first in 1517 and again in 1526. His description of judicial duels differed sharply from the procedure outlined in the 1497 Sudebnik. According to Herberstein, either of the litigants might appoint any other person to fight for him, and all arms, except a gun or bow, were permissible.

[33] Likhachev, *Sbornik*, no. 10. For other cases which record similar exchanges of judicial duel offers, see *AIu*, no. 20; *SGKE* 1, no. 76; Likhachev, *Sbornik*, nos. 9, 12.

[34] See, for example, *AFZKh* 1, nos. 259, 261; *ASEI* 1, no. 582; 2, no. 411; 3, no. 50; Likhachev, *Sbornik*, nos. 8, 9, 12; *AIu*, no. 20; Kashtanov, *Ocherki*, no. 9, pp. 354–361.

[35] See, *inter alia*, Beliaev, *Lektsii po istorii*, p. 416; Dmitriev, *Istoriia sudebnykh instantsii*, pp. 245–255; V. O. Kliuchevskii, *Sochineniia v vos'mi tomakh* (8 v., Moscow, 1959) 6: pp. 220–222; Sergeevich, *Lektsii i izsledovaniia*, pp. 605–606. Vladimirskii-Budanov particularly emphasizes the provisions of the Pskov Sudnaia gramota; *Obzor*, pp. 626–627. Others make greater use of the Sudebniki; see, for example, Marc Szeftel, "Le jugement de Dieu dans le droit russe ancien," *Archives d'histoire du droit oriental* 4 (1949): pp. 263–299; H. W. Dewey, "Trial by Combat in Muscovite Russia," *Oxford Slavonic Papers* 9 (1960): pp. 21–31.

[36] 1497 Sudebnik, article 4; 1550 Sudebnik, article 9.

[37] 1497 Sudebnik, article 5; 1550 Sudebnik, article 10.

[38] 1497 Sudebnik, article 6; 1550 Sudebnik, article 11.

[39] 1497 Sudebnik, article 7; 1550 Sudebnik, article 12.

[40] 1497 Sudebnik, article 64; 1550 Sudebnik, article 51.

[41] 1497 Sudebnik, article 7.

[42] 1550 Sudebnik, article 12.

[43] 1497 Sudebnik, article 38; 1550 Sudebnik, article 62.

[44] 1497 Sudebnik, article 48; 1550 Sudebnik, article 16.

[45] 1497 Sudebnik, articles 49, 52; 1550 Sudebnik, articles 14, 17, 19.

[46] 1497 Sudebnik, article 68; 1550 Sudebnik, article 13. The 1550 Sudebnik added that the contestants were to be evenly matched. To ensure this, the compilers added article 14, which did not correspond to any provision of the 1497 code. The article was concerned with ensuring equality of physical strength between the combatants, and left the choice of personal participation to the non-professional fighter; see commentary in *Sudebniki XV–XVI vekov*, p. 204.

[47] *PRP* 3: p. 213.

But they generally have oblong coats of mail, sometimes double, a breast-plate, bracelets, a helmet, a lance, a hatchet, and a peculiar weapon in the hand, like a dagger sharpened at each end, which they use so rapidly with either hand as never to allow it to impede them in any encounter, nor to fall from the hand; it is generally used in an engagement on foot.

Beginning with the lance, antagonists later shifted to other weapons. Herberstein reported that, for several years past, Russians fighting with foreigners—Germans, Poles, or Lithuanians—had generally been defeated. On a recent occasion, a certain Lithuanian, who was twenty-six years old, had fought a duel with a certain Russian, who had previously come off the victor in more than twenty duels. After the Lithuanian had killed the Russian, the Grand Prince "in a rage" immediately ordered that he be brought before him. "And when he saw him he spat upon the ground, and ordered that in future no duel should be adjudged to any foreigner against his own subjects." The ambassador noted that Russians loaded themselves with a great variety of weapons, while "foreigners go to an attack trusting to judgment rather than arms. They take special care not to let their hands join, for they know that the Russians are very strong in their arms, and it is only by wearying them by perseverance and activity that they in most cases conquer them." Each combatant had "many friends, abettors, and spectators," who came armed with sticks and sometimes used them.

For if any unfairness seem to be practiced upon either of them, the friends of that one immediately rush to avenge his injury, and then the friends of the other interfere, and thus a battle arises between both sides, which is very amusing to the spectators, for the hair of their heads, fists, clubs, and sticks burnt at the points, are all brought into play on the occasion.[48]

Herberstein's account sounds more like the report of some kind of tournament than the legal procedure by which cases were decided. While he presents a general impression, the ambassador does not say directly that he personally witnessed such duels, and it seems unlikely that Muscovite authorities would permit a foreign observer to attend, particularly if the Sudebnik provisions regarding "outsiders" were being enforced. Perhaps Herberstein compiled his account on the basis of a variety of tales which he heard from his interpreters and others, and somehow mixed in stories of non-judicial contests. If, on the other hand, his account is substantially correct, it illustrates that breakdown in the judicial system which is commonly believed to have been one of the reasons behind Ivan IV's issuance of a new law code in 1550.

The second report on Muscovite judicial duels is that of the Englishman Richard Chancellor, who first visited Muscovy three years after issuance of the 1550 Sudebnik. According to his account, the duel was conducted largely as the statutory regulations indicated: the combatants, who could be professional champions, were armed with war-clubs and hunting-poles, and fought on foot.[49]

A few judgment charters record cases in which the judge decreed a judicial duel, but we do not find a complete description of the event. Something always interfered with carrying out the procedure. A judgment charter issued between 1464 and 1482 provides an example, and also illustrates the use of representation in judicial duels. The Grand Prince's beekeepers had brought suit against a certain Ostafii, charging that he was depriving them of fishing rights. After the plaintiffs' witnesses had testified, Ostafii declared that they had testified against him wrongly ("not according to his deeds"). He would send his man, who would kiss the cross in the matter to support Ostafii, to fight a judicial duel to prove that the plaintiffs had no rights to the lakes. The plaintiffs agreed that, after kissing the cross, they would likewise send one person, selected from among them, to the dueling field, and the Grand Prince ordered a judicial duel. When both sides appeared at the field on the designated date, the plaintiffs declared that if four of Ostafii's servants would kiss the cross, after swearing that the plaintiffs had been given no fishing rights, they, the plaintiffs, were ready to concede. Ostafii agreed, and at the designated time, St. Peter's Day, Ostafii presented his men and, by kissing the cross, they settled the matter.[50]

We find the same pattern being repeated more than a century later. In a 1588 case, the judges decreed that the matter be resolved by judicial duel. The plaintiff petitioned, stating that he was not able to present a hired fighter, "and, Sires, I shall fight with Il'ia (the defendant) on the [dueling] field man to man (sam na sam)." The defendant petitioned in return, stating that he was sending a hired fighter; he could not fight man to man, he said, because his arm was injured. The plaintiff thereupon petitioned again, declaring that he was not able to go to the field against a hired fighter.[51] At that point both litigants requested that they be allowed to kiss the cross, and a date was set.

---

[48] Sigismund von Herberstein, *Notes upon Russia*, trans. and ed. R. H. Major (2 v., London, 1851) 1: pp. 104–105. For the original text, see *Rerum Moscoviticarum commentarii Sigismundi Liberi Baronis in Herberstein, Neyperg & Guettenhag* (Frankfurt, 1964). For a colorful literary account of a judicial duel set in the *oprichnina* period of Ivan IV's reign, see A. K. Tolstoi, *Kniaz' Serebrianyi* (Moscow, 1966), pp. 274–288 (Chapter 31, "Bozhii sud").

[49] *Chancellor's Voyage to Muscovy*, ed. J. M'Crindle and E. Goldsmid (Edinburgh, 1886), pp. 76–77.

[50] *ASEI* 3, no. 364. The defendants in a 1552 case offered to pay the sum at issue if a witness for the opposition would kiss the cross; Likhachev, *Sbornik*, no. 12.

[51] This is in accord with article 14 of the 1550 Sudebnik governing equality of strength between combatants. The provision decreed that, in case of combat between a professional fighter and a non-professional fighter, the choice was to be left to the non-professional fighter. Both litigants in a 1541 case offered to send hired fighters; *AIu*, no. 21. See also Likhachev, *Sbornik*, no. 12.

Subsequently they appeared before the judges and announced that they had become reconciled. The judges then ordered that their petition for a peaceful settlement be recorded.[52] It has been suggested that after 1550 the judicial duel was gradually being replaced by other forms of "God's justice," cross-kissing and drawing lots,[53] and the court in this case raised no objection to use of cross-kissing alone in place of a duel.

In other instances, the litigants did not quite reach the point of fighting a judicial duel because one of the combatants failed to appear at the crucial moment. After a judicial duel had been decreed between longtime residents in a 1498 case, the judge set a time for the duel and cross-kissing. The three plaintiffs and their three witnesses, along with the eight defendants and their five witnesses, were to stand on the Fedorov land on the Saturday before St. Fedor's Sunday (the first Sunday in Lent). Everyone appeared at the designated time except the plaintiffs' third witness. When the judge asked where he was, the plaintiffs replied: "Our witness, Sire, on account of our sins, left for Nizhnii Novgorod to trade, and, Sire, he has not arrived; but, Sire, give us a [new] time—when he comes, we will present him on the land for the duel and cross-kissing." The defendants, however, opposed this course of action: "Sire, do not give them a [new] time; Sire, they are delaying justice for us, they are not presenting their witness; refer this matter to the sovereign Grand Prince." The judge did as they requested, and the Grand Prince gave judgment for the defendants, because the plaintiffs' third witness had not appeared.[54] Whatever one might think of his reason for the decision, it suggests that the Grand Prince did not look upon the judicial duel as a superior method of resolving the issue.

A few plaintiffs brought suit and offered no other evidence to "prove" their claims than the demand for cross-kissing and a judicial duel. In one curious case, the defendants claimed that they, together with the plaintiff, had put a weir in the river, and that they all caught fish there. When the plaintiff denied it, the defendants declared: "Sires, it is known to the cantonal good men, but, Sires, we do not call for their testimony; give us, Sires, God's justice with Efim (the plaintiff): having kissed the life-giving cross, we, Sires, shall go out with him to the [dueling] field to fight." Efim agreed, and the judges sent the case to a higher court on *doklad*. In the higher court the defendants challenged the trial record and called for the land cadastres, claiming that the weir was registered as part of their

hamlet. The books showed otherwise, and judgment was given for the plaintiff.[55]

Another judgment charter provides a striking illustration of litigants' demanding a judicial duel as their only means of proof; in addition, the document gives somewhat more detail about duel procedure.[56] In 1525 three of the metropolitan's peasants brought suit before Grand Prince Vasilii III against three servants and five peasants of Chudin Okinfov, charging that they had stolen the plaintiffs' livestock that year, on the first Friday after St. Peter's Day. When the plaintiffs had gone to the defendants' hamlet, the defendants, they alleged, had beaten them and set dogs on them. As the plaintiffs retreated in haste, one of their comrades had been seized, beaten, and killed, after which the defendants had hidden his body, taking his horse, clothing, and money. Those defendants who appeared in court—four had fled—denied all charges, declaring that the plaintiffs had accused them falsely. The judge then asked the plaintiffs what evidence they had for their charges of assault and robbery, and they replied: "Sire, give us God's justice with them, that we, having kissed the cross, may go out with them on the [dueling] field to fight." The defendants agreed to this form of trial.

At this point the defendants' master Chudin Okinfov stepped forth, and brought a countersuit against the metropolitan's petty boiars Fedor Manuilov, Ignat Ovdeev, Gridia and Ivan Vnukov, and Olesha Matov: "They, Sire, gathered a thousand axes from the metropolitan's villages and came riding, Sire, into my hamlet Iur'ev," crossing the boundary; they plowed land, chopped down trees, and took the hamlet by force, "without trial and without bailiff," and "they swept my peasants out of that hamlet and there, Sire, they settled other peasants for the metropolitan." Okinfov declared that he had petitioned the Grand Prince's boiars for a trial over the land. He himself had appeared on the land at the time designated by the judge whom the boiars had appointed to hear the case, but the metropolitan's representatives did not come. "And this spring, Sire, that Ignat with the same Grigorii and Ivan Vnukov and many other persons with them, came riding into another one of my little hamlets, and, Sire, they beat my man Iakush and his wife and plundered his property." Iakush sent a bailiff after his attackers, and appeared at the designated time with Okinfov's son Pavlinets. But the metropolitan's men had sent a bailiff with a warrant for Pavlinets, and the village priest, and four peasants, and Okinfov's man. The boiars then decreed a judicial duel between Iakush and his attackers, and another for Pavlinets, the priest, the peasants, and Okinfov's man Sukhoi with the metropolitan's peasants. All Okinfov's people

[52] D. Ia. Samokvasov, *Arkhivnyi material* (2 v., Moscow, 1905–1909) 1, pt. 2, pp. 141–147. The document incorporates the text of the oath upon which each litigant was to kiss the cross.
[53] See *Sudebnik XV–XVI vekov*, pp. 207, 209.
[54] *AFZKh* 1, no. 117.
[55] *AIu*, no. 14. For another case in which the offer to fight a judicial duel was the only proof presented by the plaintiffs, see *AFZKh* 1, no. 222.
[56] *AIu*, no. 17.

had appeared on the field, prepared to fight, "but on the next day, Sire, my man Iakushko went out in the morning to the Neglinna [river] to fetch water and disappeared." Pavlinets had petitioned the court, requesting a postponement so that he could find Iakush, but the request was denied, and the officials gave judgment against Okinfov's people in both cases. Later, he continued, "my man Gavrilko found Iakushko after a search, in the Karashskaia canton, in a hamlet belonging to the metropolitan; and Iakush, Sire, was sitting in chains under a grain-sheaf dryer: and my man Gavrilets [sic] was going to take that man Iakushko [back with him], and, Sire, Ignat Ovdeev and Fedor Manuilov and Olesha Matov gave chase to my man Gavrilko on the road and beat him and took Iakush away from him." Okinfov's losses "connected with Iakush" had amounted, he claimed, to thirty-eight and one-half rubles.

Okinfov's man Gavrilko next brought complaint against the three petty boiars who had allegedly beaten him.[57] After Iakush had vanished from the dueling field in mid-summer, Okinfov had sent Gavrilko out to search. A week before St. Dmitrii's Day (O.S. October 26) he had found Iakush in irons under the wheatsheaf dryer, but as he tried to take Iakush away, the petty boiars caught up with him and beat him.

The metropolitan's petty boiars, when asked to answer, denied all charges, claiming that Okinfov was making false accusations in order to offset the case of the metropolitan's peasants against his men and peasants for robbery and murder, and, in addition, that Okinfov and his man Gavrilko wished to destroy the effect of the judgment charter issued in the two judicial duel cases. They then presented the judgment charter.

The judge next questioned Gavrilko, asking what evidence he had and what people knew about the matter. Gavrilko replied: "Besides my [calling for] a judicial duel with Ignat Ovdeev and his comrades there is no evidence whatever, Sire, and I did not [officially] state [my case] before anyone in the Karashskaia canton because, Sire, that Karashskaia canton is the metropolitan's territory." For the second time in this trial, a plaintiff demanded a duel and presented no other evidence.

The Grand Prince then listened to the judgment charter presented by the metropolitan's people.[58] It recorded that the metropolitan's peasants had brought suit against Okinfov's son Pavlin, his man, the priest, and the peasants, for brigandage, claiming they had beaten and robbed hamlet dwellers, stolen horses and clothing, and broken one man's arms and legs. Two of the Grand Prince's secretaries had then examined the victim, found that his injuries were as claimed, and that he named the same men as his attackers. Again the defendants denied all charges, the plaintiffs demanded a duel, and the court decreed combat. Thus we learn why the metropolitan's men had sent a bailiff after Okinfov's son—a matter which Okinfov himself had not explained. When Pavlinets agreed to the duel, he made the counter-claim on behalf of Iakush, alleging that the metropolitan's people had robbed and beaten him. The metropolitan's peasants in turn denied the charges, Pavlin requested a duel on behalf of Iakush, and the peasants agreed. The judges then ordered the central-court constable to put both parties on bond and set the date for a duel in Moscow, on Friday of the second week of St. Peter's fast (i.e., in the last week of June), in the year 7029 (1521). Pavlin, and apparently the priest, were exempted from personal participation in the duel, but Pavlin's men and peasants were to fight with the metropolitan's peasants in both matters. Both sets of litigants appeared on the designated date. Having stood at the field seven days, on the eighth day the metropolitan's petty boiar and peasants petitioned the okol'nichii, saying that Iakush had run away from Moscow. "The central-court constable Gavrilko Vorontsov and Iakush's guarantor [and] his master, Pavlin, son of Chudin Okinfov, said that Iakush had at first stood at the field but had then run off." On July 11 a judgment charter was issued to the metropolitan's petty boiar and peasants. As we have seen, the document stated that Pavlin himself had declared that Iakush had run off, and there was no reference to the request for a postponement which Okinfov had mentioned in his complaint.

After the judgment charter had been read, the Grand Prince gave Okinfov an opportunity to challenge it, asking him whether the trial had been as described. Okinfov did not repeat his earlier remarks about the previous judicial duels, nor did he himself demand a judicial duel (in this case, one would almost expect it). He simply said: "Sire, my men and peasants and the priest had such a trial as is written in that document, and, Sire, a judgment charter was issued against them in that matter."

Vasilii III gave judgment in favor of the metropolitan's peasants and petty boiars, and against the defendants, because Okinfov and his man had brought suit against the metropolitan's petty boiars to offset the peasants' charges of assault and robbery and to nullify the judgment charter, "and had brought one suit involving land and another suit against them, alleging that they had beaten Chudin's man Gavrilko and had forcibly taken his comrade, Chudin's man Iakush, from him, but he had presented no evidence against them in that matter and had not [earlier] declared

---

[57] As we have seen earlier, a slave could represent his master in court, appearing as either a plaintiff or defendant, but he lacked the capacity to appear as a formal witness (poslukh). Okinfov's strategy here was to bring his slave Gavrilko into the trial as a fellow litigant in his countersuit against the monastery—in this way Gavrilko was able to testify as a witness might; see Kolycheva, Kholopstvo i krepostnichestvo, p. 233.

[58] For the text of this judgment charter, published as a separate document, see AFZKh 1, no. 1a.

[this matter] to anyone (i.e., had not complained to the authorities at the time)."

The judgment charter really records two cases, the current one and the trial four years earlier. Both follow the same pattern: the metropolitan's people bring charges of assault and robbery, the defendants reply with similar counter-charges after denying their own guilt, and both sides present counter-demands for a judicial duel. In the first trial the Grand Prince's secretaries had verified the victim's injuries, but apart from this no evidence was offered. For some reason Okinfov never demanded that his opponents produce Iakush. This, in addition to the inconsistencies in his complaint and his failure to carry on his charges when given the opportunity, suggests that he was guilty. On the other hand, accusations on both sides could have had some basis in fact. The entire case sounds like a Russian version of a Wild West feud between cattlemen and sheep ranchers, a continuation of the old self-help principle. At the end of the case, after he had levied court costs and the sum at issue from the defendants, the Grand Prince ordered a boundary surveyor to go out and establish the boundary between the metropolitan's land and Okinfov's, although neither party had requested such action. Perhaps the Grand Prince hoped that new markers and ditches, by reminding people of their territorial limits, would discourage this type of behavior in the future.

The fourth and final form of "God's justice" which we encounter in the judgment charters is the casting of lots (*zherebii*). During the early centuries of Russian history, when the other forms of "God's justice" were commonly used, litigants resorted to lots only in deciding which party would give an oath. Yet casting of lots could also be an independent means of proof, and was used particularly by the clergy, especially as the church's opposition to the judicial duel became stronger.[59] The various types of "God's justice" gradually went out of use, one after the other, as the more complicated or more dangerous form was replaced by another which had originally been a preliminary step but had slowly acquired independent status. The judicial duel had supplanted trial by hot iron or water, then in time the oath (cross-kissing) could be used as proof in itself, without the duel, and finally in the sixteenth century cases were often decided, not even by the oath (to which lots had previously been a preliminary step), but by lots alone.[60]

Once again, the best-known description of the *zherebii* procedure does not come from Russian legal sources.[61] The classic account of justice by lots is

that written in 1560 by one Henrie Lane, an English merchant residing in Russia as an agent of the Muscovy Company. He claimed to owe "sundrie Russian marchants" the sum of 600 rubles for goods which they had exported in English ships, but the Russians demanded a double amount. Apparently the judicial duel was still alive and well in Muscovy, since the merchants obtained an order to that effect. Lane gives no account of this stage of litigation, but only reports: "For combatte I was provided of a strong willing Englishman, Robert Best, one of the companies servants: whome the Russes with their Champion refused." After this "we had the words of our priviledge put into effect, which were to draw lots." Lane apparently is referring here to Article 27 of the 1550 Sudebnik, which provided that lots were to be drawn in suits between Russians and foreigners. Lane describes the trial procedure as follows:

The day and maner of triall appointed by the Emperour at his castle in his palace and high Court of Moscovia was thus. The Emperours two Treasurers, being also Chancelours and chiefe judges, sate in court. They appointed officers to bring me, mine interpreter, & the other, through the great presse within the rayle or barre, and permitted me to sit downe some distance from them: the adverse parties being without at the barre. Both parties were first perswaded with great curtesie, to wit, I to enlarge mine offer, and the Russes to mitigate their challenge. Notwithstanding that I protested my conscience to be cleere, and their gaine by accompt to bee sufficient, yet of gentlenes at the magistrates request I made proffer of of 100 robles more: which was openly commended, but of the plaintifes not accepted. The sentence passed with our names in two equall balles of waxe made and holden up by the Judges, their sleeves stripped up. Then with standing up and wishing well to the trueth attributed to him that should be first drawen, by both consents among the multitude they called a tall gentleman, saying: Thou with such a coate or cap, come up: where roome with speede was made. He was commanded to hold his cappe, wherein they put the balles, by the crowne upright in sight, his arme not abasing. With like circumspection, they called at adventure another tall gentleman, commanding him to

---

[59] *Sudebniki XV–XVI vekov,* p. 209; Dmitriev, *Istoriia sudebnykh instantsii,* p. 262.

[60] Kliuchevskii, *Sochineniia* **6**: p. 223.

[61] Probably the most colorful example of a decision reached by casting lots occurs in a literary work, the tale of Sadko, merchant-prince of Novgorod. When his ship was suddenly becalmed one day, Sadko, after trying to appease the Sea

Tsar with gold, silver, and pearls, deduced that the sea was demanding one of his company as tribute, and decided that the victim should be chosen by lot. He ordered the members of his company to make lots (*zhereb'ia*) of wood, each man inscribing his name on one, and to cast them into the sea. He himself wrote his name in golden letters. The man whose lot sank to the bottom was to follow it into the sea. The lots of his companions "floated like ducks," but that of Sadko went straight down. Immediately our merchant decided that there had been an error in procedure (*"eti zhereb'i est' nepravil'ni"*). So he ordered his men to prepare lots with gold inscriptions, while he himself used oak. Again all the lots floated like ducks, except Sadko's. He decided that they would make a third—and final—attempt. This time his company made lots of oak, and Sadko used lime. The oak lots floated like ducks, but that of the wealthy Novgorod merchant once more disappeared under the water. Sadko then accepted the inevitable, wrote his will, put on his sables, picked up his lyre (*guselka*), walked down the gangplank, and sailed off on his chessboard, more or less ready for his meeting with the Tsar of the Sea. For the text, see N. N. Andreev, *Byliny* (Leningrad, 1938), pp. 406–422, especially pp. 416–417.

strip up his right sleeve, and willed him with his bare
arme to reache up, and in Gods name severally to take
out the two balles: which he did, delivering to either
Judge one. Then with great admiration the lotte in ball
first taken out was mine: which was by open sentence
so pronounced before all the people, and to be the right
and true parte.

Lane then paid the plaintiffs the sum of 600 rubles, out
of which "for their wrong or sinne, as it was termed,
they payd tenne in the hundred to the Emperour." Lane
also received another, unexpected benefit from the decision. "Many dayes after, as their maner is, the
people took our nation to be true and upright dealers,
and talked of this judgment to our great credite." [62]

In the judgment charters, a reference to lots is rare.
In one recently published document, however, dated
1501–1505 (or 1510), the Novgorod vicegerents used
lots to reach a decision. The plaintiff called for evidence from the Grand Prince's record books, declared
that he had a charter of grant, and presented longtime
residents, who testified that they had been mowing the
disputed land with him for seventeen years and that
no other persons had any rights in that land. The defendants had a purchase deed, which the plaintiff declared false, again calling for the Grand Prince's books.
Then the defendants presented longtime residents who
supported their claims; the witnesses could not measure
off the land, however, since it had been held jointly, and
"from olden times there has been no boundary [strip]
there." After gathering all this evidence, the lower-
court judges referred the case to the Novgorod vicegerents, Prince Danilo Vasil'evich Shcheniatev and
Prince Vasilii Vasil'evich Shuiskii. In response to the
princes' question, the litigants stated that their trial had
been as the record showed. The vicegerents did not,
as we might expect, examine the Grand Prince's land
records or call for the witnesses named in the defendants' purchase deed. Instead they ordered the lower-
court judges "to decree that both litigants—the plaintiff Shiriai Zavalishin and the defendant Onton who
also represented his brothers Gridia and Klim and his
comrades Ignash and Minia—draw lots, [and that]
whosoever lot was drawn, his longtime peasant tenants
were to measure off the [boundaries of the] land, after
kissing the cross." After this, both parties, with their
longtime residents, again stood before the judges on
the land. "And the judges cast the lot[s], and the lot
[favoring Onton, the defendant] was drawn [so that]
Onton's longtime peasant residents Gavrilo Ivanov,
and Pavel Ostaf'ev and Grisha Espov, and Grisha
Pavlov kissed the cross and measured off the boundary

line." Judgment was given against the plaintiff and
in favor of the defendants "because their longtime peasant residents' lot was drawn." [63]

Three forms of "God's justice"—judicial duel, lots,
and use of the icon in setting boundaries—figured in a
1494 judgment charter.[64] The plaintiffs, a supervisor
and priest from the Simonov Monastery, explained at
the beginning of the trial that their archimandrite had
already conferred with the defendants, and both had
agreed: "We, Sire, do not need a judicial duel." Thus
the parties, on their own initiative, had ruled out one
form of "God's justice" before court convened. In addition, they had worked out an alternative method for
settling their boundary dispute. This substitute procedure—a five-point program—was to result in the monastery's witnesses, with an icon, measuring off the land
according to the old boundaries. The litigants had
made depositions recording their use of this form of
"God's justice," and the plantiffs presented the monastery's copy before the judge.

The deposition began,

I, Archimandrite Fegnast of the Simonov Monastery, and
I, Ivan, son of Mikhailo Tveritinov, [for myself] and in
place of my stepson Ivan, son of Ostafei Sirotin, have
thrown lots concerning land [boundaries] where our
monasterial land, the hamlet Korobovskaia, comes together
with the land of Ivan and his stepson Ivan, the village
Sirotinskoe. And the lots came out in favor of me, the
Archimandrite.

Apparently, in this first step, whoever won by lot received the right to have his witnesses mark off the
boundary with the icon. As the second step, the archimandrite was to send the monasterial supervisor and
priest to the disputed land, along with the witnesses.
The third point in the procedure was the boundary
demarcation itself, during which the witnesses "are
to go on foot with the icon, the image of the Immaculate
[Mother of God]; and behind them the monasterial
supervisor Ivonia and the priest Mantyrei, along with
Ivan, son of Mikhailo Tveritinov, shall ride." Along
the way, as the fourth step, they were to dig holes and
place boundary markers on the trees. Finally, both
parties were to receive boundary-setting charters
(roz"ezhie gramoty) in accordance with this demarcation. The next section of the deposition echoes Pososhkov's faith in "God's justice":

And if the archimandrite does not send the monasterial
supervisor Ivonia and the priest Mantyrei and those witnesses to that land—Preobrazhenie Spasovo—or if any of
those witnesses shall not go behind the icon of the Immaculate [Mother of God] (i.e., if they know the boundary
being shown is incorrect and choose flight over death), then

[62] "The maner of Justice by lots in Russia, written by
Master Henrie Lane, and executed in a controversie betweene
him and one Sheray Costromitsky in Mosco," in Richard
Hakluyt, *The Principal Navigations, Voyages, Traffiques and
Discoveries of the English Nation* (8 v., London and Toronto,
1927) 1: pp. 406–408. See also Kliuchevskii, *Sochineniia* 6:
p. 224; N. M. Karamzin, *Istoriia gosudarstva rossiiskogo* (9
v., St. Petersburg, 1892) 9, *Primechaniia,* no. 788: p. 161.

[63] Anpilogov, *Novye dokumenty,* pp. 485–490. For another
edition of the text, see V. I. Koretskii, "Vnov' otkrytye
Novgorodskie i Pskovskie gramoty XIV–XV vv.," *Arkheograficheskii ezhegodnik za 1967 god* (Moscow, 1969), pp. 288–
290. See especially p. 284, n. 56, where Koretskii lists his
corrections to Anpilogov's edition of the text.

[64] *ASEI* 2, no. 409.

Ivan, son of Mikhailo Tveritinov, wins the dispute (lit. is right in that land).

If the defendant did not appear or refused to ride behind the witnesses, he was to lose. Perhaps this provision was intended to prevent stalling on the part of the man who lost at the drawing of lots. Subsequently the monastery's witnesses were to lead a judge along the boundary, without an icon, in accordance with the boundary charter. All were to appear on the land at the time designated by the judge, and both depositions were to be presented.

The judge then questioned the defendant about this agreement. Ivan, after verifying the deposition and his signature on it, declared: "And I, Ivan, had such a deposition, a copy of that deposition. But now I do not have it—it is lost." He made no attempt, however, to change or further define the agreement.

The monastery's witnesses then took the icon and measured off the land. The judge Chubar Bezobrazov had come out to the land on orders of Ivan Iur'evich Patrikeev, so he set a time for the litigants to appear before Patrikeev in Moscow. Both men declared that they had had such a boundary demarcation, and that they had written up the deposition together. Patrikeev then ordered Bezobrazov to issue them boundary-demarcation charters, thus giving legal confirmation to both forms of "God's justice" used to resolve the dispute, the lot-casting and measuring off the land with the icon.

As we have seen, litigants could present varied types of evidence and make use of several different forms of procedure. With regard to testimony or documents, they were apparently limited only by their ability to produce the witness or record in court. As a general rule, offering proof by "God's justice" was a matter of free choice, and the majority of litigants preferred to rely on the court's assessment of the facts. One other procedural step, which could affect the outcome of the case, will be discussed in the next chapter: referral of the matter on *doklad* to a court of higher instance.

VII. TRIAL PROCEDURE: *DOKLAD* AS A FINAL STEP

Approximately one-half of the extant judgment charters record cases which included *doklad* as a final procedural step. In these instances the lower-court judge did not decide the case himself but referred the matter to a court of higher instance. *Doklad* procedure usually took the following form: the judge who had conducted the original trial placed a copy of his trial record before the upper court and presented both litigants; after the upper-court judge had examined the trial record or heard a report about the trial, he questioned both parties—this was their opportunity to present any objections to the lower court's record of trial; when both sides had completed their statements, the upper court proceeded to an examination of further

evidence, if such were indicated, and then instructed the lower-court judge concerning the decision. Thus *doklad* was at the same time a continuation of the original trial and a re-examination of the evidence by the upper court. It did not, however, constitute an appeal or review process, since the lower-court judge had given no decision in the matter.

In the majority of the documents which record a trial on *doklad,* it seems to have been nothing but a formality by which the case was brought before a court of higher instance for decision. The parties themselves took no active role. Both litigants, or their representatives, simply said that the trial had been such as the record indicated, and then awaited the upper court's decision.[1]

There were a few variations from this outline. A 1498 judgment charter records an instance of double *doklad.* The case was first referred to Prince Vasilii Ivanovich Golenin. After both litigants had confirmed the trial record, Golenin ordered the lower-court judge to grant the requested judicial duel between the parties' longtime residents. Apparently Golenin thought the issue was settled, as far as his court was concerned, since he ordered that his seal be attached to the trial record and his secretary signed the document. When the plaintiffs' third witness subsequently failed to appear for the duel, the original judge again sent the case to a higher court for decision. This time the litigants appeared before Grand Prince Dmitrii Ivanovich, and the lower-court judge presented a duel and inquest record (*polevaia zajis' oprosnaia*). Rather than questioning them about the trial record, the Grand Prince asked whether they had had such a date for the judicial duel and whether the inquest record reported the facts correctly. Both parties verified the lower-court judge's account, and the Grand Prince proceeded to give judgment for the defendants because the plaintiffs' third witness had not appeared.[2]

A judgment charter issued about 1492 contains an unusual account of *doklad* procedure. In this instance, the lower-court judges apparently gave a partial decision themselves before referring the case to the upper court: "And the judges ordered a [new, official] boundary strip established along the old boundary line, where scythe had met scythe, and agreed to report to the sovereign Grand Prince on the new settlement." Then the judges placed the trial record and both sets

[1] See, for example, *ASEI* 1, nos. 430, 523, 524, 525, 557, 582; *ASEI* 2, nos. 188, 229, 285, 286, 287, 288, 332, 334, 336, 337, 370, 374, 375, 404, 405, 409, 411, 450, 483; *ASEI* 3, nos. 56, 173, 208, 276, 400; *AFZKh* 1, nos. 117, 125, 157, 248, 249, 259; Anpilogov, *Novye dokumenty,* pp. 485–490; *AIu,* nos. 16, 20, 21; Likhachev, *Sbornik,* no. 12; *RIB* 12, no. 4.

[2] *AFZKh* 1, no. 117. In Kashtanov's opinion, this case was first heard on *doklad* not by Golenin but by Ivan III's son Vasilii, the concluding stages of the legal process taking place only after Vasilii's disgrace and the coronation of Dmitrii, Ivan III's grandson; Kashtanov, *Sotsial'no-politicheskaia istoriia,* p. 56.

of litigants before the upper court, where Prince Danilo Penkov questioned the parties, who agreed that they had had such a trial. The boundary division ordered by the lower-court judges was only a part of the final decision. Two plaintiffs had charged that the defendants were taking over their meadows. When the previous holders of the meadows were questioned, however, they declared that their former land lay beyond that marked off by the defendants. The judges had then ordered that this old boundary line be established formally. The third plaintiff, however, lost all rights to a settlement which he had claimed, since the defendants had proved that he had obtained a charter by fraudulent means, and that the document had since been revoked.[3]

The course of events during *doklad* proceedings could affect the outcome of the trial decisively. This was certainly the case if one party to the suit did not show up for the proceedings in the upper court. In one instance, after both sides had presented longtime residents and the witnesses had agreed to a judicial duel, the judge ordered both litigants to appear before the Grand Prince a week before Christmas; in the meantime, neither party was to cart off the hay from the disputed land. The plaintiffs and their witnesses arrived at the designated time, but the defendant and his longtime residents did not appear. In addition, the defendant had removed the hay from the deserted village under litigation. The judge presented the plaintiffs and their longtime residents, and placed the trial record from his court before the Grand Prince, explaining that he had set a time for both sides to appear, that the defendant had not come, and that the defendant had taken the hay in violation of the court's order. The Grand Prince then gave judgment in favor of the plaintiffs, because the defendant had not appeared for the trial on *doklad* and because he had carted off the hay from the land.[4] Since both litigants had originally presented what would appear to have been roughly equal evidence, the defendant conveniently determined the outcome of the case by his own action.

A judgment charter issued between 1478 and 1485 provides another illustration. After hearing the evidence, the judge had ordered both litigants to appear in the upper court two weeks later, on Epiphany, but the defendant did not come. Again judgment was given against the defendant because he did not appear at the designated time.[5] In this case it seems probable that the defendant had decided to save himself the expense and inconvenience of going to the trial on *doklad*. Accused of mowing the plaintiff's meadowland, he had explained that he had mowed up to the boundary described by the man who had mortgaged the land to him. The mortgagor, who testified next, had declared that he could present no boundary-division witnesses

for the land and would accept the boundaries set by the plaintiff's witnesses. Since the plaintiff's longtime residents were to mark off the land, the defendant had nothing to gain by appearing for the second trial. And judgment was in fact given against the landholder who had mortgaged the land, rather than the defendant named at the beginning of the trial.

On other occasions, witnesses or documents which had not been presented in the lower court were examined during *doklad*. Vasilii Ivanovich, son of Ivan III, called in Prince Semen Romanovich to verify his donation charter before awarding the meadow in question to the Spaso-Iaroslavl' Monastery.[6] As we have noted previously, some litigants refused to present their documents in the lower court. On other occasions judges checked the land cadastre books or compared evidence from the trial record with documents in the Grand Prince's archives. In cases such as these, new evidence was introduced at the *doklad* level. The judge in a 1494 case, however, refused to allow the defendant to bring in a new issue. Before trial, the litigants had already arranged the boundary-setting procedure and recorded their agreement in a deposition. Chubar, son of Fedor Bezobrazov, had been sent out to the land by Ivan Iur'evich Patrikeev as a judge to supervise the establishment of the boundaries. After the witnesses had gone around the land, he set a time for both parties to appear before Patrikeev in Moscow. At the designated time, Chubar told Patrikeev about the demarcation proceedings, and both parties confirmed his record. Once they had agreed on this, as we would expect, Patrikeev ordered Chubar to issue the boundary charters. But at this point the defendant stepped forward and petitioned Prince Ivan Iur'evich: "Sire, the monasterial witnesses have marked off the land, and on that land we and our peasants have mown the winter wheat and hay; and how shalt thou decide, Lord? Dost thou order me and our peasants to store that grain and hay?" In Patrikeev's opinion it was too late in the trial for such a move; the defendant should have raised the question earlier, and by his failure to do so had forfeited his rights:

When thou didst write up the depositions with the archimandrite, why didst thou not write anything about that grain and hay, and why didst thou, [when on the land], say nothing in the presence of the judge about that grain? And now, when the witnesses with the icon have marked off the land along those lines, the grain and hay on that land are the monastery's.[7]

Still other litigants, when appearing in the upper court, contested the trial record of the lower court. When one defendant claimed that the trial had not been as recorded, Prince Vasilii Ivanovich Patrikeev sent for the men of court named in the trial record and postponed the hearing until their arrival. The central-

3 *ASEI* 2, no. 285.
4 *AFZKh* 1, no. 261.
5 *ASEI* 3, no. 477.
6 *ASEI* 3, no. 208.
7 *ASEI* 2, no. 409.

court constable subsequently brought them before the upper court, and also presented the lower-court judge and the plaintiff. The constable then explained that after the first hearing he had placed the defendant, Stepanko Doroga, on surety bond, "and, Sire, Ofremko Bulgak, son of Iakush, and Oleshko, son of Dmitrei Bobrovnik, secured his release from me; and, Sire, that Stepanko ran away with his sureties." Despite the defendant's absence, Patrikeev ordered that the trial record be read aloud before the men of court, so that they could verify its accuracy. The men of court then declared that they saw the plaintiff in court, but not the defendant; the litigants, they affirmed, "did have such a trial in our presence as is written in this [trial] record." [8] Thus, although the defendant had fled, the upper-court judge carried out the *doklad* procedure in full, asking the men of court to verify the trial record and identify the plaintiff as one of the parties to the lawsuit which they had witnessed.

Sending for the men of court was apparently enough to force a confession in a case tried between 1496 and 1498. Although he had no documents for the disputed land, and there were inconsistencies in the testimony on his side, and his longtime residents got lost while showing the judge the boundaries, the defendant still declared at the trial on *doklad* that he had not had such a trial as the record indicated. The upper-court judge therefore ordered the central-court constable to place the men of court before him. On the very next day both litigants appeared in court again, and the defendant said: "Sire, I do not call for the testimony of the men of court according to the [trial] record; Sire, I am guilty; and Sire, I encroached upon those lands [which are] not mine." The court gave judgment for the plaintiff. [9]

A similar situation developed in another case. When litigants appeared before Mikita Vasil'evich Beklemishev for a trial on *doklad,* the defendant first declared that the trial had not been as recorded. The judgment charter then reads: "And having left the court [and returned], again standing before Mikita, he said that the trial was such as was written in this [trial] record." The document does not indicate what happened while the defendant was not in court, nor does it give any suggestion of his reasons for changing his statement. Even after the defendant had accepted the record, Mikita did not proceed to give judgment, but ordered the lower-court judge to arrange a time for both litigants to appear before Grand Prince Ivan Ivanovich, "because Grand Prince Ivan Vasil'evich of all Rus' had ordered that land trials be deferred until his son, the Grand Prince, [returned]." The Grand Prince's secretary then summarized these proceedings and signed his notes for the record. For the second stage of this *doklad* trial, the litigants appeared before Grand

Prince Ivan Ivanovich, who questioned them concerning the trial record which had been placed before him. "And both litigants said that they had had such a trial as was written in this [trial] record, and that they had appeared before Mikita Vasil'evich; and they said: 'It was as is written in the added notation.'" After the parties had thus confirmed the trial record, the Grand Prince gave his decision for the plaintiff. [10]

Doklad proceedings in a 1510 case took yet another twist. Apparently litigants could question a part of the trial record only, rather than challenging the entire document. One defendant, speaking for this comrades, said that they had had a trial, but not such as was written in the record. After the men of court had been summoned, two other defendants explained their objection more precisely:

And furthermore, Sire, we call for [the evidence in] the [land cadastre] books, [to prove] that that weir (the property in litigation) on the Liana creek is registered with our hamlet Ievlevskaia, and, Sire, we at that time (i.e. during the trial) petitioned the judges and called for [the evidence in] the books, and they, Sire, did not put that in the [trial] record.

After hearing this complaint, rather than checking with the men of court to see whether the defendants had called for the books, the upper-court judge took the direct course and ordered that the records be brought before him. When he examined the land cadastres, however, the weir was not registered with the defendants' hamlet. Thus the defendants lost the case, "because they had called for the [evidence in the] books, and had said that their weir was registered with their hamlet, but the weir was not [so] registered in the books." [11]

Despite adverse testimony from the men of court, another litigant continued to press his contention that the lower court's record was not accurate. A 1531 judgment charter records that the defendant challenged the trial record twice. During the proceedings on the land, he had beaten his longtime residents when they were unable to lead the judges along the boundaries and had admitted that the disputed hamlet was registered for the plaintiff in the land cadastres. When he appeared before the Grand Prince on *doklad,* however, the defendant declared that the trial had not been as the record indicated and called for the testimony of both judges, Sharap Baskakov and Funik Kurtsov, and the men of court. After the bailiff had presented them, Vasilii III ordered that the trial record be read aloud, then asked: "Did both litigants have such a trial before you as is recorded in this [trial] record, and is that thy, Sharap's, handwriting on that [trial] record, and didst thou, with thy colleague Funik, send me that [trial] record on *doklad*?" Sharap identified the hand-

[8] *ASEI* 1, no. 595.
[9] *ASEI* 1, no. 607.

[10] *ASEI* 1, no. 523. Another case which follows a similar pattern may be found in Kashtanov, *Ocherki russkoi diplomatiki,* no. 9: pp. 354–361.
[11] *AIu,* no. 14.

writing as his and declared that he and Funik had sent the Grand Prince an accurate record of the proceedings. The men of court, upon kissing the cross, affirmed that such a trial had taken place in their presence.

At this point we would expect a decision, but the record continued with events occurring six months later, which gives some indication of the speed with which Muscovite justice operated. The defendant, again appearing before the Grand Prince, repeated his contention that the trial record was false. He petitioned the sovereign to order that the record not be signed, and presented what he claimed was the authentic draft trial record, written by Sharap Baskakov. In response to the Grand Prince's questions, the defendant said that "no one happened to be there" when Sharap gave him the document, and he did not remember the day on which it had taken place. Vasilii III ordered that the litigants and both judges appear before him for a direct confrontation as soon as Sharap returned from Smolensk.

When the court convened again, Sharap examined the draft trial record, denied that he had given the defendant such a document, and declared that he did not recognize the handwriting. The defendant's man, appearing in court for his master, requested a judicial duel with Sharap, to which the judge agreed, but no further evidence was presented. The other judge, Funik Kurtsov, was questioned next. He said that they had no such draft trial record, that he had not seen such a document in Sharap's possession, and that he too did not recognize the handwriting. For this part of the trial the sovereign gave judgment in favor of the judges, because, contrary to the defendant's claims, Sharap's handwriting was not on the document. In addition, the court raised another point, asking when Sharap had given the draft trial record to the defendant, since the judge had been on the road to Smolensk. This was a point which the defendant had been unable to explain satisfactorily. Finally, the defendant had not presented the document immediately but "a long time after that." The Grand Prince also ordered the judges to award the land to the plaintiff, because the defendant had declared the trial record false but had had no support for his contention.

Even at this stage the plaintiff encountered further delay in obtaining a judgment charter. The Grand Prince had given his decision in March, 1529. The record subsequently incorporated the text of his order to the judge Funik Kurtsov, dated June 24, 1530, in which the sovereign stated that he had received a petition from the plaintiff, complaining that the judges had not yet surveyed the boundary or issued a judgment charter; in the meantime the defendant's son had started ravaging the land. Since Sharap was on

military service near Kazan',[12] the Grand Prince ordered Funik to look after the land until his return. Then both judges were to survey the boundary and issue a judgment charter. The judgment charter itself, dated May 15, 1531, concluded with a record of the official boundary establishment.[13]

Apparently *doklad* did not always involve the presence of the litigants before the court of higher instance. For example, a judgment charter issued between 1462 and 1464 records that the judges agreed to refer the matter to the sovereign Grand Prince. Next the men of court are listed, indicating the end of the trial record as such. Then we find that "on the basis of this [trial] record Grand Prince Ivan Vasil'evich ordered [the joint-court judges] to give judgment in favor of the metropolitan's estate manager Vavulka and the old estate manager Serapion."[14] Perhaps this may be attributed to the abbreviated nature of early judgment charters, yet other documents suggest that such a decision by the Grand Prince, based on the judge's report alone, was an established variant of *doklad* procedure. A 1472 judgment charter states: "And before Grand Prince Ioan Vasil'evich did Iakov Tatishchev place this record of proceedings in his court. And the Grand Prince, having examined the record, ordered Iakov Tatishchev to give judgment in favor of the Simonov Monastery elders."[15] The concluding section of a 1508 judgment charter records: "And Dmitrei Volodimerovich (the original judge) told Grand Prince Vasilei Ivanovich of all Rus' about the hearing which he had conducted; and at that time the [following] boiars were with the Grand Prince: Prince Vasilei Danilovich Kholmskoi, and Iakov Zakhar'ich, and Semen Borisovich." The Grand Prince, having listened to the report of the court hearing, ordered that judgment be given in favor of the plaintiffs, "and in accordance with the instructions of Grand Prince Vasilei Ivanovich of all Rus', Dmitrei Volodimerovich gave judgment in favor of the plaintiffs."[16] Since the litigants in this case were all members of the princely Kemskii family, it seems probable that the judge would have been required to refer the matter to the sovereign for decision. A 1543 judgment charter mentions *doklad* only in passing, stating that the judges decided in favor of the plaintiffs, "having referred [the matter]

---

[12] Sharap probably accompanied the military commanders sent to Kazan' in May, 1530; see *Razriadnaia kniga*, pp. 74–75.

[13] Likhachev, *Sbornik*, no. 9. The delay until late spring may have been caused by road conditions after Sharap's return from military service. Another text, dated March 22, 1547, records that undersecretaries were to be sent to conduct an investigation concerning fishing rights "when the roads dry up"; Serebrianskii, *Ocherki po istorii Pskovskago monashestva*, p. 574. Since Sharap and Funik were to carry out a boundary survey on the land, they probably waited for better weather.

[14] *ASEI* 2, no. 285.

[15] *ASEI* 2, no. 388a.

[16] *AIu*, no. 13; see also *ASEI* 3, no. 50.

to the Sovereign Grand Prince Ivan Vasil'evich of All Rus' and with the boiars' decree."[17] Since consultation between the sovereign and the boiars was a common practice in Muscovite administration, the wording is not surprising, particularly in view of the fact that this trial took place during the period of boiar rule before Ivan IV came of age. Apparently such consultations by judges formed another variant of *doklad* procedure. Judicial *doklad* of this type, based on the essential idea of *doklad* as a report, resembles the *doklad* procedure commonly used by the Muscovite government in various administrative matters, whereby boiars and *d'iaki* were ordered to assemble the necessary information and prepare reports; the Grand Prince could then reach decisions and issue decrees upon the basis of the written reports and consultation with his investigative commission.[18]

For what reasons did a judge refer cases to a court of higher instance for decision? The judgment charters provide little information. The record simply states that a judge agreed to refer the matter to the sovereign; his reasons are not given. Two bases for such action might be suggested: either some aspect of the case placed it beyond the judge's authority to render final decision, or the judge himself, after hearing the evidence, was in doubt and wanted the opinion of his superiors in the matter.

Cases could fall outside a judge's area of competence for several reasons. On some occasions the judge who went out to the land to collect evidence had apparently been appointed to do just that and no more. He was to investigate the matter and report his findings to his superior. The plaintiffs' opening statement to the judge in a 1494 judgment charter suggests that this was Vasilii Chubar's role:

Archimandrite Fegnast of the Simonov [Monastery] did petition the sovereign Grand Prince Ivan Vasil'evich of All Rus' against Ivan, son of Mikhailo Tveritinov, and his stepson Ivan, son of Ostafei Sirotin, [complaining] that Ivan, son of Mikhailo, and his stepson Ivan had unlawfully plowed the monastery's Korobovskaia hamlet land, and had sown [it] with winter wheat, and had mown [its] meadows. And the sovereign Grand Prince ordered Prince Ivan Iur'evich [Patrikeev] to give thee as a judge [in our suit].

Although the evidence was clearly on the plaintiffs' side, Chubar referred the matter to Patrikeev for final decision.[19]

A few judgment charters record cases where *doklad* should have been unnecessary if evidence alone determined the outcome. In a document recorded between 1478 and 1485 the judge of Grand Princess Marfa, Vasilii Ushakov, tried a case in which the defendant admitted that he did not know the boundaries and agreed to accept boundaries shown by the plaintiff's

witnesses. After the plaintiff's longtime residents had demonstrated their knowledge of the boundaries, and the defendant had again affirmed his willingness to accept those lines, we might think the matter resolved. Yet the judge referred the case to the Grand Princess for final decision.[20] A 1499 judgment charter follows a similar pattern. The matter was referred to the boiars, although the defendants had declared immediately that they did not know the boundaries.[21] In cases such as these, the judge hearing the matter must have lacked the necessary authority to give a final decision.

In other instances, judges sent cases up on *doklad* when one litigant's evidence was clearly better. In a 1472 judgment charter, the defendant's witnesses knew neither the land nor the boundaries, while the plaintiff's longtime residents supported his claims and led the judge around the land; yet the judge referred the matter to the Grand Prince.[22] The defendants in a 1504 case declared that they had already moved out of the disputed settlement, since they had no proof of title, yet the judge not only heard all the plaintiff's evidence but also sent the case up on *doklad*.[23] The judge's lack of authority to render decisions would seem to be the only explanation for *doklad* in such cases. In fact, Dmitriev asserts that "all judgment charters, where it is difficult to explain the reason for *doklad,* were issued by such judges, who, one may assume, did not occupy the first (upper) rungs on the service ladder."[24]

As was noted in Chapter VI, trials which reached the judicial duel stage, once the ritual was completed and both parties had agreed to combat, usually proceeded to *doklad*. Provisions of the Sudebniki suggest that only the upper courts had the authority to order litigants to fight. Some articles list fees for duels administered by the central courts,[25] while others regulate fees for those supervised by vicegerents with full jurisdictional grants, men whose jurisdiction was equal to that of the boiars in Moscow.[26] Apparently judges of lower rank were required to refer cases which might involve a duel—or those in which one side had refused the duel—to their superiors.[27] His lack of authority to decide potential judicial duel cases, however, was not the only reason that judge Burets Skripitsyn, a local petty boiar and landholder in the Verkhdubenskii borough, referred one matter to Vasilii Ivanovich Patrikeev; earlier, the defendants had also refused to present

[17] Likhachev, *Sbornik*, no. 10.
[18] See Sergeevich, *Lektsii i izsledovaniia*, pp. 272–274.
[19] *ASEI* 2, no. 409.

[20] *ASEI* 3, no. 477.
[21] *AFZKh* 1, no. 157.
[22] *ASEI* 2, no. 388a.
[23] *ASEI* 3, no. 173; for other cases which seem to fall into this category, see *ASEI* 2, nos. 188, 332, 336, 404, 450, 483; *ASEI* 3, no. 208; *AFZKh* 1, no. 249.
[24] Dmitriev, *Istoriia sudebnykh instantsii*, pp. 19–20.
[25] 1497 Sudebnik, articles 4–7; 1550 Sudebnik, articles 9–12.
[26] 1497 Sudebnik, article 38; 1550 Sudebnik, article 62.
[27] See, for example, *AFZKh* 1, nos. 259, 261; *ASEI* 2, nos. 334, 375; *AIu,* no. 14.

their document before him.[28] It seems probable that litigants would only use this tactic when they knew that the man hearing the case did not possess authority to give judgment against them. In 1498 judge Semen Krotkoi, a servitor (*sluzhilyi chelovek*) of the Grand Prince and landholder in the Kinel'skii borough, sent a case to Prince Golenin, who ordered him to grant the duel requested by the parties.[29] A judgment charter issued between 1499 and 1502 records, however, that Golenin himself referred a case in which a judicial duel offer had been made to the Grand Prince. This time it was perhaps not a question of authority but of doubt about the decision. The plaintiffs had presented five longtime residents, who remembered from forty to sixty years, and showed the judge the boundary. The defendant had then produced six longtime residents, all remembering fifty years, who supported his claims and likewise led the judge around the land. After the plaintiffs' witnesses had declared that the defendant's men had led the judge incorrectly and both sides had agreed to a duel in support of their respective claims, Golenin sent the case up on *doklad*.[30] Since both litigants had presented roughly equal evidence, it seems likely that Golenin voluntarily requested the sovereign's decision in the matter.[31] The Grand Prince ruled in favor of the plaintiffs, because the defendant's witnesses had said that the plaintiffs' peasants had been mowing the land for twenty years. In this instance the question of authority to give a decision may have been complicated by the existence of a charter of grant from the Grand Prince, since the plaintiffs were peasants of a village belonging to the Archangel Cathedral in Moscow.[32] Depending upon the competence of the judge, *doklad* could well be required in cases where one party held a charter of grant from the sovereign.[33]

Decisions in litigation involving slaves were also reserved for the higher courts. A 1547 judgment charter records that Iakov Moklokov, deputy of the tsar, sent the case up on *doklad* even though the defendant had admitted that he was Mikhailo Kolupaev's indentured slave.[34] Moklokov's action was undoubtedly based on the Sudebnik articles which prohibited those with limited-jurisdictional grants—including deputies of the Grand Prince—from deciding matters involving slaves without report to higher authorities.[35] The same condi-

tions probably governed the use of *doklad* after an admission of guilt in a case where the defendant was finally declared a slave because he had married the plaintiffs' slave woman.[36]

It also seems likely that some judges sent cases on *doklad* to higher courts because they were uncertain of the proper decision.[37] In some instances litigants produced evidence which would appear to have been of almost equal weight. Both parties might present witnesses as their only form of proof. In a case tried between 1462 and 1505, the peasant defendants declared that the Grand Prince's estate manager had settled them on the land claimed by the plaintiffs, peasants of the metropolitan. The defendants called upon the estate manager, who said that he had settled them there because local peasants had told him the land went with their village. The estate manager in turn presented five local peasants, who remembered for over fifty-five years and declared that the land was the Grand Prince's. After the defendants' six witnesses had testified, the plaintiffs also produced six witnesses. The abbot and five longtime residents (some remembered sixty years, others forty) declared that the metropolitan's peasants had been plowing the land. At this point, with the Grand Prince's estate manager balancing the abbot and five other witnesses on each side, the judge referred the matter to the Grand Prince.[38]

In other cases, one side had documents and the opponent presented witnesses. One defendant, for example, produced a fifty-year-old purchase deed, while the plaintiff had two longtime residents who testified that the land had been the canton's for fifty years.[39] In another case, the plaintiff had two documents but could not verify them in any way, and the defendant presented two longtime residents who remembered for seventy years.[40] These cases, and others of the same type, were referred to higher courts.[41] In most of these cases, the plaintiff was bringing suit after twelve to forty years; this complication probably added to the lower-court judge's doubt concerning the decision. Yet other judgment charters record that litigants presented varied combinations of documentary evidence and testimony in support of their claims. In one case, the plaintiffs had a charter of grant and four

---

28 *ASEI* 1, no. 582.

29 *AFZKh* 1, no. 117.

30 *ASEI* 3, no. 50.

31 Golenin was one of the Grand Prince's scribes. As noted in Chapter II, the scribes could decide cases without *doklad*. Apparently this included trials in which litigants agreed to a judicial duel; see *ASEI* 2, no. 407.

32 The cathedral did have a charter of grant for another area from Vasilii II, confirmed by Ivan III, which conferred judicial privileges among others; *ASEI* 3, no. 49.

33 This would seem to be the explanation for *doklad* in several cases involving princes; see, for example, *ASEI* 1, no. 607; *AIu*, no. 13.

34 *AIu*, no. 22.

35 1497 Sudebnik, articles 20, 43.

36 *AIu*, no. 21.

37 A number of decrees from 1555/1556 take this into account. They were addressed to boiars, vicegerents, and secretaries, ordering them to attend to such matters as carrying out requests from petitioners, settling boundary questions, trying cases, returning widows' portions, and so forth. If the officials were unable to reach a decision, they were to send the matter to higher authorities on *doklad*; see *Dopolneniia k aktam istoricheskim* 1, nos. 51, 52.

38 *AFZKh* 1, no. 125. For other cases which seem to fall in this category, see *ASEI* 1, no. 557; 2, no. 388a; 3, no. 276; *AFZKh* 1, no. 248.

39 *ASEI* 1, no. 524.

40 *ASEI* 2, no. 229.

41 See, for example, *ASEI* 1, no. 525; 2, nos. 286, 287, 288.

longtime residents, while the defendants produced a purchase deed and three longtime residents.[42]

Finally, one is tempted to think, some judges referred cases to the upper court because neither side had presented sufficient evidence. One plaintiff produced a judgment charter which, he claimed, had been issued against the defendant in a previous trial. The defendant immediately declared that no such trial had ever taken place. Neither party presented any witnesses, and the judge sent the case up on *doklad*.[43] Another defendant presented two general charters which did not specifically name the disputed land, while the plaintiffs claimed that they had petitioned the Grand Prince to no avail.[44] The plaintiff in another case had only a copy of his charter, while the defendants claimed that the Grand Prince's officials had ordered them to clear the disputed forest.[45] In other cases, each side "proved" his case by leading the judge along the boundaries.[46] When such evidence was presented, it would not be surprising if a lower-court judge felt reluctant to decide the matter on his own.

The judgment charters themselves, by the evidence which they record as having been presented, thus suggest that the judges may have sent cases up on *doklad* voluntarily as well as from lack of jurisdiction. Of course, in any one of these matters, the judge may well have assessed evidence differently from the way we might. Subjective factors, which would not appear in the documents, might also have been influential. Then too, several reasons for *doklad* could arise in the same case. To consider a hypothetical example, litigants might present evidence of seemingly equal weight and then agree to a duel; if one of the parties happened to be a secular landholder or a monastery with a charter of grant, or a slave, the situation became still more complicated; in addition, the original judge could have been instructed only to hear the case and make a report. At any rate, for whatever reason they found it necessary, *doklad* was a procedural step to which judges frequently resorted.

Thus, as we have seen, Muscovite litigants and their judges had a wide range of evidence and trial procedure upon which to draw. Litigants could introduce documents of various types or testimony of witnesses—or the judge could request such evidence. The parties or their witnesses could offer to support the truth of their claims, or even to prove the entire case, by means of one or more forms of "God's justice." On the other hand, the judge could expect them to suggest such steps and hold it against them if they did not. While *doklad* appears to be a procedural step initiated for the

most part by the judge, some litigants forced him to refer the case to a court of higher instance by refusing to present documents in his court; in addition, those litigants who agreed to a judicial duel probably knew that the lower-court judge would not have authority in the case any longer— a boiar or official of equal rank would have to give the decision. Although to some extent both the court and the parties could make use of these procedures for their own ends, the surviving judgment charters indicate that each had specific responsibilities within the course of the trial, a matter which will be examined in the next chapter.

VIII. THE ROLE OF LITIGANTS AND JUDGES

In general, Muscovite courts of the fifteenth and sixteenth centuries viewed a lawsuit as a form of supervised verbal contest between the two parties. On the whole responsibility for conduct of the case and presentation of evidence lay with the litigants themselves. When a plaintiff brought charges, the defendant answered the accusation as best he could. Each party in turn then presented whatever support he had for his claim, the prevailing maxim being "the more the better."

Documentary evidence constituted the first step in the chain of proof. Those litigants who possessed documents, or claimed to have them, or declared that they had formerly had such records, generally mentioned them first, before calling for the testimony of witnesses. Next the parties named their witnesses, usually longtime residents when land litigation was the issue; these men testified after the court had examined the documents. A litigant might bring in further evidence after this, calling for an examination of the Grand Prince's record books or an inquest of "good men" or even the testimony of witnesses not mentioned earlier. Most judgment charters, however, record only the testimony of witnesses named by the parties at the outset.

Some litigants had—or claimed to have—documents but no witnesses. In a large number of cases, however, a litigant had no documents (or even assertions that he had formerly possessed them), and relied upon testimony of witnesses alone to support his claims. The judicial duel ritual—except in those cases when combat was the only proof offered—came after documents and testimony had been introduced, and, as we have noted, was often the last step before *doklad*. On the whole litigants played the active role in courtroom procedure, determining the course of the trial by the evidence which they presented. With the exception of requests for an examination of the Grand Prince's land records or in situations where the original document was in the archives or in the possession of one of the Grand Prince's officials, the parties were responsible for producing their documents and placing them before the court. When calling for the testimony of witnesses,

[42] Anpilogov, *Novye dokumenty*, pp. 485–490; for other examples, see *ASEI* 1, nos. 523, 595; *ASEI* 2, nos. 285, 400; *AFZKh* 1, no. 103.
[43] *ASEI* 2, no. 405.
[44] *ASEI* 2, no. 374; see also *ASEI* 1, no. 430.
[45] *ASEI* 2, no. 337.
[46] *ASEI* 2, no. 370, 3, no. 56.

the litigants themselves more often than not brought these men to court. Presentation of their case was not a responsibility which litigants could afford to take lightly. As we have seen, many litigants sent a representative to court on their behalf (such as a peasant hundredman, a monasterial elder, or a literate slave) who had previous experience in such legal matters.

Judges tended to limit themselves to an essentially supervisory role, ensuring each party an opportunity to counter evidence produced by the opposition with proof of his own. The judges seem to have considered it their basic function, during the trial itself, to listen to whatever support the litigants might wish to offer for their claims. The court's primary objective was to collect as much evidence as possible. Documents and testimony were usually accepted as presented. Even when a judge had seemingly reliable evidence before him, such as official documents, he nevertheless tried to get additional "new" evidence.[1] The court willingly agreed to conduct inquests, when one of the parties so desired, and, except at the time designated for a judicial duel, was very lenient in granting postponements to allow parties time to produce witnesses or documents. In fact, on some occasions judges showed admirable patience, particularly in the matter of viewing the boundaries of disputed land. It must have been a very time-consuming, and rather tedious, process, when first each litigant and then his witnesses in turn led the judge from one tree to another, down ravines and across swamps. As a rule litigants received every opportunity to present whatever proof they could muster.[2]

Yet many judges apparently felt that the court's responsibility ended there; while it was their task to examine all information offered for their consideration, the litigants were responsible for producing the evidence. In most cases the judges were content to ask the usual—and obvious—questions. If a litigant mentioned a document and did not place it before the judge, he asked where it was; then, if the man produced it, the judge examined the record and proceeded with the hearing. If witnesses were named, he questioned them. If not, the judge usually asked the parties whether anyone knew the facts and could support the claims advanced. If the plaintiff merely stated his accusations and the defendant denied them, the judge asked each man why the land in question was his, what proof—documents or witnesses sometimes specified—he could produce.

The judge's questions generally were directed toward giving each litigant an opportunity to present his side of the question to the fullest extent possible. The judge himself rarely engaged in any form of interrogation or cross-examination. When longtime residents testified, for example, they told what they knew without any interruption. Most questions about documents arose when the record did not name the disputed land specifically or did not include a precise boundary description. Yet many such documents were accepted by the court at face value. Most judges apparently operated on the assumption that the proper decision would make itself evident during the course of the trial. One litigant might challenge the other's documents or witnesses and be able to provide overwhelming support for his contention, or testimony on one side would contain contradictions or inconsistencies, or one party would eventually confess. At any rate, many judges apparently felt that it was their job only to hear the case and then render a decision based upon the overall strength of each side's argument and the specific evidence stated in the trial record. Of course, if all else failed, the issue could be referred to God or the Grand Prince for final decision.

Thus many judges confined themselves to a relatively passive role throughout the trial. The burden of proof rested with the litigants. If one party, in the court's opinion, should have taken some step, such as demanding a judicial duel or presenting another witness, and failed to do so, this could be held against the litigant in the decision, even if the court had not requested such proof specifically during the trial.

The record found in a judgment charter issued about 1472 suggests that someone should have called for additional testimony if all the available evidence was to be considered. The plaintiffs charged that the defendant was taking away half of one of their fields. To refute this, the defendant declared that the land was his prince's, and that he, the defendant, was merely in possession of the land. Each litigant in turn then led the judge around the boundaries. After this, the plaintiffs presented three witnesses who supported their claims and pointed out the same boundaries which the plaintiffs had shown. Next the defendant presented his two witnesses. Both men testified that, since they had been living elsewhere, they did not know the land or remember the boundaries, but "our father Ustin will tell [thee]." At this point one would expect that either the defendant or the judge would suggest that Ustin be summoned to court. The document records no further statement by the defendant. He may have had some reason for not wanting Ustin to appear in court, but one wonders what he had to lose. Apparently the judge felt that it was the defendant's responsibility to call for Ustin's testimony. When no such request was forthcoming, the judge referred the case to the Grand Prince for decision.[3] Since the defendant lost, we may assume that his failure to defend his cause actively by calling for another witness probably led to the adverse decision.

[1] See, for example, *AFZKh* **1**, nos. 259, 309; ASEI **2**, nos. 375, 464; *AIu*, nos. 19, 20, 24. See also Meichik, *Gramoty XIV–V vv.*, p. 30.

[2] For a discussion of the problem, see H. W. Dewey, "Judges and the Evidence in Muscovite Law," *Slavonic and East European Review* **36**, no. 86 (December 1957): pp. 189–194.

[3] *ASEI* **2**, no. 388a.

A judgment charter from the end of the fifteenth century records that the plaintiff's lack of action was the reason cited by the court for his losing the case. The plaintiff brought suit, claiming that the defendant's peasants had taken over his land fifty years earlier. The defendant replied that the disputed land was the third field of one of his villages. The plaintiff next produced two longtime residents to support his charges. One of them declared that the land was the plaintiff's but that the defendant had appropriated it thirty years before; the second said that the land had been given to the defendant fifty years earlier. Thus one of the plaintiff's witnesses disagreed about the length of time involved, while the other's testimony completely contradicted his charges. The defendant then presented nine longtime residents, all of whom supported his statement. The plaintiff lost, and, as we might expect, one reason was the principle of a statute of limitations, that he had waited for fifty years to bring suit. Yet, contrary to expectation, the judge did not refer to the conflicting testimony of the plaintiff's witnesses. He gave two other—seemingly arbitrary—reasons for his decision in favor of the defendant: the plaintiff had not petitioned the Grand Prince and his witnesses had not requested a judicial duel with the opposition.[4] The judge apparently based his decision on the plaintiff's failure to press his claims actively rather than on the specific evidence presented in court. In this case, the judge had not even asked the plaintiff to explain his long silence in the matter.

As noted earlier, the court placed great emphasis on protest activity. If, for some reason, a plaintiff could not bring suit immediately, he was expected to protest (*izvechat'*) the violation of his rights. Then, if speaking to the offender brought no result, the plaintiff was to petition the Grand Prince for justice, and apparently the court thought he should keep petitioning until he succeeded. Judges displayed the same attitude under other circumstances. In a few instances, litigants claimed that government officials previously had failed to execute administrative or judicial duties as instructed. The judge's immediate response was to ask the litigant whether he, as the injured party, had petitioned the Grand Prince against the offending official. Active defense of one's rights, by persistent protest, was apparently the standard, and expected, method to use in obtaining redress of grievances.

That the court operated on this theory could prove detrimental to a litigant. One instance is found in a judgment charter of 1505/1506. The plaintiff, the Chudov Monastery's estate manager Iakush, presented six longtime residents who supported his claim to the disputed land and showed the judge the boundary. Then the defendants, Ivashko and Fedko, for reasons which became clear later in the case, called for the testimony of two men who had already spoken on behalf

of the plaintiff. In addition, they named two other witnesses. Three of the four were present in court; "they, Sire, know the land and will show thee the boundary; and, Sire, Sukhoi (the fourth witness) is not at home now, and they say he is working." The judge then offered the defendants a postponement; he would set a new trial date, at a time when they could present Sukhoi. The defendants rejected this suggestion, declaring that their witness was not at home and that they could not place him before the court. As they gave no further explanation, we do not know how far the witness had gone or how permanent his employment there was. Perhaps the defendants themselves did not know. The judge therefore turned to an examination of the other witnesses. The two who had previously supported the plaintiff, Iakov, son of Fedor Gubin, and Ivan Zob, repeated their statement that the land was his; "and, Sire, we have shown thee the boundary between those lands." The remaining witness, Mikhal' the blacksmith, declared that he personally knew neither the land nor the boundaries; "but, Sire, I have a boundary [description] charter, and it is in Mitia Maloi's keeping, and now Mitia is in Kholopii." Then the judge offered the witness a postponement, asking when he could produce the document. Mikhal', however, refused the suggestion, declaring that he would present the charter only at the trial on *doklad*. The judge then agreed to refer the matter to a court of higher instance. After both litigants had confirmed the trial record's accuracy, the upper-court judge ordered that the boundary description charter be read aloud. The document, however, did not describe the boundary. On the other hand, it did explain why the defendants had called upon two of the plaintiff's witnesses:

Upon instructions of Grand Prince Ivan Vasil'evich of All Rus', from Grigorii Romanovich Zastolbskoi to the Grand Prince's peasants in Pleso, Mikhal' the blacksmith, and Ivashko Zob, and Sukhoi, son of Vasilii Nikonov, and Iakush Gubinskoi, and Mikhal' Orefin. Here the Pleso peasant Ivashko, son of Petelia Soloninin, petitioned me concerning the fact that under his authority are two hamlets, the Grand Prince's state [land], Timokhino and Zubkovo; and he said that his two hamlets come together with the Chudov Monastery's lands Potoploe and Kleopino at the boundaries. And that Ivashko, son of Petelia Soloninin, and the Chudov [Monastery s] estate manager Iakush, Il'ia's son, elected you, the longtime residents, and they say that ye know the boundaries [between] those hamlets of the Grand Prince, Timokhino and Zubkovo, and the Chudov [Monastery's] lands Potoploe and Kleopino. And ye should show them in God's truth that boundary of the Grand Prince's lands.

After he heard the charter, the judge asked Mikhal' the blacksmith whether he and his comrades had measured off the land and established the boundary as the document ordered. Mikhal', answering on behalf of his comrades, declared: "Sire, we did not measure off the lands according to that charter, nor did we establish boundaries." According to the record, this was the last testimony in the case. Decision against the defend-

---

[4] *AFZKh* 1, no. 114; see also *ASEI*, 3, no. 221.

ants followed. The judge gave several reasons: their longtime residents, Iakov Gubin and Ivan Zob, had said the land was part of the plaintiff's territory; Mikhal' the blacksmith had not supported them; in addition, Mikhal' and his comrades had not measured off the land nor established boundaries in accordance with the charter; finally, the defendants had said that they could not present their other witness, Sukhoi, in court.[5] Apparently the defendants had no other witnesses than those named in the boundary charter, and were forced to call for the testimony of men who had supported the plaintiff. Although the peasants had not established the boundary as ordered, the court did not go into the matter. Their failure to carry out instructions was held against the defendants.

Other judgment charters record comparable situations. And the court's attitude in these instances indicates that the defendants in the previous case should have petitioned the Grand Prince against the peasants who had failed to establish the boundary as ordered. The plaintiffs in a 1463 case declared that they had protested to the defendants and had submitted a petition against them to Grand Prince Vasilii Vasil'evich.

And the Grand Prince, Sire, sent out Mikhailo Karpov to [examine] the land. And Mikhailo, Sire, came riding out to this land and agreed, Sire, to tell the Grand Prince, but he did not tell the Grand Prince, and he obstructed justice for us and showed favor to them (the defendants), and did nothing for us. And we, Sire, again petitioned Grand Prince Vasilei. And the Grand Prince, Sire, sent out Grigorei Vasil'evich Morozov. And Grigorei, Sire, also came riding out to this land, and likewise did not bring us before the Grand Prince, and gave us no justice.

The judge's immediate response to this assertion seems indicative of the prevailing attitude: "Ye say that Mikhailo Karpov was on your land, and that after Mikhailo ye brought Grigorei Vasil'evich [Morozov] to the land; have ye petitioned the Grand Prince against Mikhailo or Grigorei, [stating] that they gave you no justice?"[6] The court apparently felt no responsibility to bring negligent officials to account or even to question them. This was the injured party's task.

The court took a similar attitude in a case recorded between 1490 and 1498. The plaintiff declared that a judgment charter had been issued against the defendants previously, and, after leading the judge along the boundaries as recorded in the charter, the plaintiff presented the document as evidence. The defendants denied that they had had such a trial: "[The judge] Karp, Sire, was on the land, but, Sire, he took no action. And prior to this, Sire, Fedor Paisov was on the same land, and surveyed the boundary, Sire, between that Polozhimatovskaia land and the Bogoroditskaia land, but, Sire, he likewise took no action." The judge apparently wondered why the defendants had

taken no action against Fedor, since he asked them how long ago Fedor had been on the land, and who had been with him during the boundary survey. The defendants replied: "Sire, it has been about twenty-five years since that boundary survey, Sire; and whatever people were [present] at the survey, Sire, those people have died."[7] Presumably the defendants' failure to take any action in twenty-five years was held against them, since the land was awarded to the plaintiff.

On other occasions, litigants charged official corruption rather than neglect. The plaintiff in a 1505 case claimed that the defendants were mowing illegally the meadowland of the Grand Prince's Mikhailovskaia hamlet, of the Ivachevo village.

"And, Sires, my brother Maliuta had a trial over this meadowland before the judges Mikhailo Shapkin and Ivan Golova and Zakhar' Mikulin; and my brother Maliuta was to appear with them in Moscow for *doklad* proceedings. And I, Sires, appeared in place of my brother at the *doklad* proceedings in Moscow, in the presence of Prince Danilo Aleksandrovich Penko[v]. And, Sires, Prince Danilo ordered judgment given in my favor, in the place of my brother; and they (the lower-court judges), Sires, took bribes from the [monasterial] elders and have not given final judgment for us.

In response the defendants, two elders from the monastery, declared that they had had no earlier trial concerning the meadowland on which they were standing. In fact, the monastery had Prince Mikhailo Ondreevich's donation charter, which was in the Grand Prince's archives, for this floodland meadow. "And, Sires, we had a trial with his (the plaintiff's) brother Maliuta, not concerning this floodland meadow but concerning the Kostinskaia meadow."[8] The judges later found the donation charter in the archives and awarded the meadow to the monastery.

A judgment charter of 1497/1498 records that, after the defendant's longtime residents had testified, the judge asked the plaintiffs whether they had petitioned the Grand Prince. Nazarik and his comrades replied:

We did petition the sovereign Grand Prince concerning that land when [vicegerent] Fedor Davydovich [Khromoi] was administering Kolomna; and the Grand Prince, Sire, gave us Fedor Davyovich as judge, and Fedor Davydovich,

---

[5] *ASEI* 3, no. 48.
[6] *ASEI* 2, no. 374.

[7] *ASEI* 2, no. 405. The defendants had not referred to this alleged survey during the earlier trial recorded in the plaintiff's judgment charter, which had been issued between 1462 and 1478 (for the text, see *ASEI* 2, no. 370). Since the documents cannot be dated precisely, the time interval between the two trials ranges from twelve to thirty-six years. It is possible that the judgment charter had been issued first, before the boundary survey had supposedly taken place.
[8] *ASEI* 2, no. 309. The elders' statement that there had been an earlier trial over the Kostinskaia meadow is supported by a reference to such a trial between the plaintiffs in this case, the Klimov brothers, and the monastery in the book recording boundaries between the monastery's lands and the Grand Prince's lands drawn up about 1492 by the Beloozero scribes, the same men named as lower-court judges by the plaintiffs; see *ASEI* 2, no. 290. The monastery had acquired the Kostinskaia meadow by a land exchange which took place between 1476 and 1482; *ASEI* 2, no. 238.

Sire, gave us a trial with the Simonov [Monastery's] peasants over that land; and, Sire, he awarded that land to those Simonov monasterial villages in return for a bribe; and, Sire, he took from them for that land a marten-skin fur coat and fifteen rubles cash.

Following the plaintiffs' statement, the judge asked them why they had remained silent after Fedor had tried the case, and they answered: "Sire, we are unable to gain access to the sovereign Grand Prince; and we petitioned the Kolomna vicegerents, Sire, more than once about that land, and they, Sire, give us no justice against the [monasterial] elders; Sire, they favor the Simonov elders." The judge then asked the defendant whether the monastery had the judgment charter issued by Fedor Davydovich. Elder Ignatii Travin replied: "Sire, when Fedor Davydovich gave judgment in our favor for that land and ordered us, Sire, to plow that land, he gave us no judgment charter, Sire." No further evidence was presented, and the court decided in favor of the defendant.[9] In this case the plaintiffs' account seems quite convincing, particularly since they were not making vague, general accusations; they stated the exact amount of the bribe allegedly accepted by the Kolomna vicegerent. In addition, the absence of a judgment charter from the previous trial is suspicious.

Charges of corruption leveled against the judges by the defendants in a 1552 document arose from an unusual twist in the case itself. The judges concerned, having just heard a case of land litigation, had left the disputed property and stopped in one of the plaintiff's hamlets. Thus they were present when the defendants in the trial they had just conducted attacked the hamlet. One of the judges was beaten, and both of them were called as witnesses by the plaintiff when he brought another complaint. After the judges had corroborated the plaintiff's account of these events, the defendants declared their testimony false, charged that it had been obtained by bribery, and requested a judicial duel. The judges agreed to the duel, but pointed out that the defendants had been willing to accept them as judges in the previous trial. Apparently there had been no doubts about their impartiality then. The defendants presented no further evidence, and did not raise the issue again during *doklad* proceedings. The defendants lost the case. Their charges of corruption had had no

effect on the outcome, especially since over two hundred men, testifying on inquest, supported the judges' account.[10]

The complaints of these litigants and others that they could not gain access to the sovereign and that Muscovite justice was governed by corruption were echoed by Herberstein. "The poor," he wrote, "have no access to the prince, but only to the counsellors themselves; and indeed that is very difficult." Official corruption was also commonplace. "Although the prince is very severe, nevertheless all justice is venal, and that without much concealment."[11] Chancellor likewise did not question the justice of the Grand Prince himself, but he reported that "wicked magistrates, nevertheless, in the strangest way pervert his decisions."[12] Fletcher returned to England with a similar opinion on corruption in the Russian administration. He reported that officials in the provinces, "comming fresh and hungrie" every year, "rack and spoile" the populace "without all regard of justice, or conscience." Their superiors tolerated such behavior "to the end they may rob them againe & have a better bootie when they call them to account: which commonly they doo at the end of their service, making an advantage of their injustice & oppression over the poore people." Therefore, he explained, the lesser officials "furnish themselves with all the spoile they can for the time of their government," so as to have enough for the sovereign and their superiors as well as to "reserve some good part for themselves."[13]

The problem of corruption was also reflected in the two Muscovite Sudebniki. The 1497 code contained only a prohibition: "And the boiars, *okol'nichie* and secretaries are not to receive bribes for judging or participation in deciding a case. Likewise no judge is to receive a bribe for judging. And no one is to use the court for purposes of [personal] revenge or favor."[14] Article 67 provided for a general public notice: "And it shall be ordered proclaimed in the markets in Moscow and all cities of the Moscow and Novgorod territories, and decreed in all cantons that the plaintiff and defendant shall not offer bribes to judges and bailiffs . . . ." Despite its decrees, the code included no provision specifying punishment for violation of these rules. Article 1 of the 1550 Sudebnik contained an order similar to the first article of the 1497 code: bribery and use of the court for personal revenge or favor were prohibited By this time, however, the necessity of providing for enforcement was recognized, and several articles dealt with the problem, giving the punishment to be exacted for various offenses by

[9] *ASEI* 2, no. 414. Peasant plaintiffs in another case leveled similar charges against the judge in a previous trial, and eventually were awarded the disputed land. We do not know how much weight their accusations carried, since the trial record does not indicate that they brought suit against the judge, and the final decision in their favor was based upon other evidence: the defendant admitted that he had made use of the disputed area on the basis of a judgment charter awarding the monastery other land, and a boundary division charter from the Grand Prince's archives supported the plaintiffs' claims; *ASEI* 2, no. 338.

[10] Likhachev, *Sbornik*, no. 12.
[11] Herberstein, *Notes upon Russia* 1: pp. 105–106.
[12] *Chancellor's Voyage to Muscovy*, pp. 74–75.
[13] Fletcher, *Of the Russe Commonwealth*, p. 32.
[14] 1497 Sudebnik, article 1; the order is repeated in articles 33 and 38.

officials of different rank.[15] Despite the cynical views of some who see only "class justice" in medieval Russia, the legal codes indicate the intent that the law should work fairly and efficiently. The problem of securing competent and honest officials, however, was one which continued to plague the Muscovite administrative system.

A 1588 document incorporates an order from the court to its agents, instructing them to conduct an investigation concerning disputed property. The plaintiff had alleged that a district elder had come to an agreement with the defendant in secret and had transferred land to him improperly. The agents were to conduct an inquest, then examine the land personally and draw up a boundary description. The decree concluded with an order to the agents that they were not to "accept bribes and gifts from anyone" nor "show favor to anyone in anything by any deeds." If they did not carry out their commission faithfully, or accepted bribes and gifts, or showed favor to anyone, they were to be punished by the tsar.[16]

Naturally the extant judgment charters do not state that a judge decided in favor of one party after accepting a bribe from him. On the other hand, as will be shown below, almost all decisions correspond with the evidence given in the trial record. Thus if we were to assume that the judgment charters record cases decided by bribery, the documents suggest that the secretaries were extremely adept at rewriting trial records to fit the desired decision. It should also be noted that the instances of objections being raised to the accuracy of the trial record during *doklad* proceedings were relatively rare. Most litigants, given an opportunity to contest the document sent from the lower court, affirmed that the trial had been as the record indicated. If evidence supporting their claims had been omitted, they should have complained at this point. Finally, it should be noted that a victorious litigant would have found it necessary to distribute bribes to numerous court officials and witnesses as well as the judges in order to secure the desired outcome of his case in this fashion.

Although litigants' charges of official negligence or corruption may have been true, the court's reaction to their complaints may be understood on procedural grounds. For example, the plaintiffs in the 1497/1498 and 1505 cases cited above, who declared that the judges in their earlier trials had accepted bribes from the opposition, were again bringing suit in the same matter against the same people. Within the Muscovite judicial system, this was not the proper method by which to gain a reversal of the decision.

As we have seen, *doklad* was not an appeal or review procedure. Review or appeal was known as *zhaloba*.[17] Appeal consisted of a complaint by a litigant of intentional injustice, and took the form of a trial with the judge or other official concerned. A litigant could bring complaint for delay or incorrect procedure during the trial, as well as for an unjust decision. He might charge that the judge had not presented the litigants for a trial on *doklad,* that he had not issued a judgment charter, or that he had issued a judgment charter without *doklad* in matters exceeding his authority. Constables might be accused of demanding bribes for the judge, or of taking bribes in matters of bond. Appeal against a judge for false judgment was usually combined with an accusation that he had taken bribes. If it turned out that the judge had decided a case unjustly through honest error, the victorious litigant was deprived of his gains and trial began anew.[18] If, however, the judge were found guilty, he had to pay the litigant's losses, plus fines.[19] Analogy with other judicial procedures of the time suggests that the matter ended here. As Dmitriev pointed out, punishment (or levying of losses and fines) "fell on the one who, so to speak, happened to be directly at hand."[20] Thus guarantors for a man on surety bond could be held responsible for his debts or obligations. They in turn would then have to bring suit against their principal to recover whatever had been assessed from them. Article 18 of the 1550 Sudebnik decreed:

And if a witness does not come before the judge (i.e., fails to appear in court), whether or not he has anything to say, then from that witness shall the sum at issue and all court fees be taken; and that witness [may have] trial with the [Muscovite] bailiff and local vicegerent's sergeant-at-arms concerning [their failure to notify him of] the trial date.

Article 21 has a similar provision. If one of several parties to a suit received the summons and did not notify the others named in the document, and a default judgment were issued against them for failure to appear in court, then they would be granted a trial against the man who had not shown them the summons. Although the default judgment would not be reversed, they would have an opportunity to receive restitution for their losses.

The Muscovite court of this period was concerned primarily with settling the issue immediately at hand. If one side's case suffered through previous misconduct of affairs by a third party, the injured litigant was apparently expected to take his losses in the current trial, and then attempt to regain what he had lost by bring-

---

[15] See the 1550 Sudebnik, articles 3, 4, 5, 8, 9, 10, 11, 28, 32, 33, 34, 41, 42, 44, 45, 47, 49, 53, 54, 62, 66, 67, 68, 69, 70, 71, 74, 99.

[16] Samokvasov, *Arkhivnyi material* 1: pp. 142–147.

[17] Vladimirskii-Budanov identifies *zhaloba* with the references to *peresud* (review) in the 1497 Sudebnik, article 64, and the 1550 Sudebnik, article 51; *Obzor,* p. 632.

[18] 1497 Sudebnik, article 19; 1550 Sudebnik, article 2.

[19] 1550 Sudebnik, article 3; see also Dmitriev, *Istoriia sudebnykh instantsii,* pp. 292–294.

[20] Dmitriev, *Istoriia sudebnykh instantsii,* p. 294.

ing suit against the offender. Such problems arose in relatively few of the trials recorded in surviving judgment charters. We find few accusations of official corruption, probably because most litigants had not had an earlier trial concerning the same issue. Even in those instances where such charges were made, the court did not give a statement of its policy, to the effect that such matters were not the court's problem. Yet the judges' questions convey the impression that it was the litigant's responsibiliy to reach a settlement by petitioning against the offending official.[21]

Most judges thus restricted themselves to a relatively passive role during the course of trial. Despite this, the judge's position was one of great power, which he apparently could exercise as he saw fit. As we have seen, a few judges did call for other witnesses or demand documents for examination on their own initiative. Occasionally a judge evidently doubted the validity of a plaintiff's charges. Under ordinary circumstances, the judge heard the complaint and immediately ordered the defendant to answer. A judgment charter issued between 1495 and 1497 provides a good illustration of the contrary situation. As soon as the plaintiff had charged that the defendant was taking away his meadow Podishcha, the judge asked him what witnesses he had. In this case, the judge's suspicions were well founded. The plaintiff's witness declared that he was not a longtime resident and did not know the name of the meadow. Then came the defendant's turn to answer. He declared that the meadow was really called Krest'tsi, and produced a document and three witnesses to verify the name of the meadow in which they were standing. In the *doklad* proceedings, however, Vasilii Patrikeev apparently had some misgivings about the defendant's evidence, since he called in the author of the defendant's document to verify his donation of the meadow in question.[22] In another case, the judge heard the plaintiff's statement, the testimony of his chief witness, and the reading of his document before asking the defendant to answer.[23]

A few judges did take a more active role in questioning litigants about their testimony. To give just one illustration, a 1547 text records that Ivan IV raised some issues which a defendant found difficult to explain. Before the trial began, the plaintiff and court officials had seized a forger and some documents at the defendants' dwelling. When the plaintiff subsequently presented one defendant's mortgage note for the half-village in dispute and also a disencumbering note, the defendant claimed that the plaintiff's promissory note was false. He declared that he had paid off the mortgage, and presented his redeemed promissory note. The tsar then asked the defendant why he had not

taken back the disencumbering note as well, if he had really redeemed his promissory note. The defendant could only allege that the plaintiff had concealed the document. Later the plaintiff presented a boundary record for the land, given to him by the defendant at the time he mortgaged the estate. The document was a record from the property division between the defendant and his brother carried out by an official land surveyor. Again the defendant denied the authenticity of the document and declared that he and his brother had had no land partition of their patrimonial property. The boundary-division witnesses and the surveyor then testified, affirming that the property division had taken place as the document indicated. After this, the tsar again raised a point which created difficulties for the defendant. How had he been able to mortgage his property if he had not first divided the estate with his brother? The defendant had to retreat from his previous statement; the brothers, he declared, had had an amicable property division. Presumably he meant one without any formal record. There was much more evidence in the case which also supported the decision in favor of the plaintiff, but the tsar's questions had brought up two important issues which the defendant was unable to explain satisfactorily.[24] According to the record, the seventeen-year-old ruler had tried the case himself. The document's concluding notation listing boiars present at the trial, however, suggests that Ivan had had competent assistance: at the court were "the boiar Ivan Petrovich Fedorov and other boiars." Fedorov-Cheliadnin was later reputed to be the only honest judge in Muscovy,[25] and the fact that he alone of the boiars present was named suggests that he probably played a leading role in the trial.

Some judges seemingly went out of their way to give the parties every chance to produce their proof. A judgment charter issued between 1494 and 1499 records that Ivan Iur'evich Patrikeev did all that he could to give the defendant an opportunity to bring his evidence to court.[26] Archimandrite Fegnast of the Simonov Monastery brought suit before Prince Patrikeev against Ivan Tveritinov, declaring that the monastery had sold its Korobovskaia land to Ostafii Sirotin for his lifetime, the land to revert to the monastery upon his death. "Now, Sire, that Ivan after Ostafei['s death] has taken his (Ostafei's) wife, and now, for the

---

[21] For examples of cases in which suit was brought against such officials, see Iushkov, *Akty XIII–XVII vv.*, pp. 216–233, and *AIu*, no. 27.

[22] *ASEI* 3, no. 208.

[23] *AFZKh* 1, no. 103.

[24] *AIuB* 1, no. 5. For other cases in which judges' questions also played an important role, see *ASEI* 2, no. 229; *AIuB* 1, no. 7.

[25] Von Staden, the German soldier of fortune who served as one of Ivan's *oprichniki*, reported: "When the Grand Prince was absent from Moscow, Ivan Petrovich Cheliadnin was the chief boyar and judge. He alone was accustomed to judge fairly, and for that reason the common people liked him." Staden, *Land and Government of Muscovy*, p. 9. Cheliadnin was executed without trial in 1567 or 1568, for supposedly conspiring with the Poles.

[26] *ASEI* 2, no. 410. For another case with numerous postponements, see *ASEI* 2, no. 493.

second year, has been ploughing that land of ours unlawfully with a bailiff's protection, and will not come to a reckoning with us."

Ivan answered the accusation, declaring that Korobovskaia was the land of his stepson Ivan. When the boy's father Ostafii died, he had left the land to his son, and therefore Ivan Tveritinov was plowing it. Patrikeev then asked whether the boy had his father's will, and Ivan replied: "I, Sire, know of no will; if there is one, my stepson Ivan knows of it and [knows] whose land that is." The judge therefore ordered Ivan to bring his stepson to court, and granted a postponement; both litigants were to appear two weeks before Christmas. At the designated time, all three came to court, and Ivan said: "My stepson, Sire, is [too] small, he is unable to answer, and he knows of no documents whatever for that Korobovskaia land." However, he declared, another man knew about documents for the land—the boy's estate manager, his grandfather Senka Shimanov (father of the defendant's wife). Since Shimanov was living in Iur'ev, the defendant requested another postponement, offering to present Shimanov in court one week before Christmas. Patrikeev agreed, and both litigants again appeared at the designated time, but the defendant produced neither witness nor document. "Now, Sire," he declared, "Senka Shimanov is ill; give me, Sire, another time—at Christmas: if Senka recovers, then I, Sire, shall bring him before thee, and he will present the documents for that land." Once again Patrikeev granted the postponement. When the litigants appeared, however, the defendant was again without evidence. "Sire, Senka Shimanov is ill, I am unable to bring him before thee, and he told me of no documents whatever for this land in his posession."

At this point Patrikeev ordered the plaintiff to explain why the land was his. The archimandrite claimed that the monastery had formerly possessed documents, but they burned up in Moscow during the hostilities with Suzdal'. He did, however, have a charter of grant from the Grand Prince. In addition, he could present a witness, Elka S'ianov, who knew that the land was the monastery's. Elka's father-in-law Terentii had purchased the land for his lifetime from the monastery's archimandrite Gerontii and the brethren. "When Terentei died, Sire, then Elka brought that charter (purchase deed) to the monastery. And here, Sire, are [both] their charter and Elka before thee."

After Prince Patrikeev had examined the Grand Prince's charter and Terentii's purchase deed, he asked the plaintiff's witness what he knew about the land. Elka S'ianov gave a detailed account of the land's history. The Korobovskaia land, he declared, had belonged to Fedor Diadkov, passing at his death to his son Ivan. Ivan had died in the great plague, leaving a small son Fedor Nepliui, who was raised by his uncles, the Kositskii princes, in Vereia. At this time

the land became deserted. When Fedor Nepliui grew up, he petitioned the Grand Prince and received a charter for his patrimony. "And, Sire, that Fedor Nepliui gave that charter of grant from the Grand Prince to my father, Gavrilo S'ianov, in order to bring in people [to settle] on that land." Because of "great brigandage and theft on the road," people had refused to settle there, and Gavrilo returned the charter to Fedor. Fedor Nepliui then gave the Korobovskaia land to Archimandrite Ivan of the Simonov Monastery. Gerontii, Ivan's successor as archimandrite, sold it to Terentii, the witness's father-in-law, for his lifetime. Terentii held the land for about twenty years, "and he, Sire, ordered that after his death that purchase deed be given back to the monastery." The witness had done as requested, and had returned the document to the Simonov archimandrite.

Patrikeev then gave judgment in favor of the plaintiff, Archimandrite Fegnast of the Simonov Monastery. In view of the evidence, his decision is hardly surprising. Yet he had certainly done all he could on behalf of the defendant.

Other judges, in cases involving promissory notes or restitution for damages, did not pass sentence until they had questioned the defeated party to see whether he required a postponement in order to redeem mortgaged property or pay off his debt. Only when the man had assured the judge that it was impossible for him to obtain the required sum did the judge award the property to the opposition or hand over the guilty party in slavery, until he had redeemed his debt.[27]

Litigants, as well as judges, seem to have felt that they had a very definite role in the courtroom. While each party bore full responsibility for presenting his case, few litigants went beyond this. Most men introduced what proof they had, answering the judge's questions and trying to counter the opponent's evidence —their legal activity amounted to an argument by demonstration. The defendant usually denied the charges completely. One party might challenge the authenticity of the other's documents, or witnesses might be accused of lying. Only on rare occasions, however, do we find one litigant questioning his opponent's case on grounds of logic, or summarizing his own in a concluding argument.[28] Perhaps this was due to the absence of lawyers and an accompanying legal tradition in medieval Russia. For the most part, however, litigants confined themselves to a simple presentation of their own claims and evidence. The judgment charters indicate that both judges and litigants marked out for themselves a definite sphere of activity. The parties were responsible for proving their claims, the judges for collecting the evidence and determining

[27] See *AFZKh* 1, no. 222; Likhachev, *Sbornik,* no. 14; *Alu,* no. 22; *AIuB* 1, nos. 4, 7.

[28] See, for example, *ASEI* 1, no. 607; 2, no. 411; *AFZKh* 1, no. 259; Iushkov, *Akty XIII–XVII vv.,* no. 220.

which side had the better case. Perhaps this attitude had developed in earlier centuries, when "God's justice" was the common method of decision. The Lord, knowing the facts in any situation, was an impartial judge and would strike down the man who tried to prove his case through falsehood. It seems likely that some elements of this belief may have been transferred, perhaps subconsciously, into the procedure of customary law. The human judge should also be able to divine the truth from the facts presented by each party. To see how successfully the judges managed to perform this duty, we shall now turn to an examination of the decisions recorded in the judgment charters.

IX. THE COURT'S DECISION

Taken together, the judgment charters provide the most valuable primary source available on questions of legal procedure and court decisions in medieval Russia. Litigants, as we have seen, might offer several forms of proof for the court's consideration. These varieties of evidence have been examined, as have the limitations imposed by the views which both litigants and judges held concerning their respective roles and responsibilities within the legal process. A final basic question arising from an analysis of the judgment charters is to determine how the court evaluated the information which accumulated during the course of a trial. To what extent did the judges base their decisions on this evidence? Would the decisions appear to be rational, in accordance with the facts, keeping in mind the attitudes and responses at work in the system? Or would the decisions appear to be largely arbitrary, to reflect class and social biases, or to be based on an intuitive approach rather than a substantive foundation?

To approach the judgment charters strictly and solely as evidence of the class struggle would be to offer the easy, convenient explanation, but would be entirely too simplistic. The documents cannot be presented as definitive proof that Muscovite courts served merely as a weapon of "class war." It does appear from the records that the church in particular made use of the courts to increase its landholdings at the expense of the peasants. In the surviving documents, the monasteries and representatives of the metropolitan almost always win. Yet it must be emphasized that most existing documents of Muscovite law from this period were originally preserved in monastery archives. It is also significant that judgment charters were issued to the victorious party; therefore a monastery would be unlikely to possess many documents directed against it. A monastery or large secular landholder would have had more familiarity with and experience in the use of written records, better facilities for storing documents, and probably greater concern for preserving them, along with a more conscious awareness of their value as legal evidence. Assume that the court had

given judgment against a peasant who had brought suit only after forty or fifty years, because he had not needed the land earlier, and who could present as evidence for title only a vague recollection that someone had once said the land had belonged to the Grand Prince at some point in the past, while his monasterial or princely opponent produced the Grand Prince's charter of grant for the land and several longtime resident witnesses who testified in support of his claims. To assert that such a decision represented unfair expropriation in the interests of the governing classes is to evaluate it in terms of philosophical point of view rather than the prevailing law. Finally, we must remember that the surviving judgment charters represent only a small fraction of the total number issued. An ordinary secular peasant could win against a prince [1] or the church [2] when the evidence was in his favor. On the basis of our fragmentary sources alone, it is impossible to prove that "class justice" was the controlling force in Muscovite courts.

If we examine the documents in terms of a contest or competition between plaintiff and defendant, those judgment charters which have survived loss and destruction may be considered to provide a fairly representative sampling of courtroom procedure and the approach used in reaching decisions. In his study of medieval Russian judicial institutions, Dmitriev asserted that Muscovite judges generally decided cases according to their own "inner convictions" rather than giving judgment on the basis of external and objective criteria presented during the course of the trial.[3] Internal evidence of the documents themselves does not support this contention. On the contrary, a study of the surviving judgment charters indicates that the majority of decisions can be explained on the basis of evidence alone. Criticism might be directed more appropriately toward the judges' attitude during the trial itself. According to the records, the court did not always examine the evidence as thoroughly as we might think necessary. Judges could have scrutinized documents more closely, and could have asked more probing questions of both litigants and their witnesses. Yet the judgment charters suggest that the judges did not view their role in this way. If the final decrees of the court are examined solely in view of the recorded evidence and the prevailing concept that such requisite procedural steps as offers to fight a judicial duel were factors which had to be considered, most judges appear to have had a factual basis, in addition to "inner convictions," for their decisions.

In slightly more than half of the surviving fifteenth-century judgment charters, the decisions include the *ratio decidendi;* that is, the judge listed one or more reasons for his decision in favor of—or more often

[1] *ASEI* 2, no. 496.
[2] *ASEI* 2, no. 334.
[3] Dmitriev, *Istoriia sudebnykh instantsii,* pp. 220–223.

against—one of the parties. As we might expect, listing of considerations became more frequent toward the end of the century. Keeping in mind that about two-thirds of the surviving documents were probably issued after 1485, more than half of those which include no reasons were granted before that date.[4] On the other hand, for judgment charters issued between 1485 and 1505, only one in four lacks considerations. During the remainder of the sixteenth century the number of documents which include no explanation for the decision drops to about one in five or one in six. The trend seems clear, and reflects the development of greater standardization and more complete record-keeping in the Muscovite administration.

To examine the effect which evidence had on the final decision, we have divided the judgment charters into two basic groups, those which include reasons for the decision and those which do not. Within each major group we have classified the documents on the basis of those elements in a trial which would appear to have been decisive. This categorization might be considered somewhat arbitrary, in that Muscovite judges gave no indication of the relative weight which they attributed to various factors. On the whole, however, analysis of the decisions on the basis of an attempt to weigh the evidence seems to provide the clearest method of examining them in a coherent manner.

I

First, we shall consider the judgment charters which include no *ratio decidendi*. A probable basis for the decision can be suggested in almost every case from the data recorded in the documents. Here we can draw upon only that information given in the trial record itself, that evidence which each party managed to produce in court. It is impossible to determine accurately those instances in which a judge would have taken into account certain negative elements, the failure of a litigant to contest his opponent's evidence at various points, which could be instrumental in determining his decision. The judgment charters in this group are of two kinds, those in which, given the evidence, the decisions seem quite clear, and those in which they are more obscure. To explain the latter point by illustration: in boundary questions, the issue might be resolved if one were able to go to the land in person and examine the claims in relation to the topography, as the judges did, whereas the written description alone is often far from clear.

In some of the judgment charters which provide no explanation, the reason for the decision is obvious: one party admitted that the claims of his opponent were true. A few defendants immediately declared that the land belonged to the plaintiff.[5] The servant boy who

confessed to inciting slaves to flee made no defense whatever, and was given to the plaintiff in full slavery, in place of the others.[6] Another man admitted that he owed the money for which he was being sued.[7] Plaintiffs might also admit that their accusations were unfounded. In one instance, a man claimed that he had been assigned a portion of communal taxes although he was not a resident of the area. Confronted with all the canton residents, who declared that he was their "brother resident" and that he and his father were debtors, he confessed that he lived there and made tax payments with the other canton people.[8] Other litigants held out a bit longer, not conceding until the opponent had produced evidence. In a 1498 judgment charter, the plaintiffs charged that peasants were taking over hamlets previously given to the monastery. The peasant elder claimed that the hamlets had always been the Grand Prince's land. After the plaintiffs produced Prince Mikhailo Andreevich's donation charter, however, the defendant admitted that the prince had given the lands to the monastery five years before his death, and since his death eleven years before the monks had held the hamlets.[9] In another case the defendants waited until the plaintiff had led the court over the area in question and pointed out his father's old drainage ditches before they declared that their land was not in this area and that they did not bring suit.[10] Still other litigants conceded after witnesses had testified against them.[11] One case had reached the point of judicial duel when the plaintiffs declared that, if the defendant's servants would kiss the cross, the plaintiffs would concede. The servants did so, and the Grand Prince gave judgment in favor of the defendant.[12] In all of the above cases, one party sooner or later acknowledged the validity of the other's claims, and the reason for the decision is evident.

In another group of judgment charters, the decision probably rested on documents presented by the victorious party. In some cases the man who lost apparently had no proof other than his own assertions. Ivashko Mezhenina, the estate manager of Prince Danilo Vasil'-evich Iaroslavskii, complained that elder Nifont, the Spaso-Evfimiev Monastery's estate manager, was tak-

[4] All documents have been categorized according to the earliest probable date.
[5] *ASEI* 3, no. 35; *AFZKh* 1, no. 204.
[6] *ASEI* 3, no. 357.
[7] Likhachev, *Sbornik*, no. 14.
[8] *PRP* 2: p. 195; see also *ASEI* 2, no. 465, a case in which the plaintiff declared that he had no means of proving his claim, while the defendant had ten years' possession and, apparently, a donation charter.
[9] *ASEI* 2, no. 416. See also *ASEI* 2, no. 483, in which the defendants first did not know the boundaries and later declared that they had no interest in the lands—after the plaintiff had presented a judgment charter from a previous trial, which awarded the lands to him.
[10] *ASEI* 1, no. 485; perhaps they hoped to avoid court costs by dropping the matter—at any rate, both sides apparently received an official boundary establishment, since four "boundary division" witnesses are named at the end of the document.
[11] *ASEI* 1, no. 522; *AFZKh* 1, no. 140.
[12] *ASEI* 3, no. 364.

ing away thirteen deserted villages and two meadows which had been given to the prince in dowry. The elder produced donation charters for the land in question and declared that, since the plaintiff had mowed the land unlawfully for the first time this year, the monastery had already petitioned the Grand Prince against him. Responding to the Grand Prince's question, Ivashko said that the prince had no documentary proof for his title, and "they say that those deserted villages and meadows go with the Niskaia free settlement which Prince Ivan [Gorbatyi] gave to my lord, Prince Danilo, as dowry." "They," however, were not named specifically. The plaintiff called no witnesses, not even his master, but declared that he had mowed the land this year on the prince's orders. The Grand Prince gave judgment for the defendant.[13] Both litigants in a case tried between 1495 and 1499 produced purchase deeds for the disputed land. Gavrilko, a priest's son, complained that the metropolitan's peasants were living unlawfully in his hamlet. The peasants, however, claimed it was the metropolitan's land, where they had been living for thirty years. The plaintiff declared that his grandfather had bought the land, and presented his purchase deed. The metropolitan's secretary, testifying on behalf of the defendants, in turn asserted that the priest Foma had purchased the disputed land from the plaintiff's grandfather, and produced Foma's purchase deed. The plaintiff then claimed that he did not know whether his grandfather had sold the land—he only knew that the peasants lived there illegally. He had not been able to concern himself with the land personally for thirty years because he had been ill for eighteen (he gave no explanation for his failure to take action in the other twelve years). The court decided in favor of the defendants, probably because the documents indicated that the plaintiff's grandfather had purchased the land about 1450 and had sold it to the priest Foma between 1464 and 1473. In addition, the plaintiff had waited thirty years to bring suit, a fact which the judge in all likelihood took into consideration.[14] Another defendant, estate manager for the Simonov Monastery, presented a purchase deed for land claimed by some plaintiffs as part of their patrimony, according to their father's will. The will, however, was being kept in the monastery's archives. The defendant then brought in the will, the plaintiffs' evidence. Judgment was given in the monastery's favor, since its purchase deed named the disputed land

but the will did not mention it among the various lands left to the plaintiffs.[15]

Witnesses' testimony, rather than documentary evidence, seems to have been the deciding factor in another group of judgment charters. The issue is very clear in a 1490 document. An estate manager of the Simonov Monastery claimed that two peasants were living in the monastery's deserted village, calling it the Grand Prince's and refusing to leave. The defendants declared that the land was the Grand Prince's. Next the plaintiff presented six longtime residents, who remembered from fifty to seventy-five years; the witnesses said that a former archimandrite, who was now the metropolitan, had settled the defendants in the village three years ago. The judge then requested confirmation from the metropolitan, who reported that he had given the defendants a three-year limited-exemption charter for the village, but that their request for a two-year extension had not been granted. The defendants subsequently named four witnesses, who all declared that the defendants had called for their testimony senselessly—they remembered that the land had been the monastery's for fifty years. The court awarded the land to the monastery, ordering that the defendants be sent out of the village.[16] In other cases, losing litigants had called upon witnesses who declared that they knew nothing about the disputed land or its boundaries, while the victor's men had supported him.[17]

On some occasions, both sides presented witnesses who supported them. The judge then had to decide, perhaps partly on the basis of his "inner convictions," which testimony was better. Of course, there were criteria which he could apply in his evaluation, such as the number of witnesses for each party and the length of time for which they could testify about events in the area. In one case the plaintiff presented three witnesses, who supported his claims and remembered for twenty years. The defendants called for the man who had sold them the land and marked off the boundaries for them. He confirmed the sale and declared that he had had an official boundary establishment with the plaintiff's father. When the plaintiff denied it, the vendor presented two longtime residents, who remembered for forty years, and two boundary-division witnesses, who declared that the plaintiff's father had been present when the land was measured off for the defendants. The court decided in favor of the defendants, and the weight of testimony supports the decision.[18] The plaintiff in another case had two witnesses who remembered for thirty years. The defendant said that the monastery's documents had burned, but that he had been plowing the disputed land for twenty years. In addition he presented four longtime residents who remembered that the land had been the monastery's since

[13] ASEI 2, no. 464. For other cases which seem to fit this category, see ASEI 1, no. 430; ASEI 2, nos. 188, 337, 381, 405; ASEI 3, no. 319.

[14] AFZKh 1, no. 129. The original purchase deeds have been published separately, in addition to being incorporated in the judgment charter; see AFZKh 1, nos. 127, 128. Strangely enough, the plaintiff's document, as incorporated in the judgment charter, contains phrases not found in the original—perhaps he made a new copy, hoping to strengthen his claims.

[15] ASEI 2, no. 387.
[16] ASEI 2, no. 402.
[17] AFZKh 1, no. 249; ASEI 2, no. 388a.
[18] ASEI 3, no. 288.

the plague, for about fifty years.[19] The defendant won, probably because he had presented more witnesses who were also residents of longer standing. The victorious plaintiff in another case produced seven witnesses, who remembered his land exchange seventeen years before and had since mowed the disputed meadow for him. The defendant, on the other hand, could not present the men who, he claimed, had previously held the land, and brought only two witnesses who testified concerning the former landholders.[20]

Judgment charters in yet another group record that litigants presented mixed forms of proof. In two cases, both parties had documents and, in each trial, both sides called upon the same witnesses to testify. Testimony in each case supported the plaintiff, who won.[21] Two defendants in other suits had purchase deeds, as opposed to the two witnesses presented by each of the plaintiffs. Both defendants won, probably in part because one plaintiff brought suit after twenty years and the other after twenty-five.[22] Yet documentary evidence was not always decisive. In another case peasant defendants with two longtime residents won. The plaintiff had produced two documents to prove that the land belonged to the monastery, but he could present no witnesses at all. When questioned by the judge, the plaintiff first asserted that the monastery had not received the documents until the former landholder had died. Then he admitted that, even after the supposed donor's death, the peasant defendants had continued mowing the land. The documents, he claimed, had only recently been found. The judge apparently suspected that the documents were not authentic. He referred the case to the Grand Prince, who decided in favor of the defendants.[23]

If any part of a litigant's evidence did not support the claims which he had advanced, this was naturally held against him. In a case tried between 1485 and 1490, both parties produced documents. The plaintiff had five witnesses, the defendant had four. All of the plaintiff's longtime residents supported him. But after one of the defendant's men said that the land belonged to the plaintiff, the defendant admitted that the plaintiff's peasants had been plowing the land, and that he had plowed it only that spring. The plaintiff won, probably because the defendant's witness had not supported him and because the defendant himself had said that he had not plowed the land before.[24] Another victorious plaintiff had presented two documents and a witness, while the defendant, despite claims of both and several postponements, could produce neither.[25]

The secular landholder who won a 1498/1499 case had presented his father's will, two purchase deeds, and three witnesses. His opponent, one of the metropolitan's estate managers, presented one witness, who testified that his father had told him twenty-five years before that the land was the metropolitan's. The manager then called for evidence from the Grand Prince's land cadastres, repeating his demand after declaring that he did not contest his opponent's documents. Since the land was not recorded as part of the metropolitan's village, this fact, in addition to his other proof, gave victory to the secular claimant.[26] The victorious plaintiff in another case had documentary evidence and six longtime residents who could show the judge the boundaries, while the defendants' two witnesses were not able to lead the judge around the land.[27]

Other plaintiffs admitted that they had not brought suit for fifteen years because they had not been concerned with the land. This, in addition to the defendants' donation charter and charter of grant from the Grand Prince clearing the land of conflicting claims, seems to have been the basis for judgment in favor of the defendants, even though they had refused to allow their four witnesses to agree to a judicial duel with the plaintiffs' five witnesses.[28] Examination of a judgment charter issued between 1490 and 1498 suggests that the plaintiff should have tried to limit the range of testimony. Eight witnesses supported him, as opposed to three for the defendant. But then the plaintiff claimed that he had spoken to the hundredman about the matter, and the hundredman denied it, adding that the land was not registered in his hundred, and that the defendant's peasants had plowed it. Next the defendant produced a charter of the Grand Prince. Finally one of the plaintiff's witnesses tried to help: he described the boundary, claiming that the plaintiff's land had a common border with the tenman's. When questioned, the tenman, who had lived there for fifty years, said that the defendant's peasants had been plowing the land along his boundary.[29] The plaintiff lost.

Judgment was finally pronounced against the defendants in a 1521 case only after the plaintiffs had been waiting at the dueling field for eight days and had petitioned to protest the delay. Failure to appear for the judicial duel was undoubtedly the reason for the adverse decision.[30]

In a final group of judgment charters where the reason for the decision seems clear, the actions of a litigant during *doklad* proceedings would seem to have been decisive, providing the immediate cause for the adverse result of his case. In one instance a plaintiff had presented a document and five witnesses in the lower court, while four witnesses had supported the defendant.

[19] *ASEI* **2**, no. 368.

[20] *AFZKh* **1**, no. 248.

[21] *PRP* **2**: p. 235; *ASEI* **1**, no. 447.

[22] *ASEI* **1**, nos. 524, 525.

[23] *ASEI* **2**, no. 229.

[24] *ASEI* **2**, no. 400.

[25] *ASEI* **2**, no. 410. The victorious plaintiff in another case was supported by documentary evidence and testimony, while the defendants' witness did not come to court; *RIB* **12**, no. 4.

[26] *ASEI* **3**, no. 105.

[27] *AIu*, no. 20.

[28] *ASEI* **2**, no. 375.

[29] *ASEI* **2**, no. 404.

[30] *AFZKh* **1**, no. 1a.

Appearing in the upper court, the defendant first claimed that the trial record was inaccurate, and then backed down. This probably cost him the case, although the plaintiff's witnesses also seem to have had more thorough knowledge of the matter.[31] In another suit the plaintiff was supported by thirteen witnesses, three of whom requested a judicial duel with the defendants' supporters. The defendants' six witnesses agreed. The defendants, however, claimed to have a charter—they did not remember who had written or witnessed it—which they would present only before the Grand Prince. On *doklad,* as it turned out, they could not produce the document. This, plus the plaintiff's superiority in witnesses, probably decided the case in favor of the plaintiff.[32]

Although the judgment charters in all these categories include no reasons for the decisions given, the decisions themselves are not difficult to explain. The court's pronouncements seem to have corresponded with the evidence recorded. The basis for the decisions in some other cases, however, is somewhat harder to perceive. Again the documents may be classified according to type of proof.

In one type of case, the defendants lost through their own actions, actions which would account for the outcome, yet, according to the record, the plaintiffs never presented any proof. Two brothers in one such suit claimed a deserted village as part of their patrimony. The defendant replied that the land was his, and declared that he had his father's purchase deed, asking for a postponement so that he could bring it to court. Appearing one week later, the defendant could not produce the document, since, he said, it had been destroyed in a fire. Judgment was then given for the plaintiffs.[33] The defendant in another case claimed that his master the prince had given him the meadow, but, despite his promises, the prince would not appear in court even after the third postponement. Again the plaintiff won without presenting any evidence.[34] Both documents have been dated as being issued in the 1450's or 1460's. The early judgment charters were much less complete records than those issued during the sixteenth century, so this may account for the lack of information. The problem is also complicated by the fact that both texts are later copies. The second document is an eighteenth-century copy, while the preceding judgment charter is an "abbreviated" seventeenth-century copy, so it is possible that the original judgment charters included a record of the plaintiffs' proof. In any event, the copies suggest that negative evidence was considered more decisive.

This basis for the decisions in certain other judgment charters is also somewhat obscure, partly because of the rather cryptic nature of the documents and the type of

evidence they tried to record. In a case tried between 1490 and 1498, the plaintiff, a monastery elder, complained that two years earlier the defendant had plowed across the boundaries and chopped down trees on the monastery's land; the elder presented a purchase deed. The defendant replied that his aunt and brothers-in-law had given him the land, and that he had chopped down no trees on monastery land. He then presented his brothers-in-law to verify that he had been plowing the land for thirty-two years. The plaintiff presented three witnesses—the monastery's boundary surveyors—and the two men, the defendant's brothers-in-law, from whom, he claimed, the monastery had purchased the land. All five men next led the judge along the boundaries, declaring that the monastery's land lay on the left and the defendant's on the right. The defendant then called upon his brothers-in-law, who testified that they had given the land to the defendant up to the boundary they had just shown the judge. The court decided in favor of the plaintiff.[35] Apparently the brothers-in-law originally held the entire area, giving part to the defendant and selling part to the monastery. Although the judgment charter describes the boundary tree by tree, its location in relation to the disputed land is not specified. While the matter was probably very clear to the judge who was there, for an outsider the record leaves much to be desired.[36]

Ivan III must have decided another case on the basis of his "inner convictions" or some evidence not recorded in the judgment charter. Each party presented six witnesses, who all supported the claims of their respective principals and remembered for approximately fifty years.[37]

In most of the surviving judgment charters where reasons are not given, however, the court's decision can be explained on the basis of evidence presented. It must also be kept in mind that proof offered by the litigants was not always the only consideration. As shall be noted below, judges occasionally listed negative factors when giving reasons for a decision: litigants had failed to take certain procedural steps which, in the judge's opinion, should have formed a part of their case. Such thinking undoubtedly played a part as well in the decisions for which no explanation was given, but it is not reflected in the judgment charters. On the whole, however, analysis of the decisions recorded in this group of judgment charters has shown that the weight of evidence alone did support the pronouncements of the court.

II

The second major group of judgment charters is composed of the documents which give reasons for the court's decision. Three different forms of decisions

[31] *ASEI* 1, no. 523.
[32] *ASEI* 1, no. 582.
[33] *ASEI* 2, no. 358.
[34] *ASEI* 2, no. 458.

[35] *ASEI* 1, no. 557.
[36] The decision in another case likewise seems to rest on the judge's viewing the boundaries; see *ASEI* 2, no. 369.
[37] *AFZKh* 1, no. 125.

which include the *ratio decidendi* occur in the judgment charters. Sometimes the judge decided in favor of one litigant, listing the evidence in his favor on which the decision had been based. At other times the court found for one party, but gave reasons for the decisions against the other. On yet other occasions, the judge listed two sets of considerations, those supporting the victor and those against the vanquished. During the sixteenth century the reasons given by the court tend to become more numerous and complicated. In some instances, the explanation of the decision itself summarizes the entire course of the proceedings, as we shall illustrate subsequently.

As with the judgment charters which did not provide explanations for the decisions, one group of documents in this second category is composed of cases in which one litigant admitted that the other's claims were valid. When the Grand Prince's beekeepers brought suit against two princes, charging that the defendants had taken the Grand Prince's bee-tree areas and were calling the lands their patrimony, the beekeepers presented their charter of grant from the Grand Prince. The princes immediately declared that the lands were the Grand Prince's, and the court decided in favor of the plaintiffs on the basis of their charter.[38] The judge in a 1499 case gave judgment in favor of the plaintiffs because the defendants had declared that they did not know the boundaries and had agreed to accept whatever line the plaintiffs' longtime peasant residents pointed out.[39]

Other litigants eventually conceded, but only after a more prolonged struggle.[40] The defendant in a case tried about 1497 finally admitted the plaintiff's claim, but certainly postponed it as long as possible. Elder Varsonofei originally brought suit against Ondreiko, Prince Boris Ivanovich Gorbatyi's estate manager, charging that he had taken nine hundred ricks of hay from the monastery's land. Ondreiko replied that he had taken the hay from the disputed land, for the first time, on the prince's orders, and requested a two-week postponement to get the prince. Two weeks later, he reported that the Grand Prince would not let Prince Boris leave Moscow, and asked for an extension. Two weeks after that, he requested a third postponement— the prince was kept in Moscow by important duties. At the next designated time, Prince Boris sent his man Pronka to testify on his behalf. Pronka declared that the lands were the prince's, given to him by his father. The prince, he claimed, had his father's donation charter (i.e., charter of gift) for the lands. The judge then turned to the plaintiff for his evidence. The elder declared that the lands had been donated to the monastery. The prince's father Ivan had tried to enter the lands earlier, and a judge had come as a re-

sult of the archimandrite's petitioning the Grand Prince. The parties, however, had become reconciled, and Ivan had ceded the land to the monastery, giving the brethren an injunction charter ordering his bailiffs not to take hay from the land. The plaintiff then named seven witnesses, and presented the donation charter and the injunction. Prince Boris's man repeated that Prince Boris had his father's charter, declared that he did not know whether the prince had witnesses, and asked for ten days in which to get the prince. Ten days later he requested an extension; Prince Boris was in Moscow attending to his affairs. After another ten days, the prince finally appeared, but without his father or the charter. Prince Boris then asked for a two-week postponement, claiming that his father had the document and would know about witnesses. The next time, Prince Boris again requested ten days—his father was ill. At that designated date, Prince Boris asked for another ten days—his father had been caught by bad roads on the way to court. After the eighth postponement in the case, the prince once more arrived alone. His father did not wish to appear on the land before the judge, and would not give Prince Boris the charter. The father, Prince Ivan, would place the document only before the Grand Prince. The plaintiff's witnesses then testified. All declared that the land had been donated to the monastery, and they showed the judge the boundaries. The treasurer Dmitrii Volodimerovich Ovtsa [Khovrin] presided at the trial on *doklad*. Apparently, before reaching a decision, he had consulted Prince Boris's father Prince Ivan. Judgment was given for the plaintiff

because Prince Boris's father Prince Ivan Ivanovich had said, in the presence of Mitrei (the judge, Dmitrii Ovtsa) that he (Prince Ivan) had given those meadows below Kholm, and the Zanemittskoi [*sic*] meadow above Kholm, along the river Nerl', to the Spaso-Eufim'ev Monastery's Archimandrite Kostiantin, and had given them such a charter for those meadows as is described in this [trial] record, and said that the charter had his seal.

In addition to considering this admission of the plaintiff's claim, the judge decided in the plaintiff's favor because his witnesses had supported him. The defendant had to pay for all nine hundred ricks of hay. We might suggest that an additional fine—for *volokita* (delay of justice)—would have been entirely appropriate.[41]

Most litigants continued to press their claims to the end of the trial. The judgment charters with explanations reveal that judges drew upon the evidence in various ways when reaching decisions. Delay before bringing suit could be a decisive factor.[42] In one case both sides presented supporting witnesses, but the

[38] *ASEI* 2, no. 496.

[39] *AFZKh* 1, no. 157.

[40] For cases in which one litigant eventually recognized the validity of his opponent's claim, see *AIu*, nos. 15, 16, 21, 22; *AFZKh* 1. no. 222; *AIuB* 1, no. 7.

[41] *ASEI* 2, no. 493. On Dmitrii Volodimerovich Ovtsa, see Alef, "Reflections," pp. 114–115. For a discussion of *volokita*, see V. I. Tagunova, "Volokita," in *Etimologicheskie issledovaniia po russkomu iazyku* 6, ed. N. M. Shanskii (Moscow, 1968), pp. 158–165. The plaintiffs in a 1492 case also admitted the validity of the defendants' claims, after the defendants had produced decisive evidence; *ASEI* 2, no. 285.

[42] *ASEI* 3, no. 56.

court decided against the plaintiff because he had said that the defendants had established the disputed hamlet fourteen years earlier, and in that time he had not brought suit or petitioned the Grand Prince or sent a constable.[43] Ivashko Sobaka, plaintiff in a 1498/1499 case, lost his suit against Vasiuk Volk because both he and his witnesses had said that the defendant's peasants had occupied the land since the plague (about seventy years).[44]

Although the idea of a statute of limitations was obviously applied by the courts, the surviving judgment charters contain no real reflection of the 1497 Sudebnik's decrees on three- and six-year limitations in bringing suit. Both before and after the code was issued, judges referred to a litigant's failure to seek justice as one reason for giving judgment against him, but the time periods involved ranged from six to fifty years. The Sudebnik apparently had no effect in preventing a man, after 1497, from initiating a suit for land forty or fifty years after it had supposedly been taken from him. Furthermore, the court never declared that the defeated party lost his suit because, according to the Sudebnik decree, he had postponed legal action for too long.

Decision might also be given against a litigant if he or his witnesses did not know the boundaries of the disputed land.[45] When one side could point out boundary markers, how could the other, not knowing the limits of his land, prove that he had not gone beyond his own border?

Documents could be the deciding factor. Judges awarded land to the man with documentary evidence when the other litigant offered nothing to support his assertions.[46] One judge made the point more specific. He gave judgment for the defendant because he had documents, and because the plaintiffs had said that their only witness was dead and they did not name any other witnesses.[47] Judges in another case decided in favor of defendants with a document, over a plaintiff with three witnesses, only after checking on the document in the Grand Prince's archives.[48] A judgment charter from an earlier trial proved decisive in a 1500 case. The plaintiff declared that the defendants had carted off hay from his meadow. The defendants admitted taking the hay, since, they claimed, the land was theirs. Next the plaintiff produced a judgment charter issued against the defendants in an earlier trial. When the defendants said that they had not had such a trial, the lower-court judge followed the procedure usually used in *doklad;* he asked them whether they called for the testimony of the men of court. The defendants then admitted that the document was accurate. Judgment was given for the plaintiff, because the defendants had taken the hay after a previous trial, in violation of the judgment charter. They were fined, and ordered to pay three rubles for the hay.[49] Documentary evidence also defeated a defendant who claimed that the plaintiffs' purchase deed was a forgery. All records produced in court proved it to be authentic, and the court decided against the defendant because he had claimed the deed was a forgery and the document he presented to prove it was in the same handwriting.[50]

Testimony could also be the decisive element. When both sides produced witnesses, it was crucial that all testimony support the claims advanced by the principals. In a case tried between 1492 and 1503, for example, each litigant named three longtime residents. The defendant's men supported his account almost line for line. The court decided against the plaintiff, however, because two of his witnesses personally did not know whose land it was or what the boundaries were, and the third man gave testimony which did not support the plaintiff.[51] Litigants also lost because their own witnesses, in addition to those of the opposition, testified that the opponent had been in possession of the disputed land for ten, twenty, or forty years.[52] One plaintiff won, partly on the basis of his charter of grant, and partly because the defendant's longtime residents refused a judicial duel and other peasants, questioned at the defendant's request, said that the meadows were the plaintiff's.[53]

A judgment charter issued between 1479 and 1481 records a series of procedural steps which led the court to base its decision on documents verified by witnesses. The plaintiff, abbot of the Trinity-Sergius Monastery, claimed that Olesha had given the monastery the disputed lands, and he presented a donation charter. The defendant, abbot of St. Cyril's Monastery, declared that Olesha's father Ofonasii, who had been a monk, had left the land to his monastery, and he produced a donation charter. Olesha testified for the plaintiff, confirming his own donation of the land, and claiming that his father had not given the territory to St. Cyril's. In addition, Olesha declared, he had not been present, as the defendant's document stated, when his father donated the land. The judge then set a new trial date, when all witnesses named in both donation charters were to appear. The defendant arrived with three witnesses, and the fourth, Prince Ivan Fedorovich Kargolomskii, who was in the Grand Prince's service in Novgorod, sent a deposition. All three

[43] *ASEI* 3, no. 221.
[44] *ASEI* 2, no. 421.
[45] *ASEI* 2, nos. 401, 411.
[46] Vladimirskii-Budanov, *Khristomatiia* 2: pp. 235–237; *ASEI* 3, no. 32; *AIu*, no. 15; *RIB* 14, no. 17; *AIuB* 1, nos. 4, 8.
[47] *ASEI* 1, no. 658.
[48] *ASEI* 2, no. 309.
[49] *ASEI* 2, no. 422.
[50] *AIu*, no. 13.
[51] *ASEI* 2, no. 407. For other cases where witnesses did not support a litigant, see *ASEI* 2, no. 287; 3, no. 48; *AFZKh* 1, nos. 103, 309; *AIu*, no. 19; Likhachev, *Sbornik*, no. 11; *AIuB* 1, no. 6.
[52] *ASEI* 2, no. 310; 3, nos. 50, 276; *AFZKh* 1, nos. 254, 259.
[53] *ASEI* 3, no. 223.

witnesses declared that they, and Olesha, had been present when Ofonasii donated his land to St. Cyril's, and one of them verified his signature on the document. The plaintiff, however, and his witnesses did not even appear in court, and judgment was given for the defendant.[54]

The judges' decisions in the preceding cases seem to correspond with the evidence presented, and the reasons given are quite comprehensive, at least with regard to one side's proof (or lack of it). In a fairly large number of judgment charters, however, the evidence recorded indicates that the court could have listed even more reasons than were given. In all probability, the practice of giving considerations at all became standardized only gradually, and judges, rather than recording such matters in full, stated those reasons which seemed most obvious to them.

Some judges apparently felt that documentary evidence was the strongest form of proof, since that was the element they stressed. One judge, for example, awarded land to the defendant on the basis of two charters of grant and a purchase deed, not mentioning that both the plaintiff and his witnesses had said that the defendant had been in possession for twenty-five years, and that the plaintiff had not brought suit in the past because the defendant had told him about the documents.[55] The plaintiff in a trial held between 1490 and 1492 also won because he had three documents; the judge did not include the fact that the defendants' witnesses had supported the plaintiff's claims.[56] A 1530 judgment charter records that Vasilii III, hearing the case on *doklad,* ordered that the land cadastres be examined and then gave judgment against the plaintiffs because the records did not support their claims. There was no reference to all the testimony in the lower-court hearing: the plaintiffs had presented four longtime residents and two men who testified on inquest, while three longtime residents and twenty-nine inquest witnesses had supported the defendant.[57]

In other instances a judge seemed to have his own special way of looking at the evidence, if we can go by what he emphasized in his decision. A judgment charter of 1498/1499 records that the plaintiff had presented a charter, dating from 1444, and twenty-two witnesses: five petty boiars, two townsmen, three city peasants, three monastery elders, one other elder, and eight longtime peasant residents, who all supported the plaintiff's claims. The defendant had only ten peasant witnesses. Yet the judge did not refer to the plaintiff's document or witnesses when deciding in his favor. The court found for the plaintiff because the defendant had brought only peasants from the one village claiming the disputed meadow as part of its land, and he had

named no "outsiders," either petty boiars or peasants.[58] A judgment charter issued between 1495 and 1497 records a decision against the plaintiffs because they themselves had said that the defendant's peasants chopped down trees in the forest. In fact, this had been their original accusation, when they claimed the forest. The decision did not mention that the plaintiffs had subsequently asserted simply that they did not know the boundary, then admitted that they had been shown the boundary (but not, they declared, the boundary indicated by the defendant). After this the boundary-division witnesses had testified that they had shown the plaintiffs the boundary, as described by the defendant, and four other men supported the defendant.[59] The judge certainly could have listed additional reasons for this decision.

A few judges included refusal to fight a judicial duel as one of their reasons, probably because the loser could not contest this indication of his failure. One judge decided for the defendant because the plaintiffs' witnesses had not supported their allegations and, when asked what proof they could offer, did not call for cross-kissing and a duel (in fact, they had said: "By what, Sires, can we swear?"). The decision did not state that the plaintiffs in their accusation had admitted that the defendant had been in possession for forty years.[60] Another plaintiff lost because his witnesses did not agree to a duel; the judge did not mention that the "longtime residents" presented by the plaintiff to show the boundary proved to be young men who knew neither the history of the land nor its boundaries.[61] A judgment charter from the end of the fifteenth century lists the following reasons for decision in favor of the defendant: the plaintiff had not brought suit for fifty years, had not petitioned the Grand Prince, and his witnesses had not requested a judicial duel. The judge did not record the fact that the plaintiff's witnesses had not supported his claims in their testimony, which would explain their failure to demand a duel.[62]

In the preceding cases, although the court may not have given the reason which would seem most decisive to us, the other evidence stated in the trial record does lead to the conclusion at which the judge arrived. The same is true of another group of judgment charters, which include a trial on *doklad.* When one party claimed that the lower court's trial record was inaccurate, and his objections subsequently proved unfounded, the court gave judgment against him for the immediate and obvious reason.[63] Litigants who did

[54] *AIu,* no. 1.
[55] *ASEI* 2, no. 307; for similar cases, see *AFZKh* 1, no. 258; *ASEI* 2, no. 288.
[56] *ASEI* 2, no. 332.
[57] Likhachev, *Sbornik,* no. 8.
[58] *ASEI* 2, no. 492; see also *ASEI* 2, no. 374. In other cases the judge did not refer to the supporting testimony offered by the victor's witnesses; *ASEI* 2, nos. 336, 406; 3, nos. 173, 208.
[59] *ASEI* 1, no. 581.
[60] *AFZKh* 1, no. 306.
[61] *ASEI* 2, no. 334.
[62] *AFZKh* 1, no. 114.
[63] *ASEI* 1, nos. 595, 607; *AIu,* no. 14; Likhachev, *Sbornik,* no. 9.

not appear for the trial on *doklad* also lost for that reason.[64]

Thus most judgment charters which include the *ratio decidendi,* as well as those where reasons were not given, show that judges did base their conclusions on the evidence. As was true with the cases where no reasons were listed, however, a few of the decisions in this group seem questionable. For example, in our case which was decided by lots, the outcome was clear: the judges decided in favor of the defendants because their longtime residents' lot was chosen.[65] Yet why did the vicegerents settle on this method of proof? During the course of the trial, the plaintiff had twice called for evidence from the Grand Prince's land cadastres. Seemingly it would have been possible—and much less arbitrary—for the judges to have examined the books to find out in whose name the disputed land was registered.

The decision recorded in a 1497/1498 judgment charter also might be questioned. The seven plaintiffs, declaring that they themselves were the longtime residents of the area, claimed that the disputed land was the Grand Prince's, and had been taken over by the Simonov Monastery after the plague, when the land became deserted. Then they led the judge along the boundaries. The defendant, steward for the monastery, presented five witnesses who all remembered from the time of the plague and declared that the land had been donated to the monastery by the widow Fedosia and her son, a monk. Asked why they had not brought suit earlier, the plaintiffs claimed that the judge in an earlier trial had accepted a bribe, and that their later petitions to the vicegerents had been unsuccessful. The defendant stated that the previous judge had decided in the monastery's favor, but had issued no judgment charter. No further evidence was offered. The judge found for the defendant, because the plaintiffs, besides themselves, had no longtime residents, and did not offer to fight a judicial duel.[66] A decision on the basis of statute of limitations would have been more logical. If we accept the plaintiffs' word, how could they produce other longtime residents? The monastery did not offer to present a donation charter for the land in question. In addition, the fact that the defendant had no judgment charter from the earlier trial would seem to be a matter requiring further inquiry. Yet the decision can probably be defended in terms of fifteenth-century Muscovite judicial practice. The plaintiffs had delayed in bringing suit, and if bribery had occurred as they claimed, they should somehow have confronted the previous judge. If the land had not been donated to the monastery, they should have contested the defendant's assertion that it had. Furthermore, the defendant's witnesses had more explicit knowledge of the

disputed land, quite detailed information about who had lived there and its transfer to the monastery, while the plaintiffs made only a general statement that the land was the Grand Prince's.

Most decisions where reasons are listed, however, reflect at least part of the evidence, while the factors not mentioned support the judgment given. In summarizing its view, the court apparently felt that it was more important to explain why one litigant lost than to account for the other's victory. Approximately two-thirds of the documents which record the judge's considerations list reasons for a decision against one party, while more than half of the remaining judgment charters include elements on each side (thus also explaining the loser's position). Judges showed a marked preference to give the negative factors, the reasons for a decision against one party. This may reflect an attempt on their part to discourage any further litigation over the same issue.

As noted above, the decisions which give the *ratio decidendi* frequently record only a few reasons and often do not include all relevant evidence. This is particularly characteristic of the fifteenth-century documents. In the sixteenth century the reasons for a decision were usually listed more completely. Possibly the best way to illustrate the "abbreviated" nature of some of the decisions we have seen is to examine a more extensive one by way of comparison. A 1543 judgment charter records that the disputed land was awarded to the monasterial plaintiff for several reasons. First, the plaintiff had presented a donation charter which recorded the natural boundaries of the land. The defendants had not declared the document false. Then the plaintiff's longtime residents had led the judge along the boundaries—the same natural boundaries described in the donation charter. Forty-two men had testified on inquest and had supported the plaintiff. Then the former estate manager of the donor, who had pointed out the boundaries at the time the land was given to the monastery, also testified in support of the plaintiff's claims. The defendants had called for evidence from the land cadastres to prove their title, but the disputed property had not been registered as they claimed. Finally, the defendants had brought a counter-suit, but only after remaining silent for nine years concerning the alleged violation of their rights.[67] Thus, in giving its decision, the court recapitulated the events of the entire trial.

Other documents provide an even more extended enumeration of reasons for a decision. In the 1547 suit where Ivan Sheremetev accused the Tokmakov brothers and Andrei Nozdrovatyi of forging a redeemed promissory note, the tsar gave judgment in favor of the plaintiff and listed nine reasons for his

[64] *ASEI* 3, no. 477; *AFZKh* 1, nos. 117, 261.
[65] Anpilogov, *Novye dokumenty,* pp. 485–490.
[66] *ASEI* 2, no. 414.

[67] Likhachev, *Sbornik,* no. 10. For other cases which summarize the entire trial in the decision, see Likhachev, *Sbornik,* no. 12; *AIuB* 1, no. 7.

decision, each of which comprises a substantial paragraph in itself.[68] The 1584 decision in favor of Timofei Shilovskii in his suit against Andrei Sherefedinov over the "extorted deed" is even more detailed—and is particularly striking in that it refers specifically to one of the substantive provisions of the 1550 Sudebnik, which decreed that, if anyone bought an estate in his own name with a third party's money and turned the property over to the third party (the arrangement between the defendant Sherefedinov and his son-in-law concerning the plaintiff's patrimony), the estate was to be returned to the vendor.[69]

Most of the judgment charters do not include such complete lists of the court's reasons. Yet, in view of the recorded data, the court's decisions were generally sound. The judgment charters as a group disprove Dmitriev's contention that judges generally made their decisions on the basis of "internal convictions." With few exceptions, decisions recorded in the documents follow logically from the evidence presented. While some cases indicate that all possible proof was obviously not considered, and that the judges' examination of witnesses and documents was certainly cursory by present standards, the source of the problem lay in the judicial system itself.

We must keep in mind the roles which judges and litigants apparently felt were appropriately theirs. The parties themselves were responsible for presenting their evidence. Judges were usually lenient in granting postponements when requested, and as a rule tried to gather all the proof which they could. The absence of lawyers and a legal tradition in Muscovite Russia probably accounts for much of the judges' uncritical attitude. What training could they receive except through practice? Both judges and their assistants were learning the trade, operating for the most part on the existing standards and procedures of customary law. Judicial duties were just one among a variety of administrative and other official responsibilities assigned to these men. Most judges took a common-sense approach to their duties, reaching conclusions after balancing the evidence presented by each side. Despite the widespread charges of arbitrary practices and corruption which have been directed at the courts, the actual records of proceedings indicate that most judges took their duties seriously. Of course, the documents may not be a faithful representation of actual courtroom proceedings, although the scarcity of complaints by litigants during *doklad* proceedings would seem to belie this. But, even if such were the case, the increasingly frequent notation and expanding enumeration of the *ratio decidendi* would reflect a developing awareness, at least in the minds of those compiling the judgment charters, that the decision had to be explained. This indicates a growing feeling that the judge must be able to account for his decision in terms of the evidence.

Some citizens too were evidently beginning to prefer a legal solution of their problems to the use of force. It is surprising in some instances that a matter even came to court. To cite just one example, in 1490 Kuzemka, the Simonov Monastery's estate manager of the Verznevskoe village, brought suit against two peasants, charging that they were occupying one of the monastery's deserted villages illegally and refused to get out.[70] It would have been much easier and quicker for him to have dispatched five or six trusty stalwarts with sticks. But perhaps the monastery wanted a judgment charter as proof of title in case the land once again became a subject of dispute.

Yet despite such examples and the decrees of the Sudebniki, the authority of the courts, particularly those in which a low-ranking judge conducted a trial on the land, seems to have been much less in actuality than it was on paper. Witnesses simply did not appear. Litigants, even peasants, showed no compunction about refusing to place their documents before the lower-court judge. Considering the difficulties which constables encountered merely in bringing defendants to trial, the court's level of efficiency in enforcing its orders was not high. On the other hand, it is imperative to remember that the Muscovite judicial system was far from being fully developed. Standardization and centralization of the courts and legal practice were only one part of the entire process of building of a unified Muscovite state administration. The rules were far from fixed. Each Sudebnik served more as a book of regulations for court personnel than a guide for judges in substantive questions. But, in view of the conditions under which it operated, we should perhaps give more credit to the level of performance achieved by Muscovite justice than do the majority of scholarly works, which stress its shortcomings with dismay.

68 *AIuB* 1, no. 5.

69 Iushkov, *Akty XIII–XVII vv.,* no. 220. The reference is to article 85 of the Sudebnik.

70 *ASEI* 2, no. 402.

MEMOIRS

OF THE

AMERICAN PHILOSOPHICAL SOCIETY

TRANSACTIONS

OF THE

AMERICAN PHILOSOPHICAL SOCIETY

TRANSACTIONS

OF THE

AMERICAN PHILOSOPHICAL SOCIETY

HELD AT PHILADELPHIA
FOR PROMOTING USEFUL KNOWLEDGE

NEW SERIES—VOLUME 65, PART 6
1975

JUSTICE IN MEDIEVAL RUSSIA: MUSCOVITE JUDGMENT CHARTERS (*PRAVYE GRAMOTY*) OF THE FIFTEENTH AND SIXTEENTH CENTURIES

ANN M. KLEIMOLA

Assistant Professor of History, University of Nebraska

THE AMERICAN PHILOSOPHICAL SOCIETY
INDEPENDENCE SQUARE
PHILADELPHIA

October, 1975

PUBLICATIONS

OF

The American Philosophical Society

The publications of the American Philosophical Society consist of PRO-
CEEDINGS, TRANSACTIONS, MEMOIRS, and YEAR BOOK.

THE PROCEEDINGS contains papers which have been read before the Society in addition to other papers which have been accepted for publication by
the Committee on Publications. In accordance with the present policy one
volume is issued each year, consisting of six bimonthly numbers, and the
price is $8.00 net per volume.

THE TRANSACTIONS, the oldest scholarly journal in America, was started
in 1769 and is quarto size. In accordance with the present policy each annual volume is a collection of monographs, each issued as a part. The current
annual subscription price is $20.00 net per volume. Individual copies of the
TRANSACTIONS are offered for sale. This issue is priced at $5.00.

Each volume of the MEMOIRS is published as a book. The titles cover
the various fields of learning; most of the recent volumes have been historical.
The price of each volume is determined by its size and character.

The YEAR BOOK is of considerable interest to scholars because of the reports on grants for research and to libraries for this reason and because of the
section dealing with the acquisitions of the Library. In addition it contains
the Charter and Laws, and lists of present and former members, and reports
of committees and meetings. The YEAR BOOK is published about April 1 for
the preceding calendar year. The current price is $5.00.

An author desiring to submit a manuscript for publication should send it
to the Editor, George W. Corner, American Philosophical Society, 104 South
Fifth Street, Philadelphia, Pa. 19106.